DATE DUE

Earth Wars

Earth Wars

THE BATTLE FOR GLOBAL RESOURCES

Geoff Hiscock

WILEY

John Wiley & Sons Singapore Pte. Ltd.

Other Wiley Editorial Offices

John Wiley & Sons, 111 River Street, Hoboken, NJ 07030, USA
John Wiley & Sons, The Atrium, Southern Gate, Chichester, West Sussex, P019 8SQ, United Kingdom
John Wiley & Sons (Canada) Ltd., 5353 Dundas Street West, Suite 400, Toronto, Ontario, M9B 6HB, Canada
John Wiley & Sons Australia Ltd., 42 McDougall Street, Milton, Queensland 4064, Australia
Wiley-VCH, Boschstrasse 12, D-69469 Weinheim, Germany

ISBN 978-1-118-15288-1 (Cloth)
ISBN 978-1-118-15291-1 (ePDF)
ISBN 978-1-118-15290-4 (Mobi)
ISBN 978-1-118-15289-8 (ePub)

Typeset in 11/13 pt, ITC New Baskerville-Roman by MPS Limited, Chennai, India
Printed in Singapore by Markono Print Media

10 9 8 7 6 5 4 3 2 1

Contents

Maps

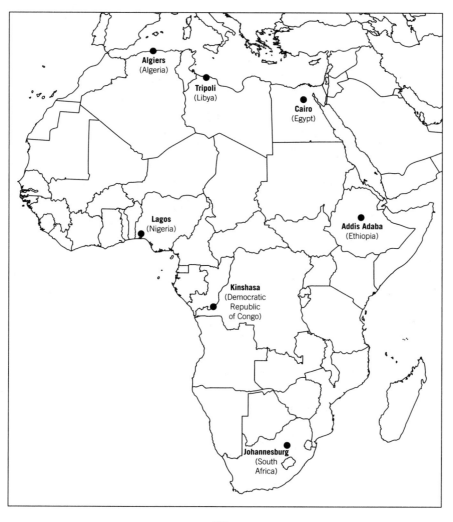

Africa

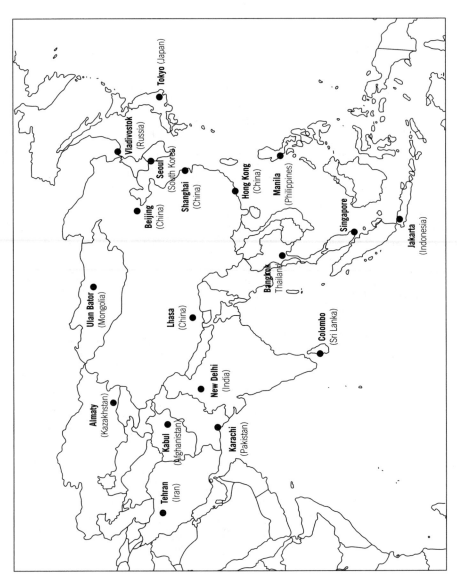

Asia

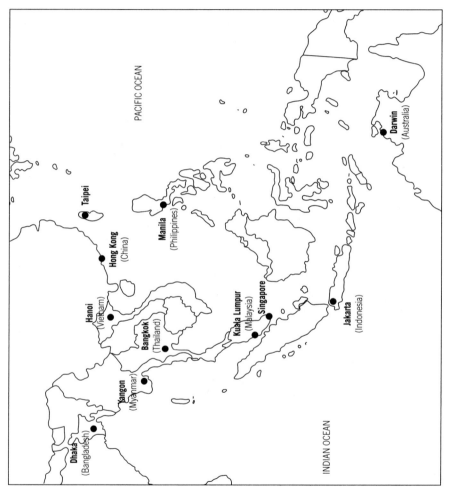

Southeast Asia

PACIFIC OCEAN

INDIAN OCEAN

Darwin
(Australia)

Taipei

Manila
(Philippines)

Hong Kong
(China)

Hanoi
(Vietnam)

Bangkok
(Thailand)

Kuala Lumpur
(Malaysia)

Singapore

Jakarta
(Indonesia)

Yangon
(Myanmar)

Dhaka
(Bangladesh)

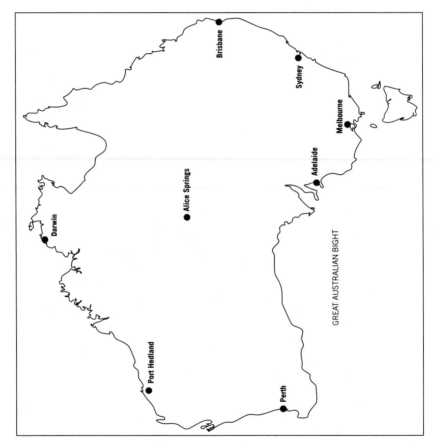

Australia

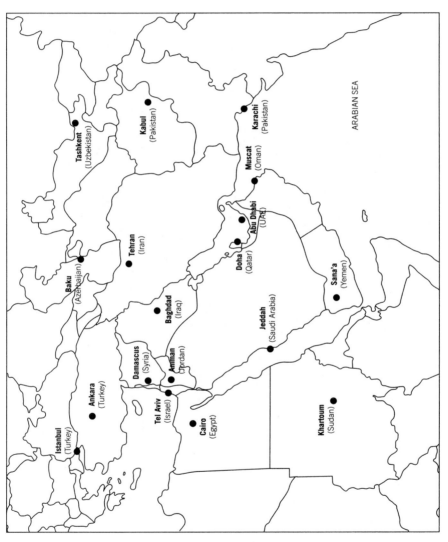

Middle East

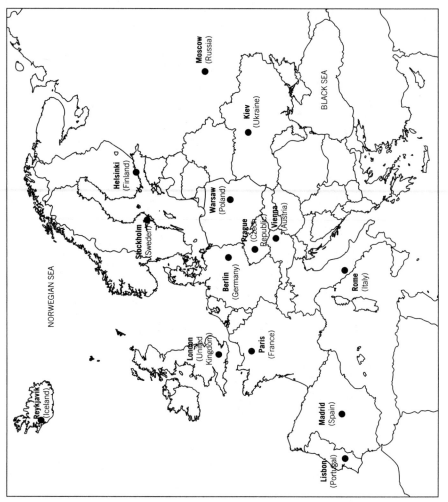

Europe

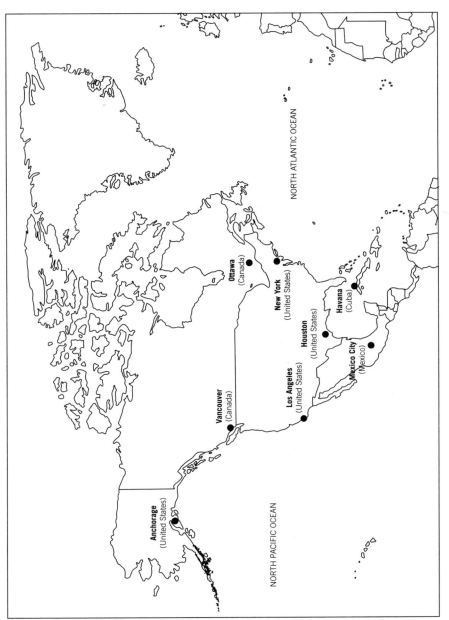

North America

Caracas
(Venezuela)

Bogotá
(Colombia)

Manaus
(Brazil)

Lima
(Peru)

La Paz
(Bolivia)

São Paulo
(Brazil)

Rio de Janeiro
(Brazil)

SOUTH PACIFIC OCEAN

Santiago
(Chile)

Buenos Aires
(Argentina)

SOUTH ATLANTIC OCEAN

South America

Introduction

What we are experiencing with the transformation of China is a once in a century or more event. It really is the start of a global rebalancing—a rebalancing that will continue to unfold over many decades.
          —BHP Billiton Chairman Jac Nasser, 9 May 2011

Six hundred years ago, China neither needed nor wanted anything from the West. It was the Middle Kingdom, the centre of the world, the seat of all that a civilization could possibly need to advance and prosper. India viewed itself through a similar prism—one rich in culture, religion, and resources. There was trading, of course: seafarers from the Mediterranean, the Persian Gulf, the east coast of Africa, and the islands of Southeast Asia bought and sold all manner of spices, timber, textiles, gems, and opium along a route that stretched from Venice to Calicut in India and on to Guangzhou in China.

Then came the great age of European exploration, as fleets from Portugal, Spain, Holland, and England sailed out into the oceans in search of new worlds to conquer. By the twentieth century, China and India were supplicants to the dominant colonialists of Europe, America, and Japan, seemingly beaten by their technology and their industrial might. After decades spent throwing off the colonial yoke and then trying to catch up economically, the two Asian giants are now poised to become the drivers of global growth in the first half of the twenty-first century. Demography is helping shape their destiny: A massive population base of 2.5 billion people, all eager to savour the full fruits of modern living, means there is increasing competition for scarce resources.

Whether it is lithium from a salt pan in the Andes, gas from the Caspian Sea, oil from a deepwater well off the coast of Brazil, coal from Africa's Zambezi River region, iron ore from the Australian outback, potash from Canada, or uranium from a Kazakhstan mine, China and India are keen to ensure the security of their future resources supply. Renewable energy from multiple sources and technologies can help, which is why the Asian duo are among the world's leading developers and users of solar, wind, and hydro power. Along with their urgent quest for control of natural resource projects around the globe, China and India know they must better nurture what they have at home. Each has substantial energy, food, and water supply capabilities, but pollution, contamination, and overuse are taking their toll of farmlands, river systems, and air quality.

In the race for global resources, tensions inevitably emerge. There are flashpoints everywhere—high food prices, for example, had a role to play in the violent political upheavals of the 2010–2011 Arab Spring. The world needs the sea lanes to stay open for trade, but maritime boundaries are a constant source of friction, and piracy adds an unwelcome element of danger for mariners. The oil and gas reserves of the South China Sea, for example, give an extra edge to China's territorial disputes with Japan, Vietnam, and other Asian neighbours over island groups such as the Senkaku, the Paracels, and the Spratlys. India has its own territorial issues with China over Aksai Chin on the Tibetan Plateau, and resource-rich Arunachal Pradesh in the eastern Himalayas. In 1953, India's then-Prime Minister Jawaharlal Nehru declared after a trip to China that the Chinese people cherished in their hearts the greatest of love for India, and wished to "maintain the friendliest of relations" with it. Nine years later, the two countries would be at war. While China–India economic ties have strengthened considerably since then, the edginess continues. At the same time, the United States, Europe, Russia, Japan, South Korea, Brazil, and half a dozen big, emerging economies such as Indonesia, Iran, Turkey, Mexico, Nigeria, and Saudi Arabia have their own interests to promote and protect.

On the political front, there are multiple changes ahead among the biggest economies. In China, Xi Jinping is likely to become chief of the Communist Party in October 2012 and president in 2013, with Li Keqiang his likely running mate as premier. Barack

Obama may well be a one-term U.S. president, while India's Prime Minister Manmohan Singh will remain until 2014 before a possible transition to Rahul Gandhi. Angela Merkel may run again for the German chancellor's job in 2013, and we have already seen massive changes in other European administrations such as Italy and Greece in 2011. As for Japan, who knows? Since the end of the Koizumi administration in 2006, it has had six prime ministers. There will be a new president in South Korea in 2013, and in Indonesia in 2014. In Turkey, Prime Minister Recep Tayyip Erdogan's term runs until 2015, as does that of Brazil's President Dilma Rousseff. In Russia, Vladimir Putin could be ensconced in the leadership until 2024.

Worldwide, energy is the key requirement to keep economies growing and living standards improving. But the era of easy energy is over. The cheap and easily accessible oil of past decades is used up or locked up in strategic reserves. Now the world has an energy choice, but what a choice. The remaining oil is too political, coal's too dirty, nuclear's too dangerous, wind's too fickle, solar's too expensive, hydro's too dislocating, geothermal is too hard to wrangle, and fracked gas is too divisive. Even so, many of the world's top resources companies see gas as the great savior over the next 20 years, in what the International Energy Agency calls the impending "golden age of gas" in its World Energy Outlook. Russia already sends Siberian gas to Germany via a 1,200 km undersea pipeline in a foretaste of how that golden era may play out. Something similar is happening in Central Asia, where gas is being piped to China from Turkmenistan, with Uzbekistan and Kazakhstan soon to follow as suppliers. Elsewhere, we're in the era of deepwater drilling in pristine Arctic environments, and getting to grips with the logistics of "pre-salt" geology off Brazil's coast in the South Atlantic. Some energy companies see potential in the tar sands of Canada and Venezuela, though this unconventional oil comes with its own set of environmental challenges. In the United States, technology investors are busy pouring molten salt into the pipes of solar concentrators to store energy overnight, or creating giant offshore wind farms that won't run out of puff at an inopportune moment. China pumps out solar panels at a rate and cost that has bitten deep into the viability of German producers. In Europe, the focus is on integrated power grids that will make the best use of renewable energy's potential. And all the time, we worry about the Pacific Ocean's volcanic ring of fire—or where best to put our next earthquake-proof and tsunami-proof nuclear power stations.

Earth Wars is an attempt to show just how interconnected our world has become in terms of the supply and demand for all sorts of resources, as living standards rise and energy consumption grows in advanced and emerging economies. As such, it is simply a snapshot of the conditions prevailing at the start of 2012, and some thoughts on where we are headed. China dominates the resources conversation, but the many challenges facing it are not to be minimised. Just keeping the country together is a constant battle for the leadership in Beijing, who must be ever mindful of the compact they have with the Chinese masses to deliver economic development in return for a delay in greater individual liberty. In India, democracy bumps up against the social frustrations of caste, color, corruption, religion, ethnicity, and gender every day, but the country's optimism about the future is undiminished.

Geoff Hiscock
January 2012

The Four Essentials

Food, Water, Energy, Metals

China has a foreign exchange reserve of $3 trillion and it is not surprising to think $1 trillion will be employed in assets outside of China within the next five to 10 years.
—Nomura China Chairman Yang Zhizhong, at the Boao Resources Forum in Perth, Australia, 12 July 2011

Food, water, energy, and metals: Keep up the supply of those four essentials, throw in some clean air and a peaceful disposition, and—short of a Hollywood-style *2012* cataclysm—the world will run smoothly forever. That's the theory, anyway, for twenty-first century optimists. The reality is that a secure supply of the first four essentials is far from assured. Big-power rivalry, surging demand for commodities, a rise in living standards for hundreds of millions of people eager to savour the delights of their first car, TV, computer, or mobile phone—or in the case of a billion poorer people, enjoy a second daily meal—means that the pressure on the planet's finite resources is rising rapidly. There is no easy safety valve to release. The 1.3 billion people in China, another 1.2 billion in India, and hundreds of millions in fast-growing, emerging economies such as Brazil, Russia, Indonesia, Turkey, Mexico, Poland, Nigeria, and

Vietnam do not want to be denied the fruits of their labours. They want what consumers in North America, Europe, and Japan already have. That is why the great battle for control of the world's resources is well and truly underway.

There are many fronts in this war. One starts deep in the desert country of the West Australian outback, where the sun beats down remorselessly on a forbidding landscape of salt pans, shifting red sand dunes, spinifex, and rocky protrusions. This is the heartland of the Yilgarn Craton, a massive block of weathered rock that takes up a vast swathe of inland Australia, underpinning its claim as the world's oldest continent. The mineral-rich craton is a crust created 2.7 billion years ago, pushed upward from the ocean floor as the earth began forming into the continents we know today.

A thousand kilometres (600 miles) by road northeast from the state capital of Perth stands one of the Yilgarn Craton's most significant place names: Mount Weld, the remnant of a volcano that blew up eons ago. At its central core, perhaps three kilometres (2 miles) in diameter, is a rich pipe of carbonatite, the host rock for something much more valuable. Mount Weld is a hot zone, repository of what may be the most important mining deposit outside of China: 24 million tonnes of rare earths resource, resulting in 1.9 million tonnes of rare earths oxide. More importantly, by the middle of 2012, it will offer one of the first new sources of rare earths supply outside China in a decade.

Around Mount Weld, the high-summer temperature regularly tops 38°C (100°F), crisping the sparse vegetation. The dry lakes are thick with salt, a legacy from millions of years of sea spray borne on the winds of the Indian Ocean and deposited hundreds of kilometres inland from the western coast.

On the surface, the land looks unforgiving and potentially fatal for a wayward traveller. But it is the treasure below ground that lures people into this harsh environment. Fortune seekers from Britain, America, and China came in their thousands in the late nineteenth century to search for gold in an area now believed to contain almost a third of the world's known gold reserves. A hundred years later, prospectors big and small pegged out claims for tenements rich in nickel, iron ore, copper, and zinc.

Now there is a new lure—rare earths: the 17 chemical elements that one day may prove the biggest mining bonanza of them all. Their names—scandium, yttrium, and the 15 lanthanides such as lanthanum and cerium—are yet to loom large in the public consciousness. But in the ongoing battle for control of the world's most valuable resources, rare earths and rare metals sit alongside oil, gas, uranium, coal, iron ore, copper, and gold as the materials that countries, companies, and consumers must have. Rare earths are in everything that is technologically hot: batteries for hybrid and electric cars, iPads, iPods, Blackberries and other smartphones, LED televisions, energy-efficient lights, lasers, camera lenses, permanent magnets, highly refractive glass, fluid catalytic cracking catalysts for oil refineries, catalytic converters for motor vehicle exhausts, X-ray machines, phosphors, computer memories, sophisticated military items such as night-vision goggles and missile guidance systems— the list goes on. In December 2010, the U.S. Department of Energy released its *Critical Materials Strategy* report that found five rare earth metals—dysprosium, neodymium, terbium, europium, and yttrium, as well as a processed rare metal, indium—were "most critical" in terms of supply for the United States over the next five years.[1] The big demand drivers are permanent magnets and battery alloy; by 2014, when global demand for rare earth oxides reaches 191,000 tonnes, about 55 percent will go to these two applications alone. The British Geological Survey's own Supply Risk List (see Exhibit 1.1) has rare earth elements as fifth on its list, with niobium behind antimony, mercury, tungsten, and the six platinum group elements (iridium, palladium, platinum, osmium, rhodium, and ruthenium). China is the leading producer of 28 of the 52 elements on the list, including antimony, mercury, tungsten, and rare earths.

Getting a secure supply of rare earths is exercising the minds of politicians, prospectors, and investors around the globe, particularly after China—which accounts for 97 percent of global production— cut back its exports in 2010 and again in 2011 to make it clear that the needs of its domestic users would take priority over exports.

1. Antimony 8.5	**4.** Tungsten 8.5
2. Platinum group elements 8.5	**5.** Rare earth elements 8.0
3. Mercury 8.5	**6.** Niobium 8.0

Exhibit 1.1   BGS Supply Risk List 2011 (1 = very low risk, 10 = very high risk)
Source: British Geological Survey, October 2011

Japanese electronics and precision equipment makers in particular are heavily reliant on rare earths. Although they are able to recycle some from discarded computers, mobile phones, and other electronic detritus, they get most of their supply from China. In fact, between 50 and 60 percent of China's rare earth exports go to Japanese buyers. But in September 2010, the buyers suffered something akin to a mini "oil shock." Their supplies from China slowed to a crawl, tied down by the sort of bureaucratic double-shuffling that the Japanese themselves once employed as a nontariff barrier against unwanted imports. There was no export ban, the Chinese declared, but the result was the same: shipments ground to a halt, and the Japanese electronics industry got very nervous. Japan's crime was to arrest the skipper of a Chinese fishing boat that collided with two Japanese coast guard vessels near a group of uninhabited islands in the East China Sea. The islands, known to Japan as the Senkaku and to China as the Diaoyu, are claimed by both sides. That there may also be oil and gas riches in the surrounding waters adds another economic dimension to their dispute.

One result from that confrontation was a quick deal by the Japanese trading house Sojitz to form a strategic alliance with the owner of the Mount Weld rare earths, the small Australian mining company Lynas Corp. Lynas, which bought the Mount Weld mining rights from global mining giant Rio Tinto in 2001, struck an agreement to supply its products to Sojitz and to accelerate its project's expansion with Sojitz's backing. It also has a joint venture with Germany's Siemens for future production of neodymium-based rare-earth magnets. According to Executive Chairman Nicholas Curtis, Lynas owns the world's richest known deposit of rare earths outside China. It claims an advantage in grade and composition over China's massive 40-million-tonne reserves at the Bayan Obo mines in Baotou, part of Inner Mongolia. According to Lynas, three of the most valuable rare earth elements—dysprosium, europium, and terbium, worth between $1.4 million and $3.8 million a tonne at January 2012 prices—are found at Mount Weld in concentrations at least double that found in the Baotou reserve.

That makes Mount Weld one of the global markers for rare earths. Apart from China, others are in South Africa, the United States, India, Mongolia, Kyrgyzstan, Vietnam, Canada, Brazil, Sweden, and Greenland, meaning that rare earths are not as rare as their name implies. But they are hard to extract economically. Many of the deposits found so far lack the concentrations that would make them a viable proposition. Others are in difficult or environmentally sensitive locations. Lead times to bring a mine into production can take up to a decade, plus the processing of rare earths ore is a dirty business, one that needs lots of water and leaves a lot of mess to clean up. Pollution is a major problem at Baotou, and few governments are prepared to sanction new projects because of the environmental issues. Lynas says its isolated Mount Weld operation, which began mining ore in mid-2011, meets international safety and environmental standards. It runs the crushed ore through a concentration plant on-site before stockpiling it for shipping to an advanced materials plant being built at Kuantan in the Malaysian state of Pahang, where it will be processed into separated rare earths products. Its first-phase production target of 11,000 tonnes in 2012 is expected to double in phase two to 22,000 tonnes.

China came close to buying Lynas in 2009, but a $500 million bid by the state-owned China Nonferrous Metal Mining (Group) Co., known as CNMC, to take a majority stake collapsed in the face of stringent conditions imposed by Australia's Foreign Investment Review Board. The Australian government insisted the Chinese company keep its stake below 50 percent and take only a minority of board seats—a stance that was unacceptable to CNMC. But why would China want to buy a smaller rival when it already has 97 percent of the market and its Baotou reserve has enough for 200 to 300 years of supply?

Clean Energy Technologies

One reason is the future demand for *clean energy* technologies. China, along with India, is fast becoming a global leader in wind and solar power. Large-scale wind turbines rely on permanent magnets, built from critical materials such as dysprosium, neodymium, praseodymium, and samarium. The same holds true for the thin films used in a solar panel's photovoltaic cells. The critical materials here are indium, gallium, and tellurium.

Lynas is not the only new candidate for a place at the rare earths top table. North American explorer Ucore hopes to have its Bokan Mountain project in Alaska, based on an old uranium mine, producing in 2015. Canada-listed Great Western Minerals has its Steenkampskrall project in South Africa, where an old Anglo-American thorium mine that closed in 1965 is to be recommissioned for its rare earth resource, with first output likely in 2013. Stans Energy has a similar plan and timetable for its Kutessay II mine in Kyrgyzstan, a past producer of heavy rare earth elements in the Soviet era. Greenland Minerals and Energy, another Australian-listed rare earths hopeful, has a multielement deposit of rare earths, uranium, and zinc at its Kvanefjeld project, on the southwest tip of Greenland. It says the reserve could sustain a large-scale mining operation for decades, with the potential to supply 20 percent of global demand for rare earths at low cost because of the revenue from uranium and zinc. But Greenland is a delicate environment, with more than its share of logistical challenges. Nothing is likely to emerge from Kvanefjeld until 2015 at the earliest.

Well before then, a U.S. contender—Molycorp's rare earths plant at Mountain Pass, California—will be back in production after being mothballed in 2002 under the weight of cut-price Chinese competition and an increasingly onerous set of environmental regulations. When Molycorp hits its stride at the end of 2012, it expects to be processing 20,000 tonnes a year of oxide, in what it calls its "mines to magnets" strategy. Molycorp also owns a rare-earth processing facility in Estonia, one of only two such plants in Europe. The United States is keen to see a steady supply of strategically critical materials coming from its own mines or from friendly nations. "Diversified global supply chains and multiple sources of materials are required to manage supply risk," the Department of Energy noted in its December 2010 report. "This means taking steps to facilitate extraction, refining and manufacturing here in the United States, as well as encouraging additional supplies around the world."[2] Industry expert Jack Lifton of Technology Metals Research says that whatever actions the United States takes, the focus must be on the security of the U.S. supply chain for rare earths, and their availability. "America has all of the technology to transform rare-earth ore concentrates, the first item in the rare-earth end-use product supply chain, into finished magnets and CFLs (compact fluorescent lamps)," he argues. "Yet we have simply abandoned these industrial steps, all of them, actually, for momentary cheaper prices."[3] Lifton also wants the world to be aware that there is a clear difference between light and heavy rare-earth elements in terms of supply. "The LREEs (light) are not rare . . . just too expensive to produce against the Chinese supply chain. On the other hand, HREEs (heavy) are scarce even in China . . . ," he wrote in December 2011.[4]

For resource seekers, a similarly strategic story is unfolding in South America, where the massive lithium deposits in the *salars* (salt pans) of the Andean plateau present what some analysts believe is the opportunity of a lifetime. Soft and silvery-white in colour, lithium is the lightest of all metals. It is used in ceramics, glasses, lubricants, pharmaceuticals, and, crucially, in lithium-ion batteries that power everything from watches, smartphones, iPods, and portable computers to hybrids and full electric vehicles (EVs). If the long-range forecasts are right, by 2020, up to 25 percent of the cars on the global auto market will be hybrids or EVs. That should mean a large market for batteries and consequent demand for lithium, though supply competition is likely to be fierce, with a likely over-supply until at least 2013.

Lithium Triangle of the Andes

In truth, there is no great shortage of lithium, but extracting it economically from salt-pan brines or hard rock can be another matter. Suppliers in South America, the United States, Australia, and China are working on a variety of resources and extraction techniques. For now, the cost advantage lies with lithium produced from brines, where the sun's evaporative power does most of the work. High in the Andes, in a part of the world subject to intense solar radiation and known as the *lithium triangle*, the flat, white *salars* that extend across Bolivia, Chile, and Argentina are deemed to be the world's richest source of lithium brines. Salar de Atacama in Chile, the adjoining Cauchari and Olaroz *salars* in Argentina and the massive 10,000-sq km Salar de Uyuni in Bolivia are the focus of global attention from investors, miners, and industrial groups keen to ensure they have a handle on lithium supply if—and this is a big if, given the recharging and recycling infrastructure required—demand for electric vehicles (EVs) takes off in the way some forecasters suggest, and if EV makers continue to use lithium in their batteries.

Lithium consumption in 2011 is around 120,000 tonnes of lithium carbonate equivalent (LCE). Only about 6,000 tonnes a year of LCE is for the batteries used in electric vehicles, but that ratio could change dramatically over the next decade if the long-awaited electric car age reaches critical momentum. In the view of metals consultancy SignumBOX, the consumption figure for the automotive industry could reach 180,000 tonnes of LCE by 2025.[5] Another analysis by the world's biggest hard-rock lithium producer, Australia-based Talison Lithium, suggests demand for all applications, including transport, could reach between 350,000 and 500,000 tonnes of LCE by 2020. According to the U.S. Geological Service, global lithium supply in 2015 will be about 250,000 tonnes of LCE. The British Geological Survey's 2011 *supply risk list* of 52 valuable metals confirms that lithium supply should not really be an issue. It puts lithium in the middle of the pack, ranked 23, equal to manganese, cobalt, gold, and cadmium, with a supply risk rating of 5.5 out of 10.[6]

The relatively plentiful supply of lithium has not stopped a cavalcade of contenders for South America's lithium brine resources. The players are many and varied, covering European, Japanese, Korean, Chinese, North American, Brazilian, and Australian interests. They include Japanese trading houses such as Toyota Tsusho, which has a stake in the Salar de Olaroz project with Australian miner Orocobre in Argentina; the South Korean trio of state-owned Korean Resources Corp. (Kores), trading house LG International and energy company GS Caltex, which are partners with Canadian explorer Lithium One in the Sal de Vida brine project in Argentina; Chilean fertiliser and mining group SQM (Sociedad Quimica y Minera de Chile), which mines Salar de Atacama in Chile and is the world's biggest producer of lithium from brine; Frankfurt-based Chemetall, which also operates at Salar de Atacama; and Chinese investment house Citic, which aims to work with state-owned Bolivia Mining Corp. (Comibol) in developing the Uyuni resource. Comibol also has Kores and steel giant Posco as potential partners in taking Uyuni lithium further to processing and eventual manufacture of lithium batteries in Bolivia.

Bolivia's Ambitious Pitch

Bolivia's President Evo Morales, who upset some of the world's biggest companies when he nationalized the country's oil and gas resources after he came to power in 2006, has consistently maintained he is not interested in Bolivia being just the starting point in the global lithium supply chain; he wants to develop a domestic battery industry and potentially a plant to make electric vehicles.

In its ambitious pitch to investors, Comibol says Bolivia holds 70 percent of the world's lithium reserves, with 100 million tonnes in the Uyuni, Coipasa, and other salt pans. It says that in comparison, Chile has 30 million tonnes, China 3 million tonnes, Argentina 2 million tonnes, and the rest of the world 7 million tonnes.[7] That's not a view shared by the U.S. Department of Energy, which in its *Critical Materials Strategy Report* of December 2010 and its update a year later, sees new low-cost lithium coming from Argentina, Chile, and the geothermal brines of the western United States, while noting that "currently and for the foreseeable future, Bolivia's lithium is only an uneconomic resource."[8]

The U.S. view tallies with the way Canadian company Lithium Americas sees its low-cost resource in Argentina on the Puna Plateau. There, Lithium Americas, which has EV maker Mitsubishi Motors and auto component supplier Magna International as its strategic partners, says its site straddling the Cauchari-Olaroz salt pans is the world's third-largest known lithium brine resource. It lies about 200 km east of the front-runner, Chile's Salar de Atacama, and about 200 km north of second-ranked Salar del Hombre Muerto, where U.S.-listed FMC Lithium operates. For now, SQM, Chemetall and FMC are the big three of brine-based lithium production, while Talison dominates hard-rock production from its Greenbushes plant in Western Australia. Between them, they account for more than 80 percent of all lithium production, though China is looking to exploit its own high-altitude salt pans in the Qaidam Basin, and the United States has its long-running Kings Mountain mine in North Carolina, plus Silver Peak and other deposits in Nevada. A host of junior miners are seeking to make an impression in the lithium marketplace, but the going is tough. In November 2010, Edward R. Anderson, the president of metals consultant TRU Group, warned: "Competition through 2020 will be increasingly fierce, making it virtually impossible for aspiring lithium businesses to ever turn a profit. Millions of dollars invested in these companies will be lost by unsuspecting investors."[9]

The lithium brine producers have the cost and quality advantage, but not time—the evaporation process can take up to 18 months. Hard-rock producers, who mine spodumene or petalite and then process the ore with heat and acid to extract lithium, can get their product into the market more quickly, but at a higher cost. And just possibly, there is something new in the lithium wings: U.S.

startup Simbol Materials aims to process brine used by geothermal power stations in California's Salton Sea and extract lithium chloride in just 90 minutes. Simbol's professed goal is to "fundamentally transform the critical materials supply chain."[10] Its partner in this ambitious undertaking is the Japanese trading house ITOCHU Corp. TRU's Anderson is skeptical of the Simbol claim, calling it a "very tall order" that does not change his view of the lithium supply-demand situation. In its 2010 report on electric vehicle batteries, the Boston Consulting Group predicted 14 million of the new cars sold in China, Japan, the United States, and Europe in 2020 would be EVs or hybrids.[11] Of these, 11 million would have lithium-ion batteries. BCG said this battery market would be worth about $25 billion. But lithium is a very small part of a battery's cost. The 20 kg of lithium likely to be found in an EV battery with a range of 160 km (100 miles) is worth about $100—hardly a critical factor in a vehicle selling for $30,000 plus. So why the rush to bring new supplies to market? The answer is that be it lithium, uranium, rare-earth elements, hydrocarbons, food, or water, everyone with a view longer than the next quarterly report wants to control the supply chain.

Multitude of Factors

Lithium and rare earths represent just a tiny part of the picture emerging in the early twenty-first century of a global struggle for resources between the big advanced economies (United States, Europe, and Japan) and the emerging economies of China, India, Brazil, and Russia. The search is breathtakingly broad in scope and geographic spread as each of the major players seeks control and security of supply over a string of valuable commodities. It reflects a multitude of factors coming together in the last few years to create a fear that someone somewhere is going to miss out. Those factors include the following:

- Very high economic growth rates of 7 to 10 percent a year in the world's two most populous countries of China and India are pushing up demand for the commodities needed to supply the twin building blocks of their industrial and agricultural economies: power and steel.
- The growth of a middle class is creating a huge demand for motor vehicles in these same two economies and in the "second

wave" of emerging economies such as Mexico, Brazil, Russia, Indonesia, Turkey, Vietnam, the Philippines, Malaysia, and Thailand.

- The global debate on climate change, emissions controls, and carbon taxes is accelerating the search for clean energy technologies such as wave, wind, and solar power, and a commitment by the coal industry and coal-fired power station operators to explore "clean coal" solutions.
- Hundreds of millions of people are being lifted out of poverty in Africa, Asia, and Latin America, allowing them to buy a second meal for the day. These higher living standards across the world mean greater consumption of food and water (and as a consequence, greater use of farming inputs such as fertiliser), raising fears that clean food and water will become scarce.
- Territorial ambitions and border disputes are intensifying as big powers jockey for potential oil and gas reserves in offshore zones of influence.
- Political upheaval in the Middle East and North Africa is changing relationships within the Organization of Petroleum Exporting Countries (OPEC).
- Big energy users such as China, the United States, India, Russia, and Japan are concerned about the security of their maritime supply lines. About 70 percent of the world's trade moves across the Indian Ocean between the Middle East and the Asia Pacific. A quarter of the world's crude oil trade passes through the Strait of Malacca, the 800-km (500-mile) stretch of water between the Indonesian island of Sumatra and the Malay peninsula that narrows to just 2.4 km (1.5 miles) wide at the Strait of Singapore, leading to the South China Sea.
- These security concerns are driving a resource diversification scramble. Africa, Indonesia, South America, the Central Asian states of Kazakhstan, Tajikistan, Kyrgyzstan, Uzbekistan, Turkmenistan, and the waters of the Arctic are all the subject of investment interest from global oil companies and miners. China is helping to build ports and rail lines in Africa, investing in Brazil's gas and power sector, and hoping to tie up more of Australia's iron ore and coal. India harbours the same ambitions.

To understand China and India's thinking, it helps to realise that an economy that grows at an average 10 percent a year doubles its size in seven years, and one that grows at 7 percent a year takes 10 years to double its size. China's average GDP growth for the seven years 2004 to 2010 was 11.0 percent, meaning its economy comfortably doubled in size during that time. For India, the figure was 8.1 percent. Brazil came in at 4.5 percent, even with a small contraction in 2009 because of the global financial crisis. Russia averaged 4.7 percent, after a 7 percent fall in 2009. For the United States and Japan, the comparable five-year figures were 1.6 percent and 0.8 percent, respectively, again with contractions in 2009. The Eurozone contains the big economies of Germany and France, but problems in Italy (and on the periphery in Greece, Ireland, Portugal, and elsewhere) leave the EU looking lacklustre at best. The old twentieth-century world order is giving way to an Asian-led expansion.

As a consequence of its rapid growth over the past two decades, China now consumes more energy, sells more cars, and produces more steel than the United States. It uses more iron ore, copper, lead, zinc, aluminium, chromium, tungsten, titanium, and rare earths than any other nation. By 2020, its high-speed rail network—even with the setbacks of its mid-2011 crash—will have likely grown to 16,000 km (10,000 miles), whisking passengers and high-value cargo at 320 km/h (200 mph) between every major Chinese city. Building this mammoth network and the rolling stock to run on it involves a huge amount of raw materials, including steel.

It is a similar growth story for India, although at a less frenetic pace. Again, steel and power are the sectors where the most activity is bubbling. Even with the push toward cleaner energy, coal will remain the backbone of India's power generation until at least 2025, meaning that its demand for coal will continue to rise. State-owned Coal India Ltd., already the world's biggest coal producer with output in 2010 of around 460 million tonnes, is scouring the world for more coal mines in Africa, Indonesia, Australia, and the United States. On the nuclear front, some of India's ambitions have been delayed because it is not a signatory to the Non-Proliferation Treaty. Despite the Fukushima nuclear crisis in Japan, India wants to build more nuclear power plants. Russia is happy to oblige India with its construction technology and is eager to stay ahead of competition from France and more recently from the United States with the signing of the U.S.–India nuclear agreements. Indeed, Russia is happy to supply India with energy (and arms) in a multitude of forms. A gas pipeline from Russia through the Central Asian nation of Turkmenistan—which has the world's fourth-largest reserves of natural gas—is a long-held dream for both parties, but the political realities of a hostile Pakistan and an Afghanistan constantly at war make this hard to achieve. The same obstacles apply for a gas pipeline from Iran to Pakistan and on to India.

According to the U.S. Energy Information Administration (EIA), Russia holds the world's largest natural gas reserves, the second largest coal reserves, and the eighth largest crude oil reserves.[12] In 2010–2011 it was the world's largest producer of crude oil, surpassing Saudi Arabia. Most of the oil it exports goes to European customers such as Germany and Holland. There is immense potential for further oil and gas developments in Arctic waters, Siberia, and the Sakhalin region, where China, Japan, and South Korea are natural customers. Japan once held half of Sakhalin, there is a large Korean population, and Chinese influence everywhere in the Russian Far East is growing.

Halfway around the world in South America, the hydrocarbons boom is picking up speed. In 2006, Brazil's Petrobras and its partners discovered the Tupi oil and gas field in the Santos Basin, an area of the South Atlantic Ocean about 250 km (160 miles) south of Rio de Janeiro. Further recent discoveries mean the area may prove to be the largest find made anywhere in the past 10 years. According to the EIA, these "pre-salt" oil deposits, found in rocks beneath the salt layer at combined water, salt, and rock depths of up to 6,700 metres (22,000 feet), have the potential to transform Brazil into one of the largest oil producers in the world.[13] Venezuela, a founder member of the Organization of Petroleum Exporting Countries (OPEC), has bigger reserves and is the world's seventh largest oil producer, but since President Hugo Chavez's nationalization of the oil industry in 2007, output has declined. Colombia, Peru, Bolivia, Argentina, Chile, and Ecuador all produce oil and are the subject of interest from national and global oil companies. Colombia is growing its role as a coal exporter, too, with more supply earmarked for China and India.

New Products for Old Trading Routes

In a sense, this scramble for resources is simply a continuation of history—only the players and the products have changed. The Romans had been trading with India since before the first century, either via the overland caravan route through Persia, or by boat through the Red Sea. Indian trade extended east to China and Southeast Asia, as well as west to Africa and beyond. In 1514, when the first Portuguese explorers sailed up the Pearl River to the port we now know as Guangzhou on the South China coast, adventurers and merchants from Africa, India, Persia, and the Arabian Peninsula had been living and trading there for more than 700 years. Spices, textiles, gems, opium, and timber were to be found in the holds of all manner of sailing craft riding the monsoon winds around the coasts of Southeast Asia and India across the Arabian Sea to Africa, Persia, and Arabia. From the port of Aden at the entrance to the Red Sea, some Asian traders ventured as far as Cairo, Alexandria, the Mediterranean and Venice. From Europe, the intrepid Franciscan monk Giovanni da Pian del Carpine had travelled overland to the Mongol court in 1246, and Marco Polo, his father, and uncle (probably) had been as far as the Chinese imperial capital of Beijing by the late thirteenth century. In the other direction, the Ming dynasty emperor Yongle had sent massive fleets from China west to India and beyond, beginning in 1405 with a 62-ship convoy that reached Calicut on the southwest coast of India. At least seven fleets under the overall command of Admiral Zheng He sailed out from the China coast in search of treasure, tribute, and geographic knowledge, reaching as far west as the coast of Africa, into the Red Sea, the Arabian Peninsula, and the Persian Gulf. The last voyage set out in 1432 and returned to Nanjing in 1434 after reaching Hormuz at the entrance to the Persian Gulf. Zheng He died in 1433 on the return leg. China clearly had the technology to mount massive voyages of discovery, but there was no religious or commercial imperative to do so. It was simply a question of prestige: to impress on other civilizations that the Middle Kingdom truly was the centre of the world and tribute was expected.

For resource-hungry Europe, it was a different matter altogether. Opening up a sea route around the southern tip of Africa to Asia at the end of the fifteenth century offered the prospect of a rich trade in spices, silks, and porcelain, and the opportunity to control new lands. The Portuguese were in the vanguard, but by 1521, seafarers from the other great European maritime power of the day, Spain, landed in the Philippines, and within 50 years had set up a Spanish capital at Manila. Under two treaties of 1494 and 1529, the

Portuguese and the Spanish had already decided how they would carve up the "new worlds" they believed they were discovering in South America and in the Asia Pacific. The Portuguese and the Spanish were just the first wave of European colonizers. By the early 1600s, the Dutch were in Java, seeking to tie up the spice trade through the Dutch East India Company. Although the Portuguese had reached Calicut and Goa in 1498, it was the British and French, along with the Dutch and the Danes, who vied to establish trading posts along the coast of India in the early seventeenth century. By the end of the eighteenth century, Britain was the dominant colonial power in India and had also been able to establish a solid foothold at Guangzhou, which was rapidly becoming one of the world's busiest trading hubs.

When British demand for tea from China rocketed in the early 1800s, there was no item the Chinese wanted from the West that would balance the trade position—until Indian raw cotton and then Indian opium took on this role. The opium trade, with its deleterious effect on Chinese users and its attraction for criminal elements, sparked trouble between Britain and China, leading to what became known as the Opium Wars of 1839 and 1856. As a consequence, China was forced to open more of its ports. Merchants, missionaries, administrators, and assorted soldiers of fortune from Europe, America, Japan, and Russia poured into these enclaves up and down the China coast, eager to make their mark. It would be more than a century before China could free itself from their advances and another 70 years on top of that before it would approach its fifteenth-century position as the centre of the world.

The World in 2050

In January 2011, the global bank HSBC—which traces its history to the formation of two bank branches in Hong Kong and Shanghai in 1865—issued a report titled "The World in 2050."[14] It concluded that by 2050, the emerging world—including China and India—will have increased its output fivefold and will be larger than the developed world. Nineteen of the top 30 economies by gross domestic product (GDP) will be countries that it currently labels as emerging. China and India will be the largest and third-largest economies, with the United States as No. 2. Japan will be fourth, followed by Germany, United Kingdom, Brazil, Mexico, France, and Canada in the top 10. Russia would rank fifteenth. HSBC predicted that "substantial progress" would be made by a host of other emerging economies, including Turkey, Indonesia, Egypt, Malaysia, Thailand, Colombia, and Venezuela, all of which would rank in the top 30.[15] China, with its massive pile of foreign reserves ($3.2 trillion at October 2011), has the money to buy virtually whatever it wants—assuming it can keep its society together. With $320 billion, India has only a tenth of China's reserves, but it is pursuing the same determined scramble for resource security. The United States, Europe, and Japan are not likely to give up easily in their own pursuit of ever-higher living standards through investments in technology and productive growth.

And what of the food, energy, water, and other natural resource constraints that might apply in 2050? HSBC says that the world is already in a period of "ecological deficit" where it is depleting natural resources faster than they can be replenished.[16] Short of a major change in the way the world operates, the depletion rate is destined to grow. This is the fundamental challenge for the biggest users, given that the impact of their decisions flows well beyond their own borders. The global resources war has a long way to run yet.

Notes

1. U.S. Department of Energy, "Critical Materials Strategy Report" (15 December 2010), http://energy.gov/downloads/us-department-energy-critical-materials-strategy-0.
2. Ibid.
3. Jack Lifton, Technology Metals Research, "Heavy Rare Earths in America, Crystal Balls and Brass Balls" (4 August 2011), www .techmetalsresearch.com/2011/08/heavy-rare-earths-in-america-crystal-balls-brass-balls/.
4. Ibid.
5. Analysis by SignumBOX, Santiago, "Lithium, Batteries and Vehicles: Perspectives and Trends" (1 October 2011). www.signumbox.com/signumbox-analysis/.
6. British Geological Service, "BGS Risk List 2011" (October 2011), www .bgs.ac.uk.
7. Bolivia Mining Corporation (Comibol) presentation at President Evo Morales press conference, La Paz, "National Strategy for the Bolivian Evaporative Resources Industrialization"(21 October 2010).
8. U.S. Department of Energy, "Critical Materials Strategy Report."

9. Edward R. Anderson, TRU Group, "Shocking Future Battering the Lithium Industry through 2020" (5 November 2010), http://trugroup .com/whitepapers/TRU-Lithium-Outlook-2020.pdf.

10. Simbol Materials media release, "Simbol Materials Advances U.S. EV Battery Material Production" (28 September 2011), www.prnewswire .com/news-releases/simbol-materials-advances-us-ev-battery-material-production-introduces-worlds-highest-purity-lithium-130682848.html.

11. Boston Consulting Group, Detroit, "Batteries for Electric Cars: Challenges, Opportunities, and the Outlook to 2020" (7 January 2010), www.bcg.com/documents/file36615.pdf.

12. U.S. Energy Information Administration, Russia Country Analysis Brief (November 2010), www.eia.gov/countries/country-data.cfm?fips=RS.

13. U.S. Energy Information Administration, Brazil Country Analysis Brief (January 2011), www.eia.gov/countries/country-data.cfm?fips=BR.

14. HSBC, "The World in 2050" (4 January 2011), www.hsbcnet.com/ gbm/global-insights/insights/2011/world-in-2050.html.

15. Ibid.

16. Ibid.

CHAPTER

Geographical Flashpoints

The Trouble with Lines on a Map

For to win one hundred victories in one hundred battles is not the acme of skill. To subdue the enemy without fighting is the acme of skill.

—Chinese military strategist Sun Tzu
(*The Art of War,* circa 500 BCE)

Deep in the western Himalayan mountains stands the high-altitude desert of Aksai Chin, one of the flashpoints that set off the short, sharp border war that India and China fought in late 1962. It is a part of the world where boundaries have never been precisely demarcated, and where the geopolitical intrigues of Russia and Britain in the nineteenth and twentieth centuries could see the borders of India, Afghanistan, Tibet, and China shift back and forth with the political tide of the day. During the British India era that ended in 1947, no military outposts marked the extent of the Aksai Chin claim—it was merely a civil servant's line on a map. Nonetheless, India sees it as an integral part of its territory, and claims that the 38,000 sq km of Aksai Chin held by China is part of Indian Kashmir and must be returned.

Although Aksai Chin has no mineral wealth, it is strategically important. China's seizure of the area allowed it to defend the

19

"secret road" it had built to connect its westernmost territory of Xinjiang with Tibet, the better to open up Tibet's mineral resources to greater exploitation. Today, a whole series of roads link Tibet with China, and Aksai Chin's importance may have more to do with keeping control of the eastern flank of the Karakoram Pass, where an old (now closed) caravan route once ran into China from Ladakh in India. The ill-defined border with India's arch-enemy Pakistan is about 100 km to the west, near the Siachen Glacier where Indian and Pakistani forces have faced off over the years on what is the world's highest, coldest, and most forbidding battlefield. Further to the northwest, China and Pakistan have their own border crossing at the Khunjerab Pass on the Karakoram Highway linking Gilgit in Pakistan with Kashgar in Xinjiang, China.

Thousands of kilometres to the east of Aksai Chin is the other main front for the 1962 war—an area in the eastern Himalayas known by India as Arunachal Pradesh. One of the Arunachal Pradesh districts occupied by Chinese troops during the war is Tawang, an important trading town that sits below the seventeenth-century Tawang Monastery. China maintains that Tawang and the other districts of Arunachal Pradesh are actually part of South Tibet, given up illegally by autonomous Tibet under the 1914 Simla Accord. This territorial agreement between Britain (represented by Sir Henry McMahon) and Tibet (represented by Lochen Shatra), but never accepted by the Chinese representative at the talks in the Indian hill town of Shimla, set out the *McMahon Line* as the notional border between India and Tibet. But its status was hazy from the outset, and it was not until 1937 that a Survey of India map for the first time showed the McMahon Line incorporating Tawang into India as the official boundary.

Up until the 1980s, there was a general view that China would acknowledge Indian sovereignty over Arunachal Pradesh if India would abandon its Aksai Chin claim. But that view no longer prevails; China more than ever seems keen to control Arunachal Pradesh. When the Dalai Lama—the Tibetan Buddhist leader who has lived in India since fleeing China in 1959—visited Tawang in 2009, China objected, and when Indian Prime Minister Manmohan Singh visited Arunachal Pradesh later the same year, the Chinese government warned India against "triggering disturbances in the disputed region."[1] However, Singh has made it clear that Tawang and the rest of Arunachal Pradesh are an integral part of India.

During a visit there in January 2008, he told a rally: "The sun kisses India first in Arunachal Pradesh. It is our Land of the Rising Sun."[2]

Unlike the icy wasteland of Aksai Chin, Arunachal Pradesh is rich in coal and hydrocarbons, and its rivers are also well-suited to hydropower. According to the Arunachal Pradesh government, it is the least explored of all Indian states, but has substantial coal reserves near Bhalukpong, which lies to the southeast of Tawang in neighbouring West Kameng district, and at Namchik-Namphuk, which is further to the east in Changlang district near the border with Burma. There are also oil and gas reserves at Kharsang and Diyun, both in Changlang district. But exploration and development of these resources face big challenges, chief among them the general remoteness from major population centres. Transport and other development costs are high and there is what the government terms "poor connectivity . . . and poor infrastructure."[3] Finally, there are the environmental and social issues of protecting the forests and the people that live within them. Against this background of remote and infrastructure-starved locations, how India and China resolve their territorial issues may well determine the course of prosperity for half the world. On the surface, things look relatively buoyant: There is a $60 billion bilateral trade relationship, growing so rapidly that Singh and Chinese Premier Wen Jiabao were able to set a 2015 target of $100 billion when they met in New Delhi in December 2010. "There is enough space in the world for the development of both India and China," they agreed.[4] But 50 years after the 1962 war, the lack of a proper border settlement drags heavily on relations between Beijing and New Delhi.

Long Trading History

Although their borders may remain in dispute, what is not in dispute is the long history of trade between India and China, going back several thousand years to when ships of the Roman Empire along with Arab and African trading vessels, propelled by the southwest monsoon, called at points on the Indian coast on their way to the great ports of Indonesia, Vietnam, and southern China. The kingdom of Aksum (modern Eritrea and northern Ethiopia), on the northeast coast of Africa facing the Red Sea, was one of the first of these ancient empires to use the monsoon to facilitate the two-way trade in spices, gold, pearls, ivory, glass, silk, and exotic animals.

The Aksumites, the Romans, the Arabs, and later the Greeks and Persians, all found their way to the harbours of Barbaricum (modern-day Karachi in Pakistan), Barygaza (Bharuch in modern Gujarat state, India), and Muziris in Kerala. Around the coast of what is now Tamil Nadu state were other ports such as Korkai, Kaveripattinam (now Puhar) and Arikamedu, where Roman pottery artifacts have been found. Arikamedu lies just south of the modern city of Puducherry, once the toehold of the French in India and still one of the few repositories of French cultural influence in the country. Puducherry (or Pondicherry, as it was known until 2006) was a French colony until 1954, the result of the inroads made 200 years earlier by Joseph-Francois Dupleix, governor general of the French establishments in India and great rival of the British trading clerk-turned-military man, Lord Robert Clive.

A thousand years ago, trading vessels would make their way from India east across that part of the Indian Ocean known as the Andaman Sea, into the Malacca Strait and on to Sumatra and the Malay Peninsula, often stopping at the capital of the Srivijaya empire (Palembang) before turning north to Tonkin and the Chinese ports of Beihai, Guangzhou, Quanzhou, Zhangzhou, and Xiamen (Amoy) and Ningbo. Guangzhou, the biggest port of them all, lies at the head of the Pearl River Delta and has a history dating back 3,000 years. As early as the Tang dynasty (618–907 CE) it was home to thriving communities of Indian and Arab traders.

Long before the great fifteenth century, Chinese armadas sailed out from Taicang (a port area near Shanghai) under the command of Admiral Zheng He to explore the "western oceans" and trade with Southeast Asia, India, Africa, the Middle East, and (possibly) the Mediterranean states. Guangzhou was the busiest entrepôt on the Chinese coast. It gained further prominence from the sixteenth century onwards as first the Portuguese and then a succession of other European seafarers came calling, looking for exotic goods to take back to their bases in India. They called the city Canton; by 1699, the British East India Company had set up a substantial commercial centre there. Traders from the United States, Scandinavia, France, Holland, Spain, Russia, and elsewhere followed suit and settled into a reasonably amicable pattern with China's Qing administration that lasted until the early nineteenth century. This was the era of the *thirteen factories,* the foreigners' quarters outside the city walls that served as business markets, rather than manufacturing centres.

But the India–China connection took a turn for the worse with the full exploitation of the opium trade in the eighteenth and nineteenth centuries. Although markets in Europe wanted an extensive range of Chinese goods, including tea, silk, and porcelain, the Chinese needed very little from the West. Only gold and silver were much in demand, plus one other commodity—opium from India. By imperial decree, the importation and smoking of opium in China was illegal, but demand was insatiable. The Portuguese were early traders in this drug, followed by the Dutch, who transshipped it to China via their East Indies capital of Batavia (Jakarta). But it was the British who turned the opium trickle into a flood, taking over Bengal in 1764 and supplanting the Indian merchants, who to this point had controlled the poppy fields of Patna, along the Ganges River. From then on, opium grown under contract to the British East India Company in Bengal was shipped to Guangzhou and distributed through the Chinese hinterland, creating millions of addicts. Further to the west in the Malwa region of what is now Madhya Pradesh state, more opium was being grown for the China trade. Much of this production was controlled by business families based in Bombay (now Mumbai). Parsi merchants such as the Jeejeebhoys, Jivanjis, Banajis, and Wadias ran ships to China, established their own companies in Guangzhou, and entered partnerships with British trading houses such as Jardine Matheson. Bombay's economy was so closely intertwined with the India-China opium trade that it was known as the "Opium City."[5]

The Opium Wars

The Chinese emperor's foreign trade commissioner Lin Zexu sought to end the trade first by diplomacy and then by force, seizing and destroying 20,000 chests of opium found in the warehouses of foreign merchants in Guangzhou in June 1839. It was not something the British were inclined to take lying down; the result was the first Opium War (1839–1842), which saw British forces occupy Shanghai and lay siege to Guangzhou and other Chinese ports. Under the terms of the Chinese surrender, five ports were opened to international trade and the island of Hong Kong was ceded to the British crown. A second Opium War followed (1856–1860), resulting in another defeat for China and the addition of land on Kowloon Peninsula to the British colony of Hong Kong. Indian opium imports, carried in the fast and graceful clipper ships that would make the return voyage with a cargo of Chinese tea, continued into the second half of the nineteenth century and reached a peak of 6,700 tonnes in 1880 before being gradually replaced by Chinese home-grown opium.[6]

Today, the giant container ships that nose their way up the Pearl River towards Guangzhou, its new Nansha terminal, and the associated container port of Shenzhen may conceivably still carry narcotics, but there is much more money in the daily to-and-fro of international commerce. Raw materials and semifinished goods of all description pour into southern China from around the world, there to be finished, packaged, and sent back out to overseas and domestic customers. Six of the world's ten busiest container ports are in China (see Exhibit 2.1), led by Shanghai with 29.1 million TEUs (20-foot equivalent units) in 2010; Shenzhen and Guangzhou between them handle 45 million a year. Nearby Hong Kong handles another 23 million. Long-time global leader Singapore (28.4 million in 2010) now ranks second in container throughput but remains the world's busiest port in total shipping tonnage. One pointer to how the world has shifted in the last 20-odd years: In 1989, the Japanese port of Kobe ranked fifth among the world's top container ports and Yokohama and Tokyo figured in the top 20. By 2010, there was not a single Japanese port among the top 20.[7]

Less than 20 years ago, state-supported piracy along the Chinese coast was a serious issue for mariners. Now, keeping the sea lanes into Hong Kong, Shenzhen, Guangzhou, and other Chinese ports open and free from piracy or terrorism is something of critical importance to China and its trading partners. All of this makes the

1. Shanghai 29.1	**6.** Ningbo-Zhoushan 13.1
2. Singapore 28.4	**7.** Guangzhou 12.5
3. Hong Kong 23.7	**8.** Qingdao 12.0
4. Shenzhen 22.5	**9.** Dubai 11.6
5. Busan 14.2	**10.** Rotterdam 11.1

Exhibit 2.1   World's Top Container Ports (millions of TEUs in 2010)

Source: World Shipping Council, 2011

South China Sea one of the most strategically important stretches of water in the world, particularly when it comes to the oil tankers and specialised bulk carriers that bring energy resources and other raw materials to China, Japan, South Korea, and Taiwan. As much as a third of the world's traded crude oil passes through these waters. China says it wants peaceful, cooperative, and mutually beneficial relations with its neighbours in the South China Sea, but rich fishery stocks and potential energy reserves make this area a place of ongoing tension. China is involved in a number of disputed sites, most notably the Spratlys (Nansha) and Paracels (Xisha), with Vietnam, the Philippines, Malaysia, Taiwan, and Brunei. Further to the north, in the East China Sea, China is in dispute with Japan over the Senkaku Islands (known by China as the Diaoyutai). A sample of the rhetoric that prevails comes from this editorial commentary in China's state-controlled *Global Times* newspaper on 21 June 2011:

> Vietnam has been taking risky actions in the South China Sea for some time. It has occupied 29 Chinese islands. It has been gaining the most benefits from undersea natural gas and oil exploitation. It is also the most aggressive in dealing with China . . . China has to send a clear message that it will take whatever measures necessary to protect its interests in the South China Sea. If Vietnam continues to provoke China in this region, China will first deal with it with maritime police forces, and if necessary, strike back with naval forces.[8]

Vietnam controls the largest number of islands in the Spratlys group, which is situated between Vietnam and the western coasts of the Philippines, Brunei, and Malaysia's Sabah and Sarawak states on Borneo. The Philippines, Malaysia, Taiwan, and China all seek to make their presence felt. Taiwan, for example, controls Taiping Island, the largest islet in the Spratly chain, and the nearby Pratas Islands (Dongsha). In 1995, the Chinese navy built an installation on Mischief Reef that brought it into conflict with the Philippines, and since then, there have been further maritime incidents between the two. The other island group, the Paracels, lies east of Vietnam and south of China's Hainan Island. Chinese and then-South Vietnamese naval forces fought a battle there in 1974 that left 18 dead and resulted in Chinese control of the islands. Another sea battle at Johnson

Reef in the Spratlys in March 1988 left 70 Vietnamese sailors dead and 6 killed on the Chinese side. Chinese patrol boats occasionally come up against Vietnamese fishing boats around the islands.

In early 1979, China briefly invaded Vietnam, ostensibly to protect ethnic Chinese in Vietnam and to protest Vietnam's occupation of the Spratly Islands. But it was also seen as a response to Vietnam's own invasion of Cambodia in 1978 that had dislodged the China-backed Khmer Rouge regime in Phnom Penh. As well, China was sending a message that the mutual defence treaty Vietnam had signed with the Soviet Union in November 1978 would not protect it from China's military might. China's invasion lasted only one month, but it destroyed significant infrastructure in the northern part of Vietnam as it withdrew. A decade of tension followed, with occasional maritime clashes over the Spratlys and Paracels, until relations were normalised in 1990. But the territorial irritant remains. In mid-2011, China announced it would substantially beef up its paramilitary Maritime Surveillance Force that patrols these waters. By 2020, it plans to have more than 500 ships and 15,000 personnel on duty—far more than any other regional claimant—while the United States continues to press what it considers its right to operate in waters off the Chinese coast. At the same time China was announcing its naval expansion plans, a report by the Australian think tank the Lowy Institute was warning that "risk-taking behaviour by Chinese naval and auxiliary forces, combined with Asia's lack of confidence-building measures, adds up to real possibilities of diplomatic crisis and armed confrontation drawing in the United States and other powers." The report's principal author, Rory Medcalf, says there is an "urgent need to improve and actually use communications channels between the Chinese and other militaries."[9]

Two Views of the 2009 *USNS Impeccable* Incident

The United States and China disagree over free navigation rights in parts of the South China Sea claimed by China as its territory. In March 2009, Chinese vessels and the *USNS Impeccable*, an ocean surveillance ship, were involved in an incident about 120 km south of China's Hainan Island.

U.S. Defense Department statement (9 March 2009):

On March 8, 2009, five Chinese vessels shadowed and aggressively manoeuvred in dangerously close proximity to *USNS Impeccable*, in

(continued)

(*Continued*)

an apparent coordinated effort to harass the U.S. ocean surveillance ship while it was conducting routine operations in international waters. The Chinese vessels surrounded *USNS Impeccable*, two of them closing to within 50 feet, waving Chinese flags and telling *Impeccable* to leave the area. Because the vessels' intentions were not known, *Impeccable* sprayed its fire hoses at one of the vessels in order to protect itself. The Chinese crewmembers disrobed to their underwear and continued closing to within 25 feet. *USNS Impeccable's* master used bridge-to-bridge radio circuits to inform the Chinese ships in a friendly manner that it was leaving the area and requested a safe path to navigate. A short time later, two of the PRC vessels stopped directly ahead of *USNS Impeccable*, forcing *Impeccable* to conduct an emergency "all stop" in order to avoid collision. They dropped pieces of wood in the water directly in front of *Impeccable's* path. The incident took place in international waters in the South China Sea, about 75 miles south of Hainan Island. It was preceded by days of increasingly aggressive conduct by Chinese vessels.[10]

Chinese Foreign Ministry spokesman Ma Zhaoxu (10 March 2009):

China has lodged a solemn representation to the United States as the *USNS Impeccable* conducted activities in China's special economic zone in the South China Sea without China's permission. We demand that the United States put an immediate stop to related activities and take effective measures to prevent similar acts from happening. The U.S. claims are gravely in contravention of the facts and confuse black and white and they are totally unacceptable to China.[11]

The United States and China each continues to maintain it was in the right in the *USNS Impeccable* incident. The broader issue of territorial claims in the South China Sea has been raised in regional discussions, such as the East Asia Summit in Bali in November 2011.

The Senkaku Islands, which lie about 200 km (120 miles) northeast of Taiwan and about 320 km (200 miles) southwest of Okinawa in the East China Sea, are administered by Japan, but both China and Taiwan lay claim to them. Japan insists the Senkakus, a group of eight uninhabited islands on the continental shelf, have been Japanese territory since 1895 and are protected under the U.S.–Japan security treaty. China's response is that it has "indisputable sovereignty" over the islands "which have been China's inalienable territory since ancient times."[12] The islands have long been used as a temporary base for fishing vessels, but conflict has only emerged since the 1970s, when it appeared that there could be substantial oil and gas reserves around the islands. The Chunxiao gas fields, for example, sit within waters where the competing exclusive economic zones of China and Japan overlap. That the islands lie in waters between China's commercial capital of Shanghai and Japan's biggest military base on Okinawa adds to the potential for friction. Various protest groups have made landings on the islands, and there have been incidents between Japanese coastguard ships and Chinese and Taiwanese fishing boats. Both China and Japan have begun oil and gas exploration and drilling programs. Although joint development of the gas fields has been proposed, no real progress has been made along these lines. In May 2011, China State Shipbuilding Corp. launched its first deepwater oil rig, a 31,000-tonne platform built at a cost of close to $1 billion. It is to be used by state-owned China National Offshore Oil Corp. (CNOOC) to explore in the deepest waters of the East and South China Seas.

In the past, China's "historic claims" also extended to part of Indonesia's Natuna Islands, an archipelago in the South China Sea about 250 km northwest of the island of Borneo, and well south of the Chinese coast. China has made no recent moves to expand its influence over Natuna, which hosts massive gas reserves that Indonesia has been tapping for two decades. Indonesia struck an agreement with U.S. oil major ExxonMobil in 1995 to develop Natuna, but it has proven to be a difficult operating environment, and in 2008 Indonesia handed over Exxon's development rights for the eastern field to state-owned oil company Pertamina. In 2011, Pertamina began developing part of East Natuna with Exxon, Total, and Malaysia's Petronas. Separately, since 2001 a 650-km subsea pipeline from the western part of the Natuna field has supplied gas to Singapore. Independent producer Premier Oil, which bought Chevron's Natuna interest in 1996, has done much of the exploring and development of fields, particularly in the west near Vietnam's offshore fields.

China's Northern Borders

China's territorial issues extend beyond these waters. In the far north of the country, Chinese border troops skirmished with their Russian counterparts in 1969 along the disputed line of the Amur and Ussuri

Rivers, near the Russian city of Khabarovsk. There were serious clashes over ownership of several islands in the river system. Inconclusive border talks dragged on for decades, and it was not until 2008 that the river border was finally demarcated to the satisfaction of both sides.

Also in the north, China shares a border with land-locked Mongolia, which gained independence from China only in 1921 and then fell under Soviet influence until a democratic revolution in 1990. The main rail line into Mongolia from China is sometimes closed at the border point of Erlianhot, usually when the Chinese are displeased at something Mongolia has done. Resource-rich Mongolia has attracted the attention of global mining companies such as Vale, Xstrata, and the Anglo-Australian giant Rio Tinto, which is developing the Oyu Tolgoi high-grade copper and gold mine in the South Gobi Desert with Canada's Ivanhoe Mines and the Mongolian government. First production should be in 2013. Even so, Russia and China are regarded as having the inside track so far in business dealings. Mongolia is already China's largest coking coal supplier, and sends virtually all of its coal and copper exports to China. That might change if Mongolia pursues a proposed rail line to Russian seaports. But given that Oyu Tolgoi is less than 100 km from the Chinese border and that the electricity to power the mine will come initially from China, production is likely to be moved out on the Chinese rail system.

Japan has its own territorial issues with Russia, and has been pressing for the return of four small islands just off the coast of Hokkaido, its main northern island. Japan calls these islands the Northern Territories. For the Russians, they are the Southern Kurils, the last part of the long Kurils volcanic island chain that runs from Kamchatka Peninsula down to Hokkaido. Russia has held the islands since the end of World War II, and its refusal to countenance their return to Japan is the reason the two nations have never signed a formal peace treaty. Potential offshore oil and gas reserves, plus the area's importance as a fishery ground enriched by the cold waters of the Oyashio current, keep the dispute simmering. The islands also have geothermal power resources.

A 45 km (27 mile)-wide stretch of water known as the Soya Strait separates the Japanese city of Wakkanai at the top of Hokkaido from the southern tip of Russia's biggest island, Sakhalin. The island, which lies just off the Siberian coast fronting the Sea of Okhostk, has been a setting for disputes with Japan over the past 200 years. Japan claimed sovereignty over Sakhalin (which it calls Karafuto) in 1807, but Russian settlers moved in and began working the coal mines there. The island was divided after the Russo–Japanese war of 1904–1905, with Japan taking South Sakhalin below the 50th parallel. At the end of World War II, the Soviet Union resumed control of the whole island. In the last 20 years, offshore oil and gas deposits have been found and are being developed in what its operators call a technically challenging and hostile subarctic environment. The first project, Sakhalin 1, is a consortium that includes ExxonMobil, Russian oil major Rosneft, India's ONGC, and Japan's Sakhalin Oil & Gas Development. Another consortium involving Gazprom, Shell, and Japanese investors Mitsui and Mitsubishi, is doing the same for the Sakhalin 2 project. This project required building two 800 km (500 mile) pipelines that take oil and gas from fields in the north of Sakhalin to the ice-free export terminal of Prigorodnoye in Aniva Bay in the south. The Sakhalin 3, 4, and 5 projects wait in the wings for what is destined to be the biggest hydrocarbon development in Asia, with a potential total investment of $40 billion. In 2006, Exxon Neftegas, the Sakhalin 1 operator, completed its own 220 km (136 mile) pipeline across the Tatar Strait from Sakhalin to the DeKastri oil terminal on the mainland, the better to ship oil and gas to customers in Japan and Korea. Japanese companies are happy to be investors in these projects, but it still rankles with some Japanese that a foreign-held island so close to Hokkaido could be so rich in energy resources.

Caspian's Strategic Significance

Another Russian energy source is the Caspian Sea, widely considered to be among the most strategically significant oil and gas basins in the world. The sea was once shared between the old Soviet Union and Iran, but now is host to five littoral states: Russia, Azerbaijan, Kazakhstan, Turkmenistan, and Iran. Russia essentially has resolved its fisheries and hydrocarbon resource-sharing with Azerbaijan and Kazakhstan, but relations between Iran and Azerbaijan (which has the oil capital of Baku in its territory) in the southern part of the sea are tense. Pipeline routes and potential maritime access for Azerbaijan, Kazakhstan, and Turkmenistan via the Volga River (which flows into the Caspian) and thence by canals to the Black Sea and Baltic Sea are also issues to be resolved with Russia. Kazakhstan and the two other Central Asian states of Tajikistan and Kyrgyzstan have settled their territorial disputes with China over the last 15 years, with China ceding territory—apparently in return for the three countries' cooperation with Beijing in its crackdown on Uighur separatists in Xinjiang province. Also in Central Asia is the setting for what is one of the world's most complicated border disputes: the Ferghana Valley, parts of which are held and claimed by Uzbekistan, Tajikistan, and Kyrgyzstan. The International Crisis Group once described this valley—home to 10 million people from various ethnic groups—as a "myriad of enclaves" where all three nations had historical territorial claims and economic interests in transport routes, rivers, reservoirs, and industries.[13] Violence broke out in 2010 between Uzbeks and ethnic Kyrgyz groups in the valley, but Almazbek Atambayev, Kyrgyzstan's prime minister since 2010 and elected as its new president in October 2011, has pledged unity as his goal. Tajikistan's porous border with Afghanistan to the south is also an issue for political stability in Central Asia.

Further to the southeast and on the other side of the mountains, India and Pakistan have a long-running dispute over Kashmir, which has seen them go to war three times since partition in 1947. Though there are no significant mineral resources in this part of the world, water for agriculture is a precious commodity that causes tensions on both sides of the border, particularly when dams are built or water is otherwise diverted. A 1960 agreement covers six key Himalayan rivers that irrigate Kashmir and the Pakistani province of Punjab, which provides much of the country's food crops. Pakistan has use of the three western rivers, the Indus, Jhelum, and Chenab, while India can use the eastern three: the Sutlej, Beas, and Ravi.

In the Middle East, the flashpoints are many and varied, particularly since the start of the Arab Spring at the end of 2010. But one that goes back for hundreds of years is the conflict in the Tigris–Euphrates river basin, which is shared mainly by Turkey, Syria, and Iraq. Iran is also involved to an extent, because some of the tributaries of the Tigris originate in Iran. Turkey's dam-building program continues to rankle with Syria and Iraq because of the impact on downstream water flows. In Africa, aside from the political confusion of the Arab Spring, the 2011 creation of South Sudan as the continent's newest nation adds another layer of complexity to the mistrust between Sudan and Ethiopia over issues such as oil, Nile Basin water, and hydropower projects. There are border disputes, too, for Africa's second-largest country, the Democratic Republic of the Congo (DRC), where armed conflict with various ethnic militias and other rebel groups has been going on for decades. It shares land borders with eight other nations and a littoral boundary (Lake Tanganyika) with Tanzania. The DRC is almost completely landlocked, but has access to the Atlantic Ocean through a 45-km stretch of coastline at Muanda, to the north of where the Congo River flows into the sea. Most of the DRC's 72 million people may be dirt-poor—more than 90 percent of them lack access to electricity—but its earth is rich in resources such as copper, cobalt, coltan (tantalum ore), gold, and diamonds, making it an attractive target for miners. Toronto-listed Katanga Mining, owned by global commodities trader Glencore, runs a copper-cobalt operation that the company says has the potential to become the largest copper producer in Africa and the world's largest cobalt producer. The DRC also has immense hydroelectric potential, but projects such as the proposed $10 billion Inga 3 dam on the Congo River face funding obstacles, opposition from environmental groups, and concerns over governance. The DRC ranks second-last (168 out of 169 nations) on the UN's Human Development Index, and 164 out of 168 on Transparency International's Corruption Perception Index.

In South America, Brazil is in dispute with Bolivia, Uruguay, and Paraguay over relatively minor islands and water resource issues. Further to the south, Argentina continues to press its claim for the Malvinas (Falklands), a group of islands 500 km off its coast in the South Atlantic Ocean, and the scene of a short but bitter war with Britain in 1982. According to a 2000, U.S. Geological Survey, the Falklands Plateau area could contain up to 17.2 billion barrels of oil and 51.2 trillion cubic feet of gas. An oil company began drilling exploratory wells off the coast in 2010.[14]

Arctic Ocean Disputes

There are scores of other resource-related disputes around the world. One example is the Arctic Ocean region, which may contain a quarter of the world's untapped oil and gas reserves and where claims over maritime boundaries and continental shelves are yet to be fully resolved between Russia, Canada, the United States, Denmark, and Norway. As the law now stands, these countries control only a 320-km (200-mile) economic zone extending from their respective coastlines. Exploration in these Arctic waters—which are becoming warmer and more accessible—runs into not only competing territorial claims, but also the rights of indigenous groups who fear their traditional way of life will be imperilled by large-scale resource extraction. Some of the Arctic indigenous peoples (Inuit, Saami, Aleut, Athabaskan, Gwich'in, and Russian Indigenous Peoples of the North, or RAIPON) maintain that the circumpolar land mass is one homeland running across national boundaries, which puts them at odds with the Arctic states. Maritime safe passage is another area of international law that is open to interpretation. The United States, for example, claims that international navigation rights prevail in Canada's Northwest Passage—a series of shipping routes that link the Pacific and Atlantic Oceans—and in some Arctic waters that Canada maintains are its territorial waters.

Symbolism is everywhere in the great Arctic resources struggle. In July–August 2007, the Russian nuclear-powered icebreaker *Rossiya* crashed its way through the Arctic Ocean icepack, providing a passage to the North Pole for the research ship *Akademik Federov*. There, as part of its Arktika 2007 expedition, two bathyscapes descended from the *Akademik Federov* to the seabed 4,200 metres (13,800 feet) below the pole, where one of them, MIR 1, left a titanium Russian flag. In the words of Russian Foreign Minister Sergey Lavrov, the aim of this exercise was not to stake Russia's claim but to show "that our shelf reaches to the North Pole"—a reference to the Lomonosov underwater ridge, which extends from the Russian Arctic coast to the pole. A year later, the U.S. Geological Survey (USGS) released its estimate of undiscovered oil and gas resources north of the Arctic Circle: 90 billion barrels of oil, 1,669 trillion cubic feet of natural gas, and 44 billion barrels of natural gas liquids. It said about 84 percent of these resources were expected to occur in offshore areas. At a notional $100 a barrel, the value of the oil resource alone is $9 trillion. And these are the estimated undiscovered reserves; the USGS said in its same 2008 report that 400 oil and gas fields north of the Arctic Circle had already been found. "These fields account for approximately 240 billion barrels of oil and oil-equivalent natural gas, which is almost 10 percent of the world's known conventional petroleum resources (cumulative production and remaining proved reserves)," it said. "Nevertheless, most of the Arctic, especially offshore, is essentially unexplored with respect to petroleum."[15] No wonder the rush for the Arctic's wealth is on.

At the globe's other pole, Antarctica's resources of coal, iron ore, and the Ross Sea oil and gas field, are protected—for now—under a treaty that bans mining until at least 2048.

Notes

1. "Foreign Ministry Spokesperson Ma Zhaoxu's Statement on Indian Leader's Visit to the Disputed East Section Area of China-India Boundary," (13 October 2009), www.fmprc.gov.cn/eng/xwfw/s2510/2535/t620094.htm.
2. Indian Prime Minister Manmohan Singh, address in Itanagar, Arunachal Pradesh, 31 January 2008.
3. Arunachal Government Department of Planning, 2010–11 Draft Annual Plan, http://arunachalplan.gov.in/html/docs/Draft_Annual_Plan10.doc.
4. Indian Prime Minister Manmohan Singh and Chinese Premier Wen Jiabao, joint communiqué, New Delhi, 16 December 2010.
5. Amar Farooqui, *Opium City: The Making of Early Victorian Bombay* (New Delhi: Three Essays Press, December 2005).
6. Leonard P. Adams, "China: The Historical Setting of Asia's Profitable Plague," in Alfred W. McCoy, *The Politics of Heroin in Southeast Asia* (New York: Harper & Row, 1972).
7. World Shipping Council, "History of Containerization," www.worldshipping.org, and American Association of Port Authorities, www.aapa-ports.org/.
8. *Global Times*, "China must react to Vietnam's provocation," (21 June 2011), www.globaltimes.cn/NEWS/tabid/99/ID/662453/China-must-react-to-Vietnams-provocation.aspx.
9. Rory Medcalf and Raoul Heinrichs, *Crisis and Confidence: Major Powers and Maritime Security in Indo-Pacific Asia* (Sydney: Lowy Institute, 28 June 2011).
10. U.S. Defense Department, "Chinese vessels shadow, harass unarmed U.S. survey ship" (9 March 2009), www.defense.gov/news/newsarticle.aspx?id=53401.
11. Foreign Ministry of China, "Foreign Ministry Spokesperson Ma Zhaoxu's regular press conference," (10 March 2009), www.fmprc.gov.cn/eng/xwfw/s2510/t541713.htm.
12. Foreign Ministry of China, "Foreign Ministry Spokesperson Ma Zhaoxu's comment on Japanese and U.S. Official's Remarks on the Issue of the Diaoyu Islands" (2 March 2009), www.fmprc.gov.cn/eng/xwfw/s2510/2535/t539811.htm.

13. International Crisis Group, "Central Asia: Border Disputes and Conflict Potential" (4 April 2002), www.crisisgroup.org/en/regions/asia/central-asia/033-central-asia-border-disputes-and-conflict-potential.aspx.
14. U.S. Geological Survey, "World Petroleum Assessment, 2000," Central Energy Resources Science Center, http://energy.cr.usgs.gov/.
15. U.S. Geological Survey, "Circum-Arctic Resource Appraisal: Estimates of Undiscovered Oil and Gas North of the Arctic Circle," May 2008.

The Key Players

Diggers, Drillers, and Dealers

*No enterprise is more likely to succeed than one concealed from the
enemy until it is ripe for execution.*
          —Italian political philosopher Niccolo Machiavelli,
                              "On the Art of War," 1520

I f we were to gather together the world's 25 top dealmakers from
the energy and mining sectors, a first guest list might include such
names as:

Rex Tillerson, ExxonMobil
Peter Voser, Royal Dutch Shell
Jiang Jiemin, China National Petroleum
Khalid Al-Falih, Saudi Aramco
Bob Dudley, BP
Marius Kloppers, BHP Billiton
Tom Albanese, Rio Tinto

Mick Davis, Xstrata*

Murilo Ferreira, Vale

Cynthia Carroll, Anglo American

Maria das Graças Silva Foster, Petrobras

John Watson, Chevron

Alexei Miller, Gazprom

Christophe de Margerie, Total

Fu Chengyu, Sinopec

Yang Hua, CNOOC

Jim Mulva, ConocoPhillips

Eduard Khudainatov, Rosneft

Zhang Xiwu, China Shenhua Coal

Zohra Chatterji, Coal India

Mukesh Ambani, Reliance Industries

Sudhir Vasudeva, ONGC

Lakshmi Mittal, ArcelorMittal

Chung Joon-yang, POSCO

Mitsunori Takahagi, JX Holdings[1]

With the exception of Saudi Aramco, the companies that these 22 men and three women represent are listed on global stock exchanges. The Chinese, Russian, Brazilian, and Indian ones (except Reliance) are largely state-owned or subject to state direction. Together, they represent the most visible part of the world's energy and minerals trade, and generally they do business in the structured way that accords with global financial norms. Just outside this top echelon sit another 200 large companies of similar scale—names like Statoil, Eni, BG Group, Pemex, Petronas, Occidental, Suncor Energy, Nippon Steel, and the mining and energy arms of the Mitsubishi, Mitsui, Marubeni, Sumitomo, and ITOCHU groups. But below them is a many-layered milieu of deep and varied connections, where thousands of influential but relatively unknown companies go about their daily business in what sometimes can be dirty, dark, and dangerous places.

---

*If a merger proposed in February 2012 between Xstrata and 34 percent shareholder Glencore International wins the approval of regulators and other shareholders, Davis will become the CEO of the combined entity, to be known as Glencore Xstrata International, in the third quarter of 2012.

In February 2007, a French businessman named Claude Dauphin issued a brief statement after he emerged with two colleagues from Maca jail in the violence-wracked West African city of Abidjan. "We went to the Ivory Coast on a mission to help the people of Abidjan," Dauphin said, "and to find ourselves arrested and in jail as a result has been a terrible ordeal for ourselves and our families."[2]

Five months spent inside a cell on pretrial detention had indeed proved an unwelcome surprise for Dauphin, chairman of the Netherlands-based commodity trading company Trafigura. He'd turned up in the Ivorian business capital of Abidjan in September 2006 to handle a toxic waste dumping accident involving a Trafigura-chartered ship, the Probo Koala. Trafigura had contracted with a local company called Tommy to dispose of the ship's waste; Tommy dumped it illegally around the city, apparently with catastrophic results: 10 people dead and thousands more affected by the fumes. Trafigura, which said it could not have foreseen Tommy's "disgraceful actions," eventually cut a deal with the Ivorian government to win the release of Dauphin and the two other executives. It would pay close to $200 million to cover the cost of the cleanup and compensation for the victims, though without admitting liability.

For a trading company that aims to keep the lowest possible profile, the Ivory Coast affair was the last thing Trafigura wanted. Like Vitol and Glencore International (until its 2011 initial public offer), its two great rivals in global commodity trading, Trafigura has never courted publicity. Dauphin and co-founder Eric de Turckheim were barely known in mainstream business before 2006, although their enterprise was founded in 1993 as a spin-off from the trading company Marc Rich + Co. that legendary commodities trader and onetime fugitive Marc Rich had set up in 1974. Rich, who fled the United States for Switzerland in 1983 after being indicted by the U.S. Justice Department on racketeering, tax fraud, and other charges, was pardoned by then-U.S. president Bill Clinton in 2001. Marc Rich + Co. eventually became Glencore, which started trading in metals, minerals, and crude oil. Agricultural commodities were added in 1987. Glencore ended its connection with Rich in 1994, when one of Rich's trading moves went badly wrong and management was able to buy him out of the company. When Glencore decided it would go public with a share offer in the first half of 2011, the world began to see the sort of grip these three companies held on the trade in commodities such as crude oil, coal, iron ore, and other metals and mineral resources.

Their combined turnover in 2010 was about $420 billion, made up of Vitol $195 billion, Glencore $145 billion and Trafigura $80 billion (see Exhibit 3.1). In its 2012 merger proposal with Xstrata, Glencore reported 2011 turnover of $186 billion. A fourth company, privately held Gunvor, is also a major player in the energy trade, handling 2 million barrels a day with turnover in 2010 of $65 billion. Gunvor, which was co-founded in 1997 by now-chairman Torbjörn Tornqvist of Sweden and Russian-born Finnish citizen, Gennady Timchenko, handles a third of sales for Russian oil company Rosneft from key offices in Amsterdam and Geneva. Also based in Geneva is the privately held Mercuria group, run by executive chairman Marco Dunand and his co-founder Daniel Jaeggi. Mercuria is a relative newcomer to the energy-trading world, having started in 2004. But it traded 117 million metric tonnes of crude and other oil products in 2010, suggesting turnover similar to Gunvor at around $65 billion. By late 2011, Mercuria said annual group turnover had risen to between $70 and $80 billion, covering oil and gas, LNG, coal, biodiesel, and power.

Another privately held energy trader is Swiss-based Addax and Oryx Group (AOG), founded by billionaire antiquities collector Jean Claude Gandur in 1987. Gandur's major focus is Africa, where his group is active in oil exploration, trading, storage, logistics, petrol retailing under the Oryx brand, and gold exploration. Gandur, who moves between bases in Geneva and London, made a fortune in 2009 when he sold Addax Petroleum to China's state-owned Sinopec for about $9 billion. Addax held oil licences in Nigeria, Gabon, and northern Iraq. Gandur is rebuilding his oil portfolio in Africa and the Middle East through Oryx Petroleum, and has a bioenergy project in Sierra Leone.

1. Vitol $195 billion	**8.** Archer Daniels Midland $62 billion
2. Glencore $145 billion	**9.** Noble $57 billion
3. Cargill $108 billion	**10.** Bunge $46 billion
4. Trafigura $80 billion	**11.** COFCO $26 billion
5. Gunvor $65 billion	**12.** Louis Dreyfus $20 billion
6. Mercuria $65 billion	**13.** Olam International $6 billion
7. Zen Noh $64 billion	

Exhibit 3.1   Top commodities traders in energy and agriculture (ranked by turnover in 2010; excludes Japanese trading companies)

Source: Company reports, 2010–2011

Standing off to one side is the diversified U.S. energy trader and manufacturer Koch Industries, run by the billionaire Koch brothers, Charles and David, the sons of founder Fred Koch. Wichita, Kansas-based Koch, a frequent target for environmental critics such as Greenpeace, is one of the world's largest private businesses, with turnover of about $100 billion and 70,000 employees in 60 countries. It trades commodities from offices in Wichita, Houston, New York, Rotterdam, Mumbai, Singapore, Geneva, Paris, London, and Calgary, dealing in crude oil, natural gas and gas liquids, refined petroleum products, coal, coke, cement, pulp and paper, and other products. Its activities go far beyond trading. It runs refineries in Rotterdam, Texas, Minnesota, and Alaska, holds a stake in the Trans-Alaska Pipeline, and runs a network of other oil and gas pipelines. Its businesses encompass chemicals, ranching, polymers and fibres, fertilisers, process and pollution control technologies and equipment, and forest and consumer products. Charles and David Koch each own 42 percent of the company. They bought out two other brothers, Frederick and William, in 1983.

Something similar takes place in the agribusiness world, where U.S. private company Cargill is the biggest farm commodities trader, with turnover of $108 billion in 2010, ahead of two U.S.-listed companies: Archer Daniels Midland ($62 billion) and Bunge ($46 billion). Their peers include the French privately held Louis Dreyfus ($20 billion), Singapore-listed Olam International ($6 billion), and the HK-based, Singapore-listed Noble Group, which defines itself as Asia's largest diversified commodities trading house. It turned over $57 billion in 2010 in agricultural, energy, metals, and mineral products. Other significant agribusiness groups are the Japanese farmers' agricultural cooperative Zen-Noh, with turnover of $64 billion (mainly in domestic business) and the Chinese oils and food importer/exporter COFCO ($26 billion). All of the agribusiness traders are building up their overseas food, plantation and other farm holdings ahead of what they see as a coming squeeze on resources.

In a somewhat separate category are the big Japanese general trading companies, known as *sōgō shōsha*, whose product range goes well beyond food, minerals, and energy into the realms of financing, investment, and deal making (see Exhibit 3.2). They are the masters of the third-party deal, which can be summarized as "my money and connections, your access or expertise, in this resource,

1. Mitsubishi Corp. $229 billion
2. ITOCHU Corp. $132 billion
3. Mitsui & Co. $129 billion
4. Marubeni Corp. $108 billion

5. Sumitomo Corp. $104 billion
6. Toyota Tsusho $70 billion
7. Sojitz Corp. $51 billion

Exhibit 3.2   Japanese general trading companies (*sōgō shōsha*) (turnover in FY ended March 2011)
Source: Company reports. Exchange rate: US$ @ 80¥

for that market." In the 1980s and 1990s, companies such as Mitsubishi Corp., Mitsui & Co., ITOCHU Corp., Sumitomo Corp., and Marubeni Corp. absolutely dominated global trade in a range of industrial and agricultural products, services, and raw materials, but their influence has waned considerably since the air whooshed out of the Japanese economic bubble in the early 1990s. Fifteen years ago, a list of the world's top companies by revenue had Japanese companies in 6 of the top 10 spots. The first three were Mitsubishi Corp., Mitsui, and ITOCHU. In fourth place was the U.S. automaker GM, followed by Sumitomo and Marubeni, ahead of Ford Motor, Royal Dutch Shell, Toyota Motor, and Exxon. Today, a top-ten revenue list would see Toyota as the only Japanese entrant. Some big *sōgō shōsha* names of the past have vanished: Nissho Iwai and Nichmen merged in 2004 to create Sojitz Corp. Even so, the top *sōgō shōsha* remain a considerable economic force; the big seven names, including Toyota Tsusho, which absorbed Tomen in 2006, turn over more than $800 billion a year. They remain major players and investors in global resource projects, particularly in Australia, South America, and North America, and with a growing interest in India, China, and Africa. Typical of their involvement is Mitsui and Mitsubishi's joint stake in the Australian North West Shelf gas project, Mitsubishi's role in the Canadian, Brazilian, and Australian iron ore and coal trade, ITOCHU's 20 percent stake in the Colombian coal operations of U.S. miner Drummond, and Sumitomo's 45 percent stake in the forthcoming Sierra Gorda copper-molybdenum mining project in Chile. Traders are not generally known for their generosity over a deal, but ITOCHU, for example, says it very much values the spirit of *sampo yoshi*, which it translates as "good for the seller, good for the buyer, and good for society."

The trading arms of the big South Korean family-run business groups (known as *chaebol*) sought to emulate the Japanese, but they, too, were forced to trim their sails after the Asian financial crisis of 1997–1998 and the *chaebol* restructuring that followed. Of those that remain, SK Networks is the biggest with turnover of $22 billion, followed by Samsung C&T, LG International, Hyundai Corp., and Hanwha Corp. Like the Japanese trading houses, they invest in overseas resources projects. SK Networks, for example, paid $700 million in 2010 for a 14 percent stake in MMX, a Brazilian iron ore miner set up by billionaire Eike Batista's EBX Group.

Commodity Trading Skills

Whether it is metals, energy, food, or other agricultural products, the top commodities traders make their money from their skill in matching supply with demand—either from their in-house resources or from their knowledge of where best to find whatever the market needs. Glencore chief executive Ivan Glasenberg,* who with Willy Strothotte led the $600 million buyout of Marc Rich in 1994 and is now a paper billionaire several times over through his 15.7 percent stake in the company, noted in a 2011 announcement about the share offer that "over many decades, we have developed Glencore into an unrivalled global integrated commodity producer and marketer, active in almost every bulk commodity market." In the document, Glencore says it believes that it is "the world's largest physical supplier of third-party sourced commodities in the majority of the metals and minerals it markets; among the world's largest non-integrated physical suppliers of crude oil and oil products; the world's largest participant in the supply of seaborne steam coal; among the world's leading physical suppliers of third-party sourced sugar; and one of the leading exporters of grain from Europe, the CIS [Commonwealth of Independent States, made up of former Soviet Union republics] and Australia."[3]

For its part, Vitol has an equally impressive record and says it is "by any standards, a major participant in world energy trading,"

---

*If the Glencore-Xstrata merger succeeds, Glasenberg will be its deputy CEO.

shipping almost 400 million tonnes of crude oil and product a year. It says it was founded in 1966 with the "focused aim of trading crude oil and oil products" and is still "resolutely an independent group of separate companies, each staffed by energy professionals."[4] Vitol Group president and chief executive Ian Taylor, a former Shell executive who joined Vitol in the 1980s, told an international oil conference in early 2011: "I have been around a long time—I have sold VLCCs (Very Large Crude Carriers) of Dubai (oil) at $7 a barrel in 1987 and sadly bought VLCCs of Nigerian at $147 a barrel in 2008."[5] Taylor's point is that volatility is here to stay, and no one really knows what the price of oil will be a year further on. As Gunvor chairman Torbjorn Tornqvist said around the same time, "The oil price is anybody's guess." Taylor also noted in 2011 that growth in demand and reduced inventories meant that OPEC producers would need to bring more supply to the market. Vitol has successfully drilled for oil and gas in Cameroon, adding to the group's portfolio of undeveloped oil and gas in its "core area around the Gulf of Guinea in West Africa." Outlining its business ethos, Taylor described Vitol as "first and foremost, a physical trading company. . . . We identify imbalances between supply and demand and act quickly to restore equilibrium, around the world. Our strength lies in anticipating and reacting to change. We don't take unnecessary risks."[6]

Glencore would say the same, though its traders have always been prepared to seek out the most lucrative commodity plays, even in difficult, dangerous, and often corrupt environments. Investments such as Katanga Mining in the Democratic Republic of Congo and the Prodeco coal mine in Colombia—bought at the height of the drug war there—attest to its stomach for the hard calls. More prosaically, it noted in its IPO prospectus that it did not control a number of its most significant industrial investments, including its stakes in Xstrata, Century Aluminum, African copper play Mutanda and alumina/aluminium producer UC Rusal. "Although Glencore has sought to take steps to protect its industrial activities where it does not exercise control (including entering into a relationship agreement with respect to Xstrata and a shareholders' agreement with respect to UC Rusal), the boards of these companies may have economic or business interests or goals that are inconsistent with or are opposed to those of Glencore," it noted.[7]

Russia's Billionaire Oligarchs

The business milieu inhabited by Trafigura, Vitol, Glencore, Gunvor, Mercuria, and Gandur's AOG is full of colourful and sometimes nefarious figures, drawn by the lure of hot prospects in emerging "frontier" economies where the rules can be changed on a political whim. Step back 20 years and the classic example is Russia, where a number of the billionaire oligarchs who made their fortunes in the chaotic Boris Yeltsin years—the free-wheeling era of the 1990s when Russia further opened up its state-controlled economy through a series of murky privatisations—have since found themselves on the wrong side of Vladimir Putin and other Kremlin bigwigs. They include one-time oil and media magnate Boris Berezovsky—who fled to London in 2001 and remains a political refugee there—and Mikhail Khodorkovsky, the former YUKOS oil company chief executive who was arrested in 2003 and jailed in 2005 for nine years (later reduced to eight) after he was convicted of fraud, tax evasion, embezzlement, and money laundering. YUKOS—once lauded as a shining example of how a Russian oil company could be transformed to meet Western standards of financial reporting and corporate governance—was seized by the Russian state in 2004 and dismantled, with various pieces going to state-owned companies Rosneft and Gazprom. Khodorkovsky once vowed to use his money to bring about political change in Russia, but he now sits in a Siberian jail and says there is "no such thing as free elections, freedom of expression, or rule of law in Russia today."[8]

Also London-based is Roman Abramovich, a former business partner of Berezovsky at Sibneft, the Russian oil company the pair created in 1995 through the privatisation of state-owned assets. Berezovsky—dubbed the "Godfather of the Kremlin" in 2000 by since-murdered journalist Paul Klebnikov—claims Abramovich paid him too little for a 21.5 percent Sibneft stake when Berezovsky fell out with the Kremlin and fled to London. A decade later, Sibneft was taken over by the giant gas company Gazprom, which bought 73 percent of Sibneft's shares for $13 billion in September 2005. Sibneft was renamed Gazprom Neft and today operates as Gazprom's oil producing and refining arm. Abramovich, who remains onside with the Kremlin (but offside with Berezovsky), owns the Chelsea football club, and is a shareholder in steelmaker Evraz Group.

Another occasional London resident is Alisher Usmanov, the Uzbek-born Russian businessman who holds a majority stake in Metalloinvest, the metals and mining company formed out of Gazprom's metals assets. Usmanov, who in 2006 bought the Kommersant newspaper once owned by Berezovsky, also has a 23 percent stake in the Arsenal football club, which Berezovsky follows. But unlike Berezovsky, Usmanov is on good terms with Putin and thinks he is good for Russia. In 2007, a Moscow court tried Berezovsky—who changed his name to Platon Elenin in 2003—in absentia and found him guilty of fraud. He was sentenced to six years in jail and ordered to pay $9 million. Another court in 2009 found him guilty of theft and sentenced him to 13 years' jail in absentia.

Almost all of Russia's current crop of billionaires have made their money in oil, metals and mining, financial services, and telecommunications. Many of them have life stories featuring an incredible mix of good luck and bad luck, depending on how well they have sniffed the political wind in Russia and its former Soviet-era territories.

An example is Kazakh-born billionaire Mikhail Gutseriev, who controls the midsized Russian oil company Russneft. Gutseriev, a decathlon athlete who also paints and plays piano and the violin, is a long-time oilman, having been a one-time president of the Belarus state oil company Slavneft. He founded Russneft in 2002, but conflict with the government over tax and licence issues prompted him to pass control to fellow billionaire Oleg Deripaska in 2006 and leave the country. He spent the years 2007–2010 living and working in the United Kingdom, where he set up oil and gas projects in Azerbaijan, Kazakhstan, and Africa and waited for the right time to return. With Russneft starting on the path to a restructure in 2010, Gutseriev was able to make a comeback in June that year as company president. Deripaska, a Putin ally and a former metals trader who is CEO and major shareholder in aluminium producer UC Rusal, returned Russneft to Gutseriev in a deal that involved another Russian billionaire, Vladimir Yevtushenkov, owner of Sistema. Sistema, a large holding company with interests in telecommunications, media, financial services, retail and oil company Bashneft, ended up with a 49 percent stake in Russneft. Gutseriev says Russneft's goal is to reach annual oil production of 18 million tonnes, aided by new investment projects. But these are troubled times for many in the oil trade. Russneft finds it necessary to carry a large warning on its site about fraudulent use of its name. The warning says fraudsters target trading

1. Gazprom	**6.** Surgutneftegas
2. Rosneft	**7.** Tatneft
3. LUKOIL	**8.** Bashneft
4. TNK-BP	**9.** Novatek
5. Gazprom Neft	**10.** Russneft

Exhibit 3.3   Russia's top 10 oil and gas companies (by turnover)
Source: Platts Top 250, company reports 2010–2011

companies in India, China, Europe, and Latin America, offering to sell oil and oil products from Russneft and its subsidiaries.

After state-run Rosneft, the biggest Russian oil company is LUKOIL, controlled by chief executive Vagit Alekperov and strategic development vice-president Leonid Fedun, whose stakes together are worth more than $20 billion (see Exhibit 3.3). LUKOIL says it is responsible for about 18 percent of Russia's crude oil production and refining, and is the world's largest privately owned oil company by proven oil reserves, with 17.3 billion barrels. LUKOIL turned over more than $100 billion in 2010 for a net profit of $9 billion. The company, which was formed in 1991 and privatized in 1993, has been led since its inception by Alekperov, who was Russia's deputy energy minister at the time. He holds the single largest stake in LUKOIL, of 20 percent. Fedun, who holds just over 9 percent, owns Russian football club Spartak Moscow.

Rosneft is held 75 percent by the Russian government (a further partial privatization is on the cards) and was chaired until June 2011 by deputy prime minister Igor Sechin, Putin's oil industry insider and the man dubbed "Darth Vader" by Russian media. Sechin left after Russian President Dmitry Medvedev earlier in the year said ministers should not be on the boards of state-own corporations (before becoming president in 2008, Medvedev had served as chairman of Gazprom for seven years). Rosneft says on a company basis it holds the world's largest hydrocarbon reserves of 22.9 billion barrels of oil equivalent, at June 2011.[9] It produces about 2.5 million barrels a day and is looking to develop vast Arctic shelf oil and gas fields—the East Prinovozemelsky 1–2–3 blocks in the South Kara Sea—that could contain as much as 5 million tonnes of oil and 10 trillion cubic metres of gas. Rosneft had planned to have global energy leader BP as its partner for the development, but the deal collapsed in the wake of trenchant opposition from a group of billionaire tycoons who make up BP's partner AAR in their Russian joint venture TNK-BP.

The AAR Connection

TNK-BP, which was created in 2003 and has faced its share of corporate intrigues since then, is Russia's third-largest oil producer behind Rosneft and LUKOIL. AAR stands for Alfa-Access-Renova, representing the business empires of four of Russia's richest men. They are Alfa Group chairman Mikhail Fridman, Renova Group chairman Viktor Vekselberg, Access Industries chairman Leonard Blavatnik (who is now a U.S. citizen), and German Khan, who was one of the original founders of Alfa Group. Their combined wealth on paper is close to $50 billion, with Fridman and Vekselberg regarded as the most influential. Vekselberg set up aluminium group SUAL and merged it with Rusal and Glencore's aluminium assets in 2007 to create the global aluminium powerhouse UC Rusal. "Resource nationalism" and "kick out the foreign managers" are common refrains in modern Russia, but after the BP-Rosneft deal lapsed, Fridman said[10] AAR was a long-term strategic investor and "remains dedicated to the success of TNK-BP" in Russia and abroad. So is BP—the joint venture contributes about a quarter of its global profits. The *TNK* in the joint venture's name stands for "Tyumenskaya Neftyanaya Kompaniya," or Tyumen Oil Company. It was set up in 1995 and was largely state-owned until a privatization program beginning in 1998 led to the AAR Group gaining control. Tyumen takes its name from the city on the Tura river, 2100 km east of Moscow in West Siberia, that is the industrial and transport hub for much of the Russian oil industry.

It's been hard going for some of BP's staff in Russia. There was a serious dustup with the AAR oligarchs over strategy and control in 2008 that led to BP's then representative in Russia, Bob Dudley, fleeing the country after what he called sustained harassment. Dudley, who was grilled by tax investigators at the Interior Ministry, would later take over from Tony Hayward as chief executive of BP following the Gulf of Mexico oil spill disaster in 2010. For his part, Hayward joined the TNK-BP board.

Behind TNK-BP is Gazprom Neft (the former Sibneft, taken over in 2005 by Gazprom) and then the conservatively run

Surgutneftegas, which since its creation as a private company in 1993 has been led by CEO Vladimir Bogdanov, known as the "Surgut Hermit" for his seeming reluctance to leave the company's head-quarters in the Western Siberia city of Surgut. A study of Russian oil industry figures by Dr Nina Poussenkova for the James Baker Institute described him thus: "The key difference between the two tycoons is that Vladimir Bogdanov literally 'minded his own business' by improving operations of Surgutneftegas and taking care of its workers and the local community. He was a success. By contrast, Mikhail Khodorkovsky represents a case study of business trying to influence authorities to improve the situation beyond the immediate scope of his company. In the process, Khodorkovsky has destroyed himself and brought YUKOS to the brink of ruin."[11] Surgutneftegas was formed from the merger of a number of state-owned oil and gas enterprises, and by 2011 was producing almost 13 percent of Russian crude output and 25 percent of its gas. Its massive Kirishi refinery in Leningrad Oblast in northwestern Russia accounts for 9 percent of total domestic refining throughput.

Russia's sixth largest oil company is Tatneft, which dates its founding back to 1950 and in which the government of Tatarstan holds a 36 percent stake plus a "golden share." As well as produc-ing and refining oil and gas, Tatneft has a retail network of about 450 filling stations. Most of its oil and gas production is in Tatarstan, a republic of the Russian Federation between the Volga River and the Ural Mountains, about 750 km southeast of Moscow. It had total proved reserves of crude oil and condensate of just under 6 billion barrels at the start of 2011. Tatneft holds a stake of almost 9 percent in the Ukrainian oil and gas processor Ukrnafta, but this is subject to dispute after some corporate manoeuvring. A key shareholder in Ukrnafta is the prominent Ukrainian billionaire Igor Kolomoisky, who runs PrivatGroup.

Another significant oil company is Bashneft, controlled by Vladimir Yevtushenkov, owner of the diversified conglomerate Sistema. Yevtushenkov, who made his fortune in the early 1990s in Russian telecommunications (he also has an Indian telecoms company, Sistema Shyam), subsequently moved into the oil and gas sector in the following decade through his stakes in Bashneft and Russneft, which now contribute about 30 percent of the group's $20 billion revenue. In March 2009, Yevtusheknov paid $2.5 billion for Bashkir Oil and Energy Group, which gave him a

76.5 percent stake in Bashneft, based in Ufa, capital of the republic of Bashkortostan, about 1,500 km east of Moscow. In the first quarter of 2011, Bashneft was producing crude oil at a rate of 291,000 barrels a day. Bashneft has three oil refineries in Ufa (Ufaneftekhim, Ufa Oil Refinery, and Novoil) and the petrochemicals producer Ufaorgsintez. Together, these plants have crude refining capacity of 24.1 million tonnes.

Among the pure gas players, second behind Gazprom in gas production is Novatek, based in West Siberia, where it operates in the Yamal-Nenets region. Novatek says this region is the world's largest natural gas producing area, accounting respectively for 83 percent and 16 percent of Russian and world gas production. Its billionaire chief executive and major shareholder is civil engineering graduate Leonid Mikhelson, while among its other key shareholders is Volga Resources, the Luxembourg investment vehicle of Gennady Timchenko, owner with Torbjörn Tornqvist of the oil trading firm Gunvor. Gazprom also holds about 10 percent of Novatek, while French oil major Total became a significant shareholder in 2011 and is looking to increase its involvement, particularly in Novatek's Yamal LNG development in the Arctic.

Another powerful company in the oil and gas industry is Transneft, the state pipeline that handles Russia's oil exports. Overseas, state-owned Zarubezhneft runs various ventures, including VietSovPetro, its long-running and profitable 50–50 partnership with Petro Vietnam covering Vietnam's offshore oil fields. In 2011, Zarubezhneft and PetroVietnam formed RusVietPetro to exploit oil fields in Russia's Nenets autonomous region.

Money in Metals

Apart from LUKOIL's Vagit Alekperov and the AAR Group four-some of Fridman, Vekselberg, Blavatnik and Khan, most of Russia's top echelon of billionaires have made their money in metals (see Exhibit 3.4). They include men like Vladimir Lisin, a one-time metal works foreman who now chairs the steelmaker Novolipetsk Steel (NLMK); Alexei Mordashov, chief executive and major shareholder of Severstal, one of Russia's biggest steel and mining companies with interests in Russia, Kazakhstan, and Africa; Vladimir Potanin, chairman of Interros, which has a major stake in the Siberian nickel

1. Evraz Group	6. UC Rusal
2. Severstal	7. Mechel
3. Novolipetsk Steel (NLMK)	8. Magnitogorsk Iron & Steel (MMK)
4. Norilsk Nickel	9. Ural Mining & Metallurgical Co.
5. Metalloinvest	(UGMK)

Exhibit 3.4   Major Russian metals companies
Source: Company reports 2010–2011

company Norilsk Nickel; his one-time partner and political aspirant Mikhail Prokhorov, who sold out of Norilsk in 2008 for a stake in aluminium producer Rusal plus cash that he used to buy more assets for his investment fund ONEXIM Group; Alisher Usmanov of Metalloinvest; the well-connected Oleg Deripaska, owner of Basic Element, whose major assets include Rusal; Igor Zyuzin, who chairs another big metals company Mechel, which operates in mining, steel, ferroalloy, and power; and Suleiman Kerimov, owner of investment company Nafta Moskva, with stakes in Russia's biggest gold producer Polyus Gold and fertiliser company Uralkali. Three others who have made their money in metals are Viktor Rashnikov, chairman of Russia's third largest steelmaker Magnitogorsk Iron & Steel Works (MMK); Iskander Makhmudov, an Uzbek-born businessman who controls two large coal companies and chairs Russia's second largest copper producer, Ural Mining and Metallurgical Co.; and Alexander Abramov, chairman and major shareholder of Russia's largest steelmaker Evraz Group, an integrated producer with mills in Russia, the Ukraine, Europe, South Africa and the United States, and iron ore, coal, and vanadium interests. Abramov's Evraz co-founder, Alexander Frolov is CEO and also holds a significant stake, as does Roman Abramovich.

The Russian minerals and energy sectors may have created a swag of billionaire oligarchs in the past 20 years, but the global market has yet to value their companies as highly as those of China's many state-owned corporations. China National Petroleum Corp.(CNPC), China Petroleum and Chemical Corp. (known as Sinopec), and China National Offshore Oil Corp. (CNOOC) have wide-ranging aspirations in their search for oil and gas, and market caps that reach giddying heights.

World's Most Valuable Companies

Among all listed companies, PetroChina (which is held 86.3 percent by parent CNPC) is ranked third in the world by market value ($275 billion at 19 January 2012), behind only ExxonMobil and Apple. In fourth spot is the Industrial and Commercial Bank of China, followed by Royal Dutch Shell, Microsoft, IBM, and Chevron. Rounding out the top 10 are Anglo-Australian mining house BHP Billiton and China Mobile:

- Five of the top 10 are energy and/or mining companies, 3 are high-tech and 1 each is a bank and mobile phone carrier.
- By location, 5 of the top 10 are U.S. companies, 3 are Chinese, and 1 each is Anglo-Dutch and Anglo-Australian.

The first Russian company, Gazprom, sits in the twenty-first spot with a market capitalization of about $140 billion. South Korea's Samsung Electronics and Japan's Toyota Motor rank as the biggest non-Chinese companies from Asia, both with a market value that puts them just into the top 25. The rise in value of the Chinese banks and oil producers stands in sharp contrast to India, where the biggest company by market cap ($55 billion) is Reliance Industries, the diversified energy, petrochemicals, and retailing group controlled by India's richest man, Mukesh Ambani. State-owned oil and gas producer ONGC ranks second in India with a value of $47 billion, while Coal India Ltd. is third at US$44 billion and the nation's biggest power producer, state-owned National Thermal Power Corp. is valued at $30 billion.

The world's most valuable company overall is regarded as the unlisted state-owned oil producer Saudi Aramco, which had output in 2010 of about 8.5 million barrels of oil a day and claims oil reserves of 264.5 billion barrels. Saudi Aramco does not release financial information, but based on output figures, its annual revenue for oil exports is at least $150 billion. On top of that, there is income from oil refining, distribution, shipping and marketing, plus gas sales. The world's top 10 oil companies ranked by reserves of oil and gas are all state-run corporations. Along with Saudi Aramco, the largest include the National Iranian Oil Co. (NIOC), the Qatar General Petroleum Corp. (QGPC), which has substantial gas fields on its books, the Iraq National Oil Co. (INOC), Petroleos de Venezuela

(PDVSA), Abu Dhabi National Oil Co., Kuwait Petroleum Corp. (KPC), Nigerian National Petroleum Corp., National Oil Co. of Libya and Sonatrach of Algeria. Estimates of reserves can be a hazy area, particularly as OPEC takes members' assessments at face value. That allowed Venezuela to surpass Saudi Arabia in 2010, with claimed proven reserves of 296.5 billion barrels.[12]

Ranked by revenue, five of the world's top six listed companies are oil majors—Royal Dutch Shell, ExxonMobil, BP, Sinopec, and PetroChina. They stand ahead of Chinese utility State Grid, two more oil producers in Total and Chevron, and Japanese automaker Toyota. But they are still no match for the biggest money-mover, U.S. retailer Wal-Mart, which had turnover for the year to 31 January 2011 of $419 billion. Apart from the companies just listed, other big players in the oil and gas sector are Pertamina of Indonesia, Petronas of Malaysia, Pemex of Mexico, Petrobras of Brazil, and Sonangol of Angola. Japan's biggest oil and gas explorer Inpex and producer-refiner Nippon Oil—which with Nippon Mining makes up JX Holdings—also are big investors in overseas production opportunities. Inpex, for example, is working on a $34 billion LNG project off the Australian northwest coast with France's Total that aims to produce more than 8 million tonnes of LNG a year, primarily for Japanese power utilities. JX Holdings has earmarked 70 percent of its planned $10 billion of business investment in 2011–2012 for the oil and gas sector, and has identified China as a key market. With oil demand declining in Japan, JX says it is streamlining its refining operations there, converting a refinery in Osaka in a joint venture with PetroChina to serve export markets. JX is not alone. Many of the top international oil companies are quitting the downstream business of refining and marketing oil to concentrate on the more lucrative upstream business of exploring for and producing oil.

Chinese Miners on the Prowl

It's not just about oil and gas when it comes to the earth wars. In the mining and energy sector a whole host of Chinese companies are on the prowl for global resources (see Exhibit 3.5). They include China Shenhua Energy, Datong Coal, China Coal Energy, Yanzhou Coal Mining, Xishan Coal, Inner Mongolia Yitai Coal, Hebei Iron & Steel, Baoshan Iron & Steel, Anshan Iron & Steel, Wuhan Iron &

1. BHP Billiton $62.6 billion	**7.** China Shenhua Energy $23.2 billion
2. Rio Tinto $60.3 billion	**8.** Chinalco $21.0 billion
3. Vale $46.5 billion	**9.** Norilsk Nickel $15.0 billion
4. Xstrata $30.5 billion	**10.** JX Nippon Mining $11.5 billion
5. Anglo American $27.6 billion	**11.** Coal India $11.2 billion
6. China MinMetals $26.0 billion	**12.** Rusal $11.0 billion

Exhibit 3.5   World's top mining companies by revenue

Source: Company statements for 2010–2011FY

Steel, Shandong Iron & Steel, Jiangsu Shagang, China Minmetals Corp., Aluminum Corp. of China, Jiangxi Copper, Zijin Mining Group, Fosun International, and Maanshan Iron & Steel. And they play the game hard. State-owned Aluminum Corp. of China (Chinalco), is the world's No. 3 aluminium producer and has long had an interest in overseas resources beyond alumina. With a 9 percent stake, it is the single biggest investor in Anglo-Australian miner Rio Tinto, which has extensive iron ore, coal, uranium, diamond, and copper operations in Australia, plus interests in North America, South America, Africa, Asia, and Europe. Chinalco sought to double its stake in Rio Tinto in 2009, but the deal collapsed in the wake of opposition from other shareholders and a likelihood the Australian government would rule against it. Instead, Rio Tinto opted for a joint venture with BHP Billiton to combine their iron ore operations in Western Australia—a deal that itself was scrapped less than 18 months later because of anticompetition concerns among European and Asian customers.

Despite that setback, Chinalco and Rio Tinto are pushing ahead with a large iron ore joint venture in Guinea (the Simandou project) that will produce its first ore in 2015, and have formed another joint venture to explore for copper and coal within China. Rio Tinto is the world's second largest miner behind BHP Billiton and ahead of Brazil's Vale, and counts Chinese companies among its biggest customers. Indeed, Rio Tinto chief executive Tom Albanese called the exploration joint venture "an important milestone" in its expanding ties with China. But things are not always rosy. Barely a month after the Chinalco deal collapsed, the head of Rio Tinto's Shanghai office, Stern Hu, was arrested on charges of bribery and stealing business secrets from the China Iron and Steel Association, in connection with iron ore price negotiations. Hu and three colleagues were subsequently jailed and fined; Hu's sentence, handed down in March 2010, was 10 years. Rio Tinto immediately sacked all four and said their acceptance of bribes was "deplorable behaviour."

Corruption is not, of course, unique to China, but a damning 2011 report by the antimoney laundering unit of the central People's Bank of China found that as many as 18,000 government officials and executives of state-owned enterprises had fled the country or disappeared over a 20-year period up to 2008, taking with them up to $120 billion of illegal money.

Rapid Emergence on the Global Stage

To understand how rapidly China's biggest companies have evolved as global players, we need only look back a decade to the 2001 Fortune Global 500 list, when only 10 Chinese companies made the revenue list. Today there are 46. India, too, has seen a significant scaling-up. There was only one Indian name in 2001: state-owned energy company Indian Oil Corp., compared with eight on the 2011 list. In 2001, Brazil had three entries—oil and gas company Petrobras and two banks, Banco Bradesco and Banco do Brasil. From Russia there were three: Gazprom, LUKOIL, and the now defunct YUKOS. There were none from Turkey or Saudi Arabia, but a decade later, they each have a single representative on the 2011 list (Turkish conglomerate Koc Holding and Saudi petro-chemicals giant Sabic), and Russia has six. The United States, as expected, still leads the way with 139 companies on the 2011 list, while Japan has 71, France has 39, Germany has 37, South Korea has 10, and Brazil has 7. One name not on Brazil's list is that of OGX Petroleo & Gas. The company has barely begun to produce oil, but has already delivered a paper fortune to its billionaire owner, flamboyant mining tycoon Eike Batista. OGX, which holds licences for deepwater fields off the coast of Brazil, hopes its first oil will flow from one of its Colombian wells in 2012, and its first natural gas from its Parnaiba Basin field in Brazil in 2013. Batista, son of Eliezer Batista da Silva, a former head of mining company Vale (1979–1986, when it was known as CVRD), has amassed a substantial fortune from investments in Brazil's mineral riches via Canadian miner TVX Gold and in setting up Brazilian companies in logistics, mining, and power generation. His holding company is EBX.

The big international mining companies have substantially longer histories than Batista's EBX, but like Fortescue Metals Group, the Australian iron ore newcomer created by Andrew "Twiggy" Forrest, it is a name to watch. Fortescue claims it is now the new force in global iron ore trade, with output of 50 million tonnes a year from its West Australian mines and plans to triple that to 155 million tonnes by mid-2014. It comes as no surprise that Fortescue's potential was spotted from afar: it won early funding from two U.S. hedge funds, and one of its key shareholders is Russian steelmaker Magnitogorsk Iron & Steel (MMK); another cornerstone investor is Hunan Valin, a provincial Chinese steelmaker that holds a 15 percent stake in Fortescue. Three other Australian names who are at the forefront of deal making in the minerals and energy trade are multibillionaire Gina Rinehart of Hancock Prospecting, horse breeder and car-racer Nathan Tinkler of Tinkler Group, and Clive Palmer of Mineralogy/Resourcehouse. Rinehart in particular has such a rich revenue stream from her holdings in West Australian iron ore and Queensland coal that she is likely to rise to the very top tier of the world's billionaires in the next 5 to 10 years.

Notes

1. Executives in place at February 2012.
2. Statement by Trafigura, "Release of Trafigura executives," 15 February 2007.
3. Glencore International Plc, initial public offer prospectus, 14 April 2011.
4. Statement by Vitol Group on its website, www.vitol.com.
5. Ian Taylor, presentation at International Petroleum Week conference, London, 22 February 2011.
6. Ibid.
7. Glencore prospectus.
8. Quoted in Anne Jolis, "Putin's Personal Enemy," *Wall Street Journal* (20 June 2011).
9. Rosneft corporate profile, www.rosneft.com/about/Glance/.
10. BP and AAR joint media release, "BP and AAR Reaffirm Commitment to Growth and Success of TNK-BP" (17 May 2011), www.bp.com/genericarticle.do?categoryId=2012968&contentId=7068993.
11. Dr Nina Poussenkova, "The Energy Dimension in Russian Global Strategy," study for the James Baker III Institute of Public Policy, Rice University, Houston, Texas (October 2004).
12. Organization of Petroleum Exporting Countries, "Annual Statistical Bulletin," Vienna (18 July 2011), www.opec.org/opec_web/en/publications/202.htm.

CHAPTER

Food and Water

Where the Rivers Run

If the wars of this century were fought over oil, the wars of the next century will be fought over water—unless we change our approach to managing this precious and vital resource.

—Ismail Serageldin,
then vice president of World Bank, August 1995

Long before the *great bend*, the point where China's Yarlung Zangbo River flows around the Namcha Barwa mountain, beginning its sharp curve south into India and an eventual name change to the Brahmaputra, this sacred river has well and truly made its mark on the cold Tibetan Plateau. Fed by melting snow from the northern face of the Himalayas, the first trickles of the Yarlung Zangbo gather volume as the river pushes east through southern Tibet toward the start of its own Grand Canyon 1,500 km (930 miles) away near the town of Pe. Cutting deeper and deeper into the valley floor, the Yarlung Zangbo River drops 2,700 metres (9,000 ft) in 250 km (155 miles), cascading over rocks and waterfalls to create white-water heaven for intrepid adventurers with the money, courage, skill, and perseverance to tackle it. It is an experience with sometimes-fatal consequences: expeditions from Japan in 1993 and the United States in 1998 both lost experienced kayakers in the churning waters of the Yarlung Zangbo. In 2002, a team from the U.S. adventure magazine *Outside* made the first whitewater descent of the Zangbo upper gorge, travelling 70 km downstream in a journey that took them past the abandoned Tibetan monastery of Pemakochung into country that few people had ever seen. They were keen to go further, but the dangers of the lower gorge with its towering cliffs and huge waterfalls made further descent impossible.

Although the river is sacred for Tibetans, the real allure for Chinese authorities is its hydropower potential. There is talk of a massive dam in the gorge that would generate 40,000 MW of power, and be bigger than the Yangzi River's Three Gorges project. Already China has begun work on a pilot project, the Zangmu Dam, that is due for completion in 2015. Associated with this is a long-term water diversion scheme that would see part of the Yarlung Zangbo's flow redirected to the Yellow River, which flows for more than 5,000 km from western China to northeast China's Bohai Sea. It is this sort of project that alarms downstream users in India and Bangladesh and renders the Yarlung-Zangbo-Brahmaputra just one of many global flashpoints in the world's water wars. There are scores of others, most notably between India and Pakistan (the Indus), in Africa (the Nile), the Middle East (the Tigris-Euphrates, the Jordan), Central Asia (the Aral Sea), South America (the Amazon, the Parana) and Europe (the Danube). Wherever there is a river or freshwater lake that has more than one claimant to its water, the potential for conflict exists.

There have always been wars over water, dating back 4,500 years to when the Sumerian city-states of Lagash and Umma fought for control of irrigated farming land in the fertile valley of the Tigris and Euphrates in what is now southern Iraq. But with 7 billion mouths to feed, the world is more conscious than ever of the unbreakable nexus between water and life. No water, no food, no life, is the simple equation.

Farming accounts for 70 percent of global water use, and half the world's population relies on water from the great rivers that rise in the Himalayas, the Tibetan Plateau, and the Tibetan ethnic areas of China.[1] The way the most important of these rivers—the Indus, Ganges, Brahmaputra, Salween, Yangzi, Yellow, and Mekong—are being used carries the potential for twenty-first-century water wars as countries struggle with the challenges of rising populations, pressure on farming and food supplies, diminishing water quality, and demand for hydropower. The Mekong, for example, runs through and between six Asian countries—China, Myanmar, Laos, Thailand, Cambodia, and Vietnam—on its journey of almost 5,000 km from the snowbound "Three Rivers" area in Tibet to the steamy delta lowlands of Vietnam, where it flows into the South China Sea. Its use is supposed to be regulated by the four-nation Mekong River Commission (MRC), but Chinese dam-building for hydropower and the blasting of rapids in an attempt to make the river more navigable has provoked consternation among downstream nations. Falling water levels, loss of fish and animal species as riverside industrialisation and fertiliser runoff increases pollution and algae infestation, and the enforced migration of people either from dam-building or loss of livelihood are all pointers to how Asian societies may live or die on the way they treat the continent's great rivers. The scholar Milton Osborne, who has written extensively about the Mekong over the past 30 years, fears that the dam-building plans of China, Laos, and Cambodia will end the river's role as a "bounteous source of fish and guarantor of agricultural richness, with the great river below China becoming little more than a series of unproductive lakes."[2]

Challenge for India, Pakistan

Though the Mekong and the Brahmaputra are two important examples, China is not alone when it comes to water envy among Asian neighbours. India has its own conflict to resolve with Pakistan over the Indus River, which rises on the Tibetan plateau in China and flows for more than 3,000 km through India and Pakistan before emptying into the Arabian Sea near Pakistan's port city of Karachi. India and Pakistan have a troubled relationship. Since independence and partition in 1947, they have gone to war with each other three times, and came close to nuclear conflict in 1999 at Kargil and again in 2002. The disputed territory of Kashmir—through which the Indus flows—remains one of the most dangerous flashpoints on earth. In November 2008, the deadly attack on India's commercial capital Mumbai by Pakistan-based terrorists added a new, worrying dimension to the way these two South Asian nations interact.

Within this volatile milieu, the Indus provides a living for 180 million people along its basin. Indeed, the fertile Indus valley has been one of the world's "cradles of civilisation" for 5,000 years, dating back to the Harappa and Mohenjo-daro era, when the first canals were dug. A network of modern canals and dams built from 1850 onward extended the valley's agricultural value, but also laid the seeds of future discord over water use when "British India" gave way to two very separate nations.

After almost a decade of torturous negotiation, in 1960 the World Bank brokered the Indus Waters Treaty, which set out how India and Pakistan could share the river and its tributaries. That treaty gave the waters of the Ravi, Sutlej, and Beas rivers (known as the Eastern Rivers) to India, and the waters of the Indus, Jhelum, and Chenab (known as the Western Rivers) to Pakistan. The treaty also gave Pakistan a financial settlement for loss of water from the Eastern Rivers, and allowed India, as the upper riparian neighbour, some right to use the Western Rivers for domestic use, agriculture and hydropower. For half a century, the treaty worked well. But in recent years Pakistan has become concerned that too much Indus water is being diverted inside India. In particular, it is opposed to India building a hydropower project on the Neelum River, a tributary of the Jhelum known as Kishanganga in India. Pakistan is working on its own Neelum-Jhelum hydropower scheme. With groundwater supplies declining in its Punjab and Sindh provinces— where most of Pakistan's food is produced—it worries about an over-dependence on river water for irrigation, even as accelerated melting of the Himalayan glaciers puts more water into the system. Adding to Pakistan's woes were the devastating Indus River floods of mid-2010, which left half a million people homeless and land in southern Sindh province waterlogged. The challenge for Pakistan and India is how to harness the power of their big Himalayan rivers in a way that is fair and sustainable.

Taming the Yangzi

Chairman Mao Zedong, leader of the People's Republic of China until his death in 1976, knew the symbolic power of bending the big rivers to his will. In 1956, he braved the waters of the Yangzi and penned a poem he called "Swimming." In it, he wrote how great plans were afoot to build a bridge spanning north and south, "turning a deep chasm into a thoroughfare." Upstream, walls of stone would hold back the clouds and rain of Wushan, creating a "smooth lake" in the Yangzi's narrow gorges.[3]

China has always been prepared to move mountains (and people) to achieve its economic and social goals—the $25 billion Three Gorges project (built 1994–2011) was testament to that, with 1.3 million people relocated so the dam could be built on the Yangzi River, both to generate power and as a flood mitigation measure. Its full ecological impact is yet to be determined. Now there is something even bigger on the horizon—the $60 billion China South-North Water Diversion Project that involves China's two most important rivers—the Yangzi and the Yellow—plus numerous tributaries, canals, and other rivers such as the Huai and Hai. It is one of the biggest civil engineering projects yet conceived anywhere in the world. First formulated by Mao Zedong in 1952 as a way to move water from the southern half of China to the dry but heavily populated north, the three-part scheme took its first steps forward in 2002 when work began on the 1,155-km (716-mile) eastern route. This part of the project, scheduled for completion in 2013, will take water from the Yangzi River via channels to Shandong province, and then by a tunnel under the Yellow River and onward to the coastal city of Tianjin.

Work on the central route began late in 2003. This 1,267-km (785-mile) diversion is designed to take water from the Danjiangkou Reservoir on the Han River (a tributary of the Yangzi), along new canals and on to Henan and Hebei provinces, and finally to Beijing. A trunk line will also serve Tianjin. After various delays prompted by environmental concerns, the central route is now likely to be finished by 2014.

The western route is the one that causes the most concern outside China, as it involves diverting water from three tributaries of the Yangzi—the Tongtian, the Dadu, and the Yarlung Zangbo River—across the Bayankala Mountains to the Yellow River, to supply northwest China. The Yarlung Zangbo River flows for 1,700 km (1,050 miles) across the southern Tibet plateau before entering India. Work has already started on a small hydropower project, the Zangmu Dam (due for completion in 2015) on the Yarlung Zangbo. China maintains that any dams it builds on the river will have little downstream impact, but Zangmu and the associated western route diversion are a concern for India because of the importance of the Brahmaputra to many millions of its people, particularly in eastern India. That concern is heightened by the knowledge that India and China have yet to draw up a water-sharing treaty along the lines of the Indus Waters Treaty.

China has more irrigated land than anywhere else in the world: 51 million hectares (197,000 square miles), compared with 46 million hectares for India and 20 million hectares for the United States, according to China's Ministry of Water Resources. Indeed, the world's three biggest water users by volume are India, China, and the United States. Following them in the top 10 are Pakistan, Japan, Thailand, Indonesia, Bangladesh, Mexico, and Russia.[4] Increasing prosperity in China means that farmers want more water, not just to meet the demand for more food but also for better-quality food that consumes more water in the production process. Industry and mining also need large quantities of water. With an economy growing at double-digit pace, one consequence is that China is drawing on its groundwater faster than rainfall can replenish it.

China's unsustainable water use has increased the pressure to find new water sources, such as river diversion from the west, or perhaps from a transboundary aquifer (an underground water source) such as the Heilongjiang-Amur aquifer that runs from northern China into the Russian Far East. The Amur River, which in places marks the Sino-Russian border and which joins the Ussuri River at the gritty Russian city of Khabarovsk, was the setting for a series of heavy clashes between Chinese and Soviet Union troops in 1969 that left hundreds dead. Although the reasons for those hostilities have long been resolved by border demarcations, there is a marked imbalance in development momentum between China and Russia in this part of the world, and that affects water usage. China's northeastern provinces of Heilongjiang, Jilin, and Liaoning are home to more than 100 million people. In contrast, there are only a couple of million Russian citizens living in this part of the Russian Far East. As Chinese cities mushroom along the Amur River, the demand for water for crops, industry, and drinking is expected to rise rapidly. According to a recent study of the Heilongjiang-Amur aquifer by the UNESCO initiative ISARM (Internationally Shared Aquifer Resources Management), it is "in balance," meaning the current discharge rate of the groundwater is matched by the recharge rate.[5] But China's water usage from the aquifer is twice that of Russia's, and in 2005 an accident at a petrochemical plant in Jilin province polluted the Songhua River (part of the Heilongjiang-Amur) and potentially put at risk the water supply of Khabarovsk city downstream. Although containment measures by both China and

Russia allayed the threat, it highlighted how accidents could have an impact beyond national boundaries.

Aral Sea's Damage

Sometimes those accidents—or in the case of Central Asia's Aral Sea, a deliberate policy—can have far-reaching consequences. The Aral Sea was once the world's fourth largest lake with a surface area of 68,000 sq km (about 26,250 square miles). But the Soviet Union's desire in the 1960s to create a cotton export industry using water that previously flowed into the Aral Sea almost completely destroyed it and the livelihoods of thousands of people, mainly the farmers and fishers who depended on it. Only in recent years have parts of the lake made something of a comeback. Even so, according to a case study by the UN's World Water Assessment Program, the unsustainable use of water has caused irreversible damage to water quality and the ecosystem of the Aral Sea basin. There is heavy pollution of surface water and groundwater from untreated wastewater containing high concentrations of pesticide, fertiliser, and industrial runoff. According to the case study, mass migration away from the basin, as well as malnutrition and extreme poverty for many of the people who remain there, are consequences of Soviet policy.

The Soviet Union is long gone; in its place since 1991 are five Central Asian republics—Uzbekistan, Turkmenistan, Kyrgyzstan, Tajikistan, and Kazakhstan—with an interest in the Aral Sea's health because of the rivers that flow through the basin. The two most directly affected are Kazakhstan and Uzbekistan, which share a border through the middle of the lake area. Since the end of World War II, the Soviet Union had been using water from the basin's two main rivers, the Amu Darya (which rises in Kyrgyzstan) and the Syr Darya (which originates in Tajikistan), for irrigation and hydropower as part of its regional development plans. In what is regarded as one of the world's worst postwar environmental catastrophes, from the 1960s onward, the volume of water diversion for irrigation was stepped up as the Soviet Union set out to increase cotton crops in what is now Uzbekistan. As a result, the Aral Sea shrank dramatically. The loss of inflow was so severe that in 1986 the lake divided into northern and southern parts, leaving fishing boats stranded as the shoreline receded. In 2003, the South Aral Sea split into eastern and western halves, with the eastern portion almost completely drying out in 2009 before meltwater in 2010 gave it another lease of life. The North Aral Sea was dammed in 2005 by Kazakhstan in an attempt to preserve its fishing industry and restore the heavily polluted lake to some semblance of health. Since then, its water level has risen and salinity has dropped. The need to balance the competing claims of hydropower, irrigation, environmental protection, and sustainable fishing remains a constant challenge for the area's inhabitants and governments.

Further to the west, Turkey has been involved in a long-running water war with Syria and Iraq over the Tigris-Euphrates basin. All three countries depend on water from these rivers, and with their populations and water usage growing, shortages over the next two decades are a distinct possibility. Both the Tigris and Euphrates rise in the mountains of eastern Turkey before flowing through Syria and into Iraq, where they are joined by several tributaries (including some from Iran) and merge, eventually to drain into the head of the Persian Gulf through the marshes of the Shatt al-Arab water- way. Turkey, as the dominant upstream nation, has the advantage over its vulnerable downstream neighbours in controlling the water flow, but faces its own security concerns over Kurdish sepa- ratists active in southeast Anatolia. In January 1990, Turkey briefly stopped the flow of the Euphrates as part of its construction of the Ataturk Dam, which is the centerpiece of its Southeast Anatolia Development (GAP) program, one of the world's largest dam, hydropower, and flood mitigation projects. That stoppage signaled to downstream Syria just what was possible should relations take a turn for the worse. At the time, Syria was supporting the Kurdish rebels, while Iraq was still recovering from its eight-year war with Iran (1980–1988) and would soon find itself in the first Gulf War. Along with the Ataturk Dam, Turkey is committed to building the Ilisu Dam on the Tigris about 50 km (30 miles) from the Syrian border. But this dam, due for completion in 2015, will submerge the ancient town of Hasankeyf, regarded as a cultural relic of all the major civiliza- tions that have existed in upper Mesopotamia over the past 4000 years. Once all 22 dams in Turkey's massive GAP project are built, the result is likely to significantly reduce per capita water availability in both Syria and Iraq.

Similar problems prevail in the Jordan River valley, where Jordan, Syria, Lebanon, and Israel each have claims on water from the Jordan. Israel, which built a pumping station on the Sea of Galilee to take water to its settlements, is regularly accused of stealing "Arab water."

Waters of the Nile

Israel's neighbour to the west, Egypt, is involved in a tussle with Ethiopia, Sudan, and the new nation of South Sudan over the waters of the Nile, which at 6,500 km (4,030 miles) is the world's longest river. Other African countries with an interest in the Nile or its tributaries include Uganda, Rwanda, Burundi, Tanzania, Kenya, Eritrea, and the Democratic Republic of Congo. The two arms of the river, the White Nile and the Blue Nile, rise respectively in Uganda (at Jinja, on Lake Victoria, though this is disputed) and in the Ethiopian highlands at Lake Tana. The rivers join at Khartoum, the capital of Sudan, before flowing through Egypt and into the Mediterranean at Alexandria. The Blue Nile accounts for about 85 percent of the water flow reaching Egypt. The Aswan High Dam, completed in 1970, provides power and flood mitigation for millions of Egyptians living in the Nile valley. But its creation has also led to a host of changes, including the relocation of thousands of villagers and the destruction of eco-systems, fisheries, and archaeological treasures from thousands of years ago. Egypt is the primary user of the Nile's water, followed by Sudan, which uses only about a third as much as Egypt. Ethiopia, the source country for much of the Nile's flow, uses only a tiny fraction of it, but in the past has been too weak to make a stand against Egypt. In 2011, Ethiopia sought to push ahead with its Great Millennium Dam, a 5,200 MW hydropower project on the Blue Nile that Egypt and Sudan want to block.

In Libya, a project begun in 1984 by the late Colonel Muammar Gaddafi is the "Great Man-made River" or GMR, which pipes water from aquifers in the sparsely populated south to the more populous but arid northern coast. The $25 billion project, completed in 2007, is based on a 4,000 km (2,500 mile) network of underground pipes, some of which draw water from aquifers close to the Egyptian border. Gaddafi, who was overthrown by rebels and subsequently killed in October 2011, called it the Eighth Wonder of the World.

In March 2011, Brazil began work on its own mega-project, the $11 billion Belo Monte dam on the Xingu River, a tributary of the Amazon, in Pará state. When completed, the dam will generate 11,000 megawatts, making it the third largest hydroelectric dam in the world behind the Three Gorges and the Itaipu Dam, which sits on the border of Brazil and Paraguay. But the Belo Monte project has incurred the wrath of environmentalists and local communities, who say 400 sq km (150 square miles) of Amazon rainforest will be flooded, 20,000 people will have to be moved, and many other indigenous people who live in the Xingu region will be negatively affected.

Some water conflicts are more perceived than real. Although Canada's massive lakes and rivers make it water-rich—globally it ranks third behind Brazil and China in terms of annual fresh water available per head of population—many of its citizens worry about the possible depredations of its water-hungry neighbour, the United States. About 40 percent of Canada's 8,800 km (5,450 mile) border with the United States runs through waters such as the Great Lakes, where levels have declined in recent years to the point where Council for Canadians chairperson Maude Barlow declared in March 2011 that scientists were saying the Great Lakes could be bone dry in 80 years.[6] Longstanding U.S. proposals for bulk water shipments or pipelines from Canada, plus overuse of the Ogallala aquifer by farmers in the U.S. Midwest, serve as a constant irritant to the Canadian conservation movement. Even though bulk sales are highly unlikely over the next decade, water usage is one of the touchiest subjects in the relationship. Under the 1909 U.S.-Canada Boundary Waters Treaty, an International Joint Commission has been set up to resolve disputes over water and other environmental issues along their border.

The Floating Garbage Patch

Greenpeace calls it the *trash vortex*. Others call it the Great Pacific Garbage Patch—an area in the North Pacific between Hawaii and the California coast where plastic garbage and other debris swirl around and around, carried by the system of rotating ocean currents known as the North Pacific Gyre. The plastic bottles and their caps, along with toys, shoes, plastic bags, nets, and other bits and pieces are choking birds and killing fish and other marine life that try to ingest them. According to the U.S. government's National Oceanic and Atmospheric Administration, the exact size, content, and location of the garbage patch are difficult to predict accurately, but it lies within the North Pacific Subtropical High—an area that moves and changes. "Contrary to what

(continued)

(*Continued*)

its name implies, the area is not a concentration of trash visible in satellite or aerial photographs," NOAA says, but confirms it does contain many small bits of floating plastic debris, fishing nets, and other litter. There is a similar garbage patch floating in the North Atlantic Gyre, in an area known as the Sargasso Sea, to the north of the Caribbean Sea. Scientists think it likely that the three other major ocean gyres—in the South Atlantic, the South Pacific, and the Indian Ocean—also host an accumulation of non-biodegradable plastic garbage.

Source: U.S. National Oceanic and Atmospheric Administration, Marine Debris Program, "What we know about the 'garbage patches,'" http://marinedebris.noaa.gov/info/pdf/patch.pdf.

Whether in the Americas, Africa, or Asia, drought and floods have long been part of the cycle of rural life. And despite the often-lavish food consumption that typifies life for many wealthy people on China's prosperous east coast in cities such as Beijing, Shanghai, and Guangzhou, China's desperate and ongoing thirst for water is predicated on a history of suffering. China has seen its share of famine as a result of crop failure from drought, floods, or other natural disasters such as earthquakes. But its greatest food catastrophe of all was manmade; tens of millions of people died of starvation and other privations between 1958 and 1962 as a consequence of Mao Zedong's disastrous "Great Leap Forward" in agriculture. Instead of the full bellies that the Chinese leadership believed would follow from mass mobilization, quota setting, collective production, and centralized food distribution, the result was famine of almost unimaginable proportions, along with social dislocation, corruption, and oppression. The full death toll will never be known, although detailed research by the Hong Kong-based author Frank Dikotter in his 2010 book *Mao's Great Famine* suggests a figure of at least 45 million deaths, 50 percent higher than previous estimates of 30 million. Certainly it is hard to dispute Dikotter's judgment that it was "the worst catastrophe in China's history."[7] These days, there is an unwritten pact between China's 1.3 billion people and their leaders in Beijing: Give us economic progress, give us food security, give us freedom from hungry ghosts, and we will leave some of our other freedoms on the table for a later day.

High Food Prices

Food is a constant concern for half the world, with more than a billion people going to bed hungry in the second decade of the twenty-first century—a figure not seen since the poverty-wracked 1970s. According to the UN's Food and Agricultural Organization, food prices are at their highest in 20 years, with food inflation a major concern for India, China, and Africa. A return to the food riots of 2008–2009 that hit some developing economies is an ever-present possibility, particularly given the dramatic political changes that shook parts of North Africa and the Middle East in the first few months of 2011. Leaders fell, in part, because their citizens were suffering from high prices for such basics as bread.

Shenggen Fan, director general of the International Food Policy Research Institute in Washington, is one expert who advocates setting up an emergency grain reserve to help counter food crises around the globe. He says the reserve should be owned and managed by an institution such as the World Food Program, which already has a global food management system in place. In Fan's view, the reserve should be created "through grain stock donations from large food exporters, such as the United States, and large food producers, such as China and India." It should be positioned in these countries and, for easy access, in poor countries that import food, such as Bangladesh. Fan recognises the challenges of running such a system, so he has suggested it be started on an experimental scale with relatively small reserves.[8]

Unlike China's Great Famine of 1958–1962, when the burden was borne most acutely by rural peasants, urban food security is the big challenge today. There are now more than 400 cities in the world with a population above 1 million, including 160 in China alone and 45 in India. That compares with less than 20 such cities globally 100 years ago. In the emerging world, megacities such as Shanghai, Beijing, Guangzhou, Mumbai, Kolkata, Delhi, Dhaka, Manila, Sao Paulo, Jakarta, Cairo, Istanbul, Tehran, Mexico City, Lagos, Karachi, Rio de Janeiro, and Buenos Aires all have populations of 10 million or more. By 2050, when the world's population reaches 9 billion, 6 billion people will live in cities.

According to agricultural scientist Professor M. S. Swaminathan, the father of India's first Green Revolution of the 1960s–1970s, the rapid urbanisation of the Third World has brought food security front and centre of global concerns. "Managing urbanisation is a key contemporary challenge across the developing world," Swaminathan noted in a report on Urban India Food Insecurity.[9] According to the Food and Agriculture Organization (FAO), most urban expansion over the next 20 years will be in the developing world, and feeding the poorest of these city-dwellers will be a real challenge. One solution: increased harvesting of rainwater in cities to support more urban agriculture—the old backyard vegetable garden revisited.

Experts agree that food production and the supply chain has to become more efficient—for example, in India as much as 30 percent of food is spoilt in the long journey from farm gate to consumer. Most of all, the world has to be smarter about how it uses water— not just once, but how it captures and recycles this most valuable resource.

Frozen Fresh Water

Actually, the world has plenty of water—1.4 billion cubic kilometres in total, but 97 percent of it is salt water, unfit for human consumption without the expensive process of desalinization. According to the U.S. Geological Survey, the remaining 3 percent is fresh water, but almost 70 percent of this is frozen in glaciers and the polar ice caps and thus—short of major climatic change—economically inaccessible. The 30 percent of fresh water left is almost entirely groundwater, stored in massive aquifers such as the Great Artesian Basin of Australia, the Guarani Aquifer of South America, and the Ogallala Aquifer of North America. Some of this groundwater, particularly in the driest parts of the world—the Nubian Sandstone Aquifer in Libya, the Disi-Saq in Jordan/Saudia Arabia, and the Sanaa basin in Yemen—is "fossil water," meaning that it is not replenished by seasonal rainfall. It is much older, and it is finite. Once it is gone, that's it. After the frozen water and the groundwater, there is the fresh water found in the world's lakes, swamps, and rivers. It makes up just 0.33 percent of the total.

The way the world currently uses water, a shortage is inevitable as the population, life expectancy, and food demand all increase. According to the Sweden-based international water security network Global Water Partnership, China's per capita water availability will drop from 2,195 cubic metres in 2000 to just 1,760 cubic metres in 2030 when the population reaches 1.6 billion. By the reckoning of the United Nations, that will make it "water stressed."

Agriculture is the biggest user of fresh water, taking 70 percent of it, followed by industry with 22 percent. The remaining 8 percent is for human consumption, where the key demand determinants are clean, safe, and affordable drinking water. But that is not so easily achieved. India's "mother river," the Ganges, rises in the pristine environment of the Gangotri Glacier on the southern face of the Himalayas, but before it completes its 2,500 km (1,550 mile) journey to the Bay of Bengal, it becomes so polluted by industrial effluent, untreated sewage, and other types of human waste that it is unfit for drinking, bathing, and agriculture along several parts of its length.

> Every day, millions of tons of inadequately treated sewage and industrial and agricultural wastes are poured into the world's waters . . . Every year, more people die from the consequences of unsafe water than from all forms of violence, including war. . . . Water contamination weakens or destroys natural ecosystems that support human health, food production, and biodiversity. . . . Most polluted freshwater ends up in the oceans, damaging coastal areas and fisheries . . .
>
> —*United Nations World Water Day statement,*
> *22 March 2011*

Water quality is crucial, because while starvation in Africa and Asia is an ever-present fear for many millions of people living below the poverty line, more people die every year from bad water than any other cause. Waterborne diseases such as diarrhoea, jaundice, typhoid, cholera, polio, and gastroenteritis are the killers. Children in particular are vulnerable. According to the World Health Organization's director of Public Health and Environment, Dr. Maria Neira, dirty water, inadequate sanitation, and a lack of hygiene take the lives of about 2.2 million children under the age of 5 every year. Of these, 1.5 million die from diarrhea. In India alone, about 400,000 children die annually from diseases spread by contaminated water. With the right measures, these are preventable deaths. And there is a significant economic benefit from providing clean water and better sanitation to people. This one measure can add as much as an extra 2 to 7 percent to a country's gross domestic product, according to the World Health Organization.

When water is polluted, purification can make it potable. But in a country like India, many rural inhabitants have no access to power or running water, meaning that a water purifier must be able to operate in the most basic environment. Boiling water on a regular basis is not feasible for many people, which has prompted some of India's biggest business houses to pursue the water-purification fortune at the bottom of the pyramid. Tata Group, for example, sells its Swach purifier for about $20. The purifier uses rice-husk ash impregnated with nano-silver particles to deliver about 3,000 litres of filtered drinking water, with replacement cartridge filters costing about $6.

Pressure on Prices

There is no doubt that the push for cleaner energy, particularly biofuel, is putting pressure on water, food production, and food prices. According to the UN World Water Development Report of 2009, more than a third of U.S. maize production in 2008 was used to produce ethanol, while about half of the European Union's vegetable oil production went into biodiesel fuel. "Although the impact is extremely difficult to assess, bioenergy production is estimated to have caused as much as 70 to 75 percent of the rise in the global prices of some food stocks, including 70 percent of the increase in maize prices," the report concluded.[10] To this could be added the bizarre way that politics drives agribusiness. As Goldman Sachs' global head of commodities research Jeffrey Currie told an oil and gas conference in London, the United States is the bread basket of the world, and is to agriculture what Saudi Arabia is to oil. But political restrictions prevent most optimal investments, which is why the United States turns farmland into oil (via ethanol production) and Saudi Arabia turns its oil into fertiliser to use on its deserts to grow food.[11]

Notes

1. UN World Water Development Report No. 3, "Water in a Changing World," Paris, UNESCO, 2009.
2. Milton Osborne, "Mekong Dam Plans Threatening the Natural Order," *The Australian* (29 June 2011).
3. Mao Zedong, poem "Swimming," June 1956, in *Selected Works of Mao Tse-Tun* (Peking: Foreign Language Press, 1972).
4. UN World Water Development Report 2009.
5. UNESCO, Internationally Shared Aquifer Resources Management, Report on Heilongjiang-Amur Aquifer in "Transboundary Aquifers in Asia with Special Emphasis on China," Beijing, October 2006.
6. Media release, Council for Canadians, "Protect the Great Lakes as a Commons, says Council of Canadians," 22 March 2011.

7. Frank Dikotter, *Mao's Great Famine: The History of China's Most Devastating Catastrophe, 1958–1962* (London: Bloomsbury, September 2010).
8. Shenggen Fan, International Food Policy Research Institute, Washington, "Urgent Actions Need to Prevent Recurring Food Crises," East Asia Forum (1 May 2011).
9. Professor MS Swaminathan, "Urban India Food Insecurity," *MS Swaminathan Research Foundation*, Chennai (September 2010).
10. UN World Water Development Report 2009.
11. Jeffrey Currie, Goldman Sachs, presentation to Platts Crude Oil Markets Conference, London, 13 May 2011.

CHAPTER

"Going Out" for Energy

China and India Stake Their Claims

*As two billion more people start consuming more goods, and
driving more cars, and using more energy, it's certain that demand
will go up a lot faster than supply.*
—U.S. President Barack Obama, 30 March 2011
(energy policy speech, Georgetown University,
Washington DC)

For the next 20 years at least, coal-fired power stations will continue to dominate the world's electricity generation, while oil products (gasoline, diesel, jet fuel) will still be the lifeblood of the transport sector. In the words of the International Energy Agency (IEA), a "golden age" for natural gas is on its way, as the gas pipeline grid spreads ever further across Europe and Asia, and Russia boosts its already substantial gas output. In the United States, cheap shale gas gives it a hefty cost advantage for now. Oil and gas fields in the Caspian will assume a bigger role ahead, as will liquefied natural gas (LNG) from Qatar and Australia. The IEA expects that conventional crude oil output will reach a plateau by 2020 while production of gas and unconventional oil—notably Canadian oil sands—grows strongly.[1]

Essentially, the era of cheap, easy oil is over. The days when a rig could hit the jackpot anywhere in the Middle East or North America are long gone. Now comes the hard stuff—the offshore drillers with their attendant dangers in the Gulf of Mexico (see BP's Deepwater Horizon disaster in 2010), the sheer climatic challenge of the Arctic waters above Russia, the environmental hazards of Canada's Athabasca tar sands, the ultra-deep and ultra-long-range technology Brazil must master to tap its "pre-salt" bounty hundreds of kilometres offshore in the South Atlantic Ocean, the upgrades needed to get Iraqi oil flowing freely again, the geopolitical risks that have to be weighed for existing and new ventures in Africa, the Middle East, Central Asia, and beyond—not to mention the clashes that may intensify when Vietnam, China, Japan, the Philippines, Indonesia, and Malaysia cross paths as they probe the oil and gas riches of the South China and East China Seas. The exploration, logistics, and security challenges are huge, even for the biggest of the oil companies. And yet the demand is there. Europe and the United States may be able to get by with less, but China wants more oil and gas, as does India, the Middle East, Japan, South Korea, Brazil, and a dozen fast-growing economies behind them. In 2012, the U.S. Department of Energy expects that the world's consumption of liquid fuels will reach 90 million barrels a day (b/d).

Most of the world's incremental oil over the next two decades will come from just five countries—Saudi Arabia, Iraq, Brazil, Kazakhstan, and Canada—if the IEA's "new policies" central scenario for 2035 proves correct. Saudi Arabia and Iraq will be the two heavyweights, lifting output by 5 million and 4.5 million barrels a day, respectively. Brazil will lift by 3.2 million, Kazakhstan by 2.4 million, and Canada by 2.2 million. Venezuela and the United Arab Emirates will also be important contributors to what the IEA calls the world's incremental production. As oil demand grows steadily from 84 million b/d in 2009 to 99 million b/d by 2035, the IEA says crude oil production will plateau at about 69 million b/d by 2020, with the remainder coming from unconventional oil such as Canadian oil sands, and natural gas liquids.[2]

So where does that leave Russia, currently the world's biggest producer (ahead of Saudi Arabia and the United States), with daily output above 10 million barrels of crude? (See Exhibit 5.1.) If the IEA's outlook is right, Russian output will remain steady until 2015

1. Russian Federation 12.6	**7.** Venezuela 3.8
2. Saudi Arabia 11.9	**8.** Mexico 3.6
3. United States 8.5	**9.** Nigeria 3.3
4. Iran 5.7	**10.** UAE 3.2
5. China 5.0	Rest of world 38.4
6. Canada 4.0	

Exhibit 5.1   World's biggest producers of crude oil (by percentage share)
Source: IEA Key World Energy Statistics October 2011

and then decline to about 9 million barrels a day by 2035. Russian oil reserves may not be as well-defined as those of Saudi Arabia, Iraq, Iran, and Venezuela, yet there are plenty of energy-hungry countries and companies prepared to bet big money that they can find and exploit more oil in the Russian Far East on Sakhalin Island, in the frozen tundra of Eastern and Western Siberia, in the icy waters of the Arctic Ocean, or in the ethnically volatile region of the Caucasus/Caspian Sea. For example, Nikolay Tokarev, the president of Russian pipeline operator Transneft, expects Russian production to grow to 11 million barrels a day after 2012 as new fields such as Rosneft's Vankor extension in Eastern Siberia and TNK-BP's Uvat project in Western Siberia come onstream.[3]

Unlike oil, there will be no plateau for Russian gas. Russia is already the world's largest gas producer and, with reserves estimated at 48 trillion cubic metres (1,695 trillion cubic feet), will also be the main source of gas supply growth. According to an IEA projection in April 2011, Russian gas production is expected to reach 800 billion cubic metres (28.2 trillion cubic feet) in 2035, a rise of 215 billion cubic metres (7.59 trillion cubic feet) compared with 2009. That will make Russia by far the biggest contributor to incremental supply, well ahead of Qatar, Iran, China, Turkmenistan, Australia, and Nigeria.

> Today, I'm setting a new goal: one that is reasonable, achievable, and necessary. When I was elected to this office, America imported 11 million barrels of oil a day. By a little more than a decade from now, we will have cut that by one-third.
> —*U.S. President Barack Obama, 30 March 2011 (energy policy speech, Georgetown University, Washington, DC)*

U.S. Gas Revolution

In the world's biggest economy, the United States, something quite different is going on in gas—the shale gas revolution has sent gas prices plunging to one-tenth that of oil. This domestic gas glut is driving out imported LNG, in the process creating what the IEA calls a segmented "island" market in North America where the low prices stimulate demand, particularly in power generation and chemicals. Aside from this cheap gas, the United States also consumes a billion tonnes a year of thermal coal, and the equivalent of about 20 million barrels a day of oil and petroleum products, of which just under half is imported. The single biggest supplier of crude is Canada, with a 21 percent share, followed by Mexico (12 percent), Saudi Arabia (12 percent), Nigeria (11 percent), and Venezuela (10 percent). The United States itself produces about 5.5 million barrels a day of crude and about 2 million barrels of natural gas liquids. The United States also has the world's largest reserves of oil shale deposits, estimated at between 1.5 and 2 trillion barrels. But extraction is complex and costly, and the economic viability of oil shale is haphazard. Estonia, China, and Brazil are the only current producers of any size. Russia has oil shale reserves of 250 billion barrels, and Israel may have about the same.

Against this backdrop, oil executives from around the world gathered in the ballroom of London's Waldorf Hilton Hotel in May 2011 for an important update on the latest market information. Russia, Brazil, China, Africa, and the North Sea were all on the agenda, but it was the recent cataclysmic events in North Africa and the Middle East—and the likely response from the oil cartel known as OPEC (the Organization of Petroleum Exporting Countries)—that figured high in their calculations of where oil demand and oil prices were headed.

Tunisia Heralds Arab Spring

It had started in Tunisia six months earlier, in December 2010. On a Friday morning in the rural town of Sidi Bouzid, 250 km south of the capital Tunis, a 26-year-old fruit and vegetable seller named Mohammed Bouazizi found himself in dispute with municipal authorities over his lack of a street vendor's licence. His goods were seized, his family insulted. Bouazizi, humiliated by the officials and stripped of his sole source of income, made his way to the governor's office to complain. When he was turned away without a hearing, he set himself alight in protest. His action, which led to his death in the hospital 18 days later on January 4, was the spark for a firestorm of public protest against food inflation, unemployment, and government repression.

Tunisia's autocratic President Zine El-Abedine Ben Ali visited Bouazizi in the hospital, but the damage was done. Within weeks, Ben Ali was gone, and the shock waves that would become known as the Arab Spring began to radiate out across the region. By February, Egypt was convulsed by prodemocracy demonstrations that led to the ouster of long-time military ruler Hosni Mubarak. Protesters took to the streets in Yemen, and then in Bahrain. The agitation spread to Libya and Syria, where Muammar Gaddafi and Bashar al-Assad, respectively, chose to meet rebellion with old-fashioned military might. That spelt disaster for Libya, where full-scale civil war erupted. NATO sent in aircraft to bomb Gaddafi's forces under a "responsibility to protect civilians" rationale. By October 2011, Gaddafi was dead and his regime was well and truly over. In March, Saudi Arabia had sent troops across the causeway to crush the Bahrain protests, and splurged with $130 billion at home for jobs, housing, and pay rises for millions of its citizens. By the end of 2011, Yemen's President Ali Abdullah Saleh had renounced his powers and was out of the country, with an interim government tasked with staving off civil war. In Syria, Assad's brutal crackdown continued, prompting thousands of Syrians to seek refuge in Turkey. The only thing certain about the Arab world in the months ahead was that more chaos would follow.

For the wider world, the loss of Libya's 1.4 million barrels a day of high-quality crude for six months or more, plus the general instability generated across the Middle East and North Africa as Morocco, Algeria, Jordan, and Sudan worried about their own domestic politics, signaled a new volatility in the energy trade. Until Iraq's oil infrastructure is rejuvenated over the next decade, only Saudi Arabia has enough oil-pumping capacity to make a significant difference among Mideast suppliers. And despite the momentum gathering for renewable energy sources, oil is still the lifeblood of global commerce and transport.

After a fumbled midyear meeting in Vienna of the Organization of Oil Producing Exporters (OPEC) and with oil prices above $100 a barrel, the IEA at the end of June 2011 announced the release of emergency oil reserves for only the third time since its formation in 1974. While the 60 million barrels—half of which was from the U.S. strategic reserve—covered less than two months of lost Libyan production, it was a symbolic statement of intent and a soothing sign for emerging energy consumers such as China and India. By the start of January 2012, Libyan output was above 800,000 b/d, and OPEC members were able to pump close to 31 million b/d, comfortably above the 30 million output ceiling they had agreed to at their December 2011 meeting.

China the Biggest User

China is now the world's biggest energy user, having overtaken the United States in 2009. Every day, it chomps through the equivalent of 10 million barrels of oil, 350 million cubic metres of natural gas, and 5 million tonnes of thermal coal, plus assorted inputs from its nuclear, hydro, and renewable energy sectors. More than half its oil and much of its gas and coal must be imported from suppliers in the Middle East, Africa, Central Asia, Russia, Southeast Asia, and Australia.

China's energy demands are so intense and so fundamental to its continued survival and development that it has embarked on a series of extraordinary measures over the last decade to secure its future energy supplies. Its own resources of oil, gas, and coal are not enough to keep its economy growing. Its solution has been a multipronged strategy:

- Rework its own resource base to see if it can be more efficient and extract more value from existing coal mines, oil wells, gas fields, and associated logistics such as pipelines, processing, storage, and transport.
- Embark on a massive technological effort to see how big a role renewables such as wind and solar energy might play.
- Step up its hydro and nuclear power plant programs.
- Assiduously search offshore for investments, partners, and projects that will give it access to reliable energy supplies, be they hydrocarbons, uranium, steaming coal, or some other form.

"The proportion of non–fossil fuels in primary energy consumption should reach 11.4 percent; energy consumption and

CO₂ emissions per unit of GDP should be reduced by 16 percent and 17 percent, respectively."

—*Premier Wen Jiabao sets out energy targets in China's twelfth five-year plan, covering 2011–2015, on 14 March 2011.*

In its five-year plan unveiled in March 2011, the Chinese government said it aimed to reduce energy intensity (the amount of energy consumed per unit of GDP) by 16 percent over the next five years. Even so, energy use will continue to grow—the automotive market alone will see to that. And because China's domestic oil and gas production is at or near its peak, as the IEA points out, "virtually every incremental barrel of oil or cubic metre of gas consumed must be imported." By 2020, oil demand alone is likely to reach 12 million barrels a day. Until pipelines from Russia, Kazakhstan, and Myanmar are open and operating at full capacity, more than three-quarters of China's oil imports will continue to move through the chokepoint that is the Strait of Malacca and into the contested waters of the South China Sea.

Although India's energy demands might not yet be as intense as China's, its young population, fast-growing car ownership rates, and desire for higher living standards puts it on the same trajectory as China. And it too has embarked on a remarkably similar energy strategy involving more oil and gas exploration, cleaner coal, a greater emphasis on renewables such as wind and solar, expanded hydro and nuclear programs, greater efficiencies in energy production, storage and distribution, and a push for offshore investments in resources and energy. It feels the same vulnerabilities and insecurities as China, with the added drawback of a neighbourhood in perpetual, dangerous chaos, and nowhere near the transport infrastructure capabilities that China enjoys. And then there is the matter of financial firepower. When India goes looking for offshore energy projects, often it finds itself in competition with China. But India's foreign exchange reserves are only $300 billion, compared to more than $3 trillion for China. Money talks and the loser walks.

We should hasten the implementation of our "going out" strategy and combine the utilisation of foreign exchange reserves with the "going out" of our enterprises.

—*Premier Wen Jiabao, 20 July 2009 (quoted in* Financial Times *article, "China to Deploy Foreign Reserves," 21 July 2009)*

China's National Energy Commission, headed by Premier Wen Jiabao, says that one of its key targets is "securing energy supply through international cooperation" under the "Going Out" policy.[4] Most of China's crude comes from Saudi Arabia, with state-owned Saudi Aramco identifying itself as China's "largest and most reliable supplier" and pointing to the kingdom's ability to be a calming influence on oil markets because of its spare supply capacity. Saudi oil exports to China topped 1 million barrels a day in 2009 and continue to account for almost 20 percent of its supply. Angola, Iran, Russia, Sudan, Oman, Iraq, Kuwait, and Kazakhstan are other substantial suppliers to the Chinese market. Japan, South Korea, Taiwan, and India also are big Asian buyers of Saudi crude. In contrast, Saudi Arabia is only the third largest supplier to the world's No. 2 energy consumer, the United States, behind U.S. regional neighbours Canada and Mexico (see Exhibit 5.2).

In its quest for energy security, China has made some big investments overseas, primarily through its three main national oil companies—China National Petroleum Corp. (CNPC), China Petroleum & Chemical Corp. (Sinopec), and China National Offshore Oil Corp. (CNOOC). Although they are state-owned (with listed arms in Hong Kong, New York, and Shanghai), they are not necessarily "state-run," in the view of the International Energy Agency. According to a February 2011 report by the IEA on Chinese oil companies' overseas investments, the big three show "independent, commercially driven behaviour," particularly when it comes to upstream exploration and production investments. But as the IEA also notes, the top leaders of the oil companies are appointed by the Communist Party of China (CPC) and are alternate members of the party's central committee.[5]

1. United States 510	7. Italy 80
2. China 199	8. France 72
3. Japan 179	9. Netherlands 57
4. India 159	10. Spain 56
5. South Korea 115	Rest of world 477
6. Germany 98	

Exhibit 5.2   World's biggest importers of crude oil (in millions of tonnes)

Source: IEA Key World Energy Statistics Oct 2011

Each company has a favoured sector: CNPC dominates exploration and production, plus pipeline construction and operation. Sinopec is by far China's largest refiner, while CNOOC operates mainly in offshore upstream production. The Chinese oil companies operate in more than 30 countries and have equity production in 20 of them. Four countries account for most of the equity shares: Kazakhstan (23 percent) and Sudan, Venezuela, and Angola (each around 15 percent). Syria, Russia, and Tunisia are the next most important.

CNPC was the first overseas investor, starting in the early 1990s in Sudan, Peru, and Kazakhstan. Since then, it has made large investments in Syria, Australia, Canada, and Singapore, Indonesia, Angola, Chad, and Ecuador. More recently, in mid-2011, CNPC began work on stage one of its $3 billion Iraqi oil field project at Al-Ahdab, 180 km southeast of Baghdad. CNPC's controversial deal, first struck with Saddam Hussein in 1996, was renegotiated with the Iraqi government in late 2008 as a technical service contract after protracted talks. It is the first major new oil project in Iraq for 20 years, with a daily production target of 115,000 b/d after six years. CNPC's listed arm, PetroChina, has invested $2.5 billion in Canada's Athabasca oil sands, moving to 100 percent ownership of the MacKay River project in northern Alberta in early 2012.

Sinopec has been an aggressive investor in recent years. In 2010, it spent $7.1 billion to buy 40 percent of Repsol Brasil, the Brazilian subsidiary of Spanish oil company Repsol. It also paid $4.7 billion for a 9 percent stake in Canadian oil sands company Syncrude and made another foray into Latin America, paying $2.45 billion for all of the oil and gas assets in Argentina held by U.S.-based Occidental Petroleum Corp. In late 2011, it struck a $5 billion deal to buy 30 percent of Portuguese company Galp Energia's assets in Brazil, giving it potential exposure to pre-salt technology there, and followed that in January 2012 with a $2.5 billion deal with Devon Energy covering a one-third share in several U.S. shale field developments. Earlier, in 2009, it paid a total of about $9 billion to buy Africa-focused Addax Petroleum from the Swiss-based oil trader Addax & Oryx Group (AOG). The deal, which delivered a handsome profit to AOG founder Jean Claude Gandur, gave Sinopec key oil assets in Nigeria, Gabon, and the Kurdish part of Iraq. The Addax transaction remains the single biggest purchase by one of the Chinese national oil companies, aside from their long-term gas deals in Qatar and Australia.

Facing Political Pressure

In March 2010, CNOOC bought 50 percent of Argentine oil company Bridas Corp. for $3.1 billion, calling it a "very good beachhead" to enter Latin America. Bridas, owned by the family of Argentine tycoon Carlos Bulgheroni, at the time held 40 percent of hydrocarbons producer Pan American Energy, with the remainder in the hands of BP. In 2006 CNOOC had paid $2.7 billion for a stake in Total's Akpo field in Nigeria. That followed its 2005 failure to buy U.S. oil company Unocal in the face of American political pressure. This is the political reality the Chinese energy companies sometimes face: when they go looking to buy overseas assets, be it oil, gas, coal, iron ore, or some other mineral resource, there is always the chance of a knockback by the target country's investment regulator—often on "national security" grounds that seem to be more strongly asserted when the money is coming from the East rather than the West.

All three of the major Chinese oil companies are active in Iran, a country that is off limits for most of the international oil companies because of UN and U.S. sanctions. In 2009, CNPC signed a $4.7 billion deal to develop the next phase of the South Pars field in the Persian Gulf, and may buy gas from a future phase of the same field. CNOOC is working on a deal for the North Pars field, while CNPC and Sinopec are involved in at least three other Iranian oil and gas projects, including in Iran's Caspian Sea territory. Outside of the Middle East, some of the biggest Chinese investments have been in Africa in the shape of roads, railways, ports, storage, and other logistics. A fourth Chinese company, Sinochem, paid more than $3 billion to Norway's Statoil in 2010 for a 40 percent stake in Brazil's Peregrino oilfield. China's sovereign wealth fund, the China Investment Corporation (CIC), has bought other big oil and gas assets in Canada, Russia, and Kazakhstan.

Pipelines Open New Markets

Chinese oil companies also are investing in transnational oil pipelines to bring in supplies from Central Asia, Southeast Asia, and Russia. An example is the 1,830-km Central Asian gas pipeline, which opened in December 2009 and runs from Turkmenistan through Uzbekistan and Kazakhstan to China's Xinjiang province. Built at a cost of $7 billion by CNPC, the line has initial gas capacity of 10 billion cubic metres (353 billion cubic feet) a year from Turkmenistan—a figure that will quadruple to 40 billion cubic metres (about 1.4 trillion cubic feet) by 2012. A connection from Turkmenistan into Iran means there is now a pipeline link between China and Europe. Separately, a 2,200-km (1,360-mile) oil pipeline runs from Atyrau on the Caspian Sea in Kazakhstan to Alashakou on the Chinese border and on to Urumqi in Xinjiang. CNPC and Kazakh oil company Kazmunaigas are equal shareholders in this line.

The first half of Russia's East Siberian Pacific Ocean (ESPO) pipeline running from Taishet in eastern Siberia to Skovorodino in the Amur region, bordering China, began pumping oil to China in early 2011. A spur pipeline takes the oil from Skovorodino to Daqing. Far away to the southwest, CNPC has begun work on a $2 billion twin gas and oil pipeline project that will run from a deep-water port in the Bay of Bengal in Myanmar (Burma) to Kunming in southwestern China and eventually on to Chongqing in central China. These 1,100-km (680-mile) pipelines, due for completion in 2013, will bring in gas from Myanmar's offshore reserves and allow oil from Africa and the Middle East to be transhipped to China without transiting the Strait of Malacca. More than 75 percent of China's total oil imports now enter via the Strait of Malacca. That figure could drop to 54 percent as the pipelines change the market dynamic, though the volume of oil shipped through the strait will continue to rise. China became a net oil importer in 1993, and its import dependence is unlikely to decline substantially because its oil fields are ageing, and production is nearing its peak. But what is changing is the primary energy mix. In 2011, China's mix was 18 percent oil, 4 percent gas, 68 percent coal, and 10 percent renewable/other sources. Natural gas is becoming increasingly important; its share of China's energy mix is expected to more than double to above 8 percent by 2015. China became a net importer of gas in 2006, and despite an expected expansion of domestic production to 150 billion cubic metres (5.3 trillion cubic feet) by 2015, it will still need to import about 80 billion cubic metres (about 2.8 trillion cubic feet). LNG is sourced mainly from Australia, Qatar, and Indonesia, while piped gas comes from Central Asia. Qatar gas still goes through the Strait of Malacca, but gas from Australia is able to take a different path, through the Ombai, Sunda, or Lombok Straits. Some of the wild cards in the gas mix are possible imports from

North America or Russia's Arctic region, and the economics of China tapping into its own shale gas reserves.

India Makes Modest Forays

In contrast to the big spending by Chinese companies abroad ($70 billion in oil and gas deals since 2002), India's overseas investments have been relatively frugal, at about $12.5 billion. There are five majority-state-owned oil and gas companies in the mix—ONGC Videsh Ltd. (OVL), Bharat Petroleum Corporation Ltd. (BPCL), Indian Oil Corporation Ltd. (IOCL), Oil India Ltd. (OIL), Gas Authority of India Ltd. (GAIL), plus India's largest private enterprise company, Reliance Industries Ltd. (RIL), a smaller rival, Essar Oil, and a UK newcomer with Indian origins, Vedanta Resources.

OVL, the international arm of India's main national oil company Oil and Natural Gas Corporation Ltd. (ONGC), invested about $2.1 billion in 2009 to buy UK-based Imperial Energy Corporation, which has oil assets in the Tomsk region of Russia's Western Siberia. OVL is also working on 40 oil and gas projects in Iran, Iraq, Syria, Sudan, Egypt, Libya, Nigeria, Colombia, Venezuela, Brazil, Vietnam, Myanmar, Kazakhstan, Uzbekistan, and elsewhere in Russia with a variety of partners including BP, PetroVietnam, and—in the case of Sudan—CNPC. OVL's parent ONGC has a large number of domestic energy assets and produces about 30 percent of India's crude oil requirement. It also runs a pipeline network in India covering more than 11,000 km (6,800 miles). In early 2011 it reported India's first shale gas discovery, in West Bengal state—possibly an encouraging portent. As New Delhi strives to lift its oil and gas self-sufficiency, ONGC has more than half the new exploration blocks awarded by the Indian government in recent years.

Separately, Bharat Petroleum is working with other companies in 26 exploration blocks, of which nine are in India and the others are in Australia, the United Kingdom (North Sea), Mozambique, and East Timor. It also has interests in existing blocks in Oman, the United Kingdom, Australia, East Timor, Indonesia, and in Brazil's challenging deep-water Campos Basin. Indian Oil Corp. has invested in 11 oil exploration blocks in Libya, Iran, Gabon, Nigeria, East Timor, Yemen, and Venezuela. It farmed into an exploration block in Gabon along with Oil India as the operator. As part of a consortium, IOCL has been awarded Project -1 in Venezuela's Carabobo heavy oil region. Domestically, IOCL has a pipeline network covering just under 11,000 km. It also has agreed to jointly develop a deepwater pipeline from Oman to India, to give it access to cheaper gas. Oil India has a mainly domestic focus, with most production coming from Assam state in India's northeast, plus Rajasthan in the west. Its overseas exploration blocks, usually in partnership with IOCL and/or OVL, are in Iran, Gabon, Libya, Egypt, Nigeria, Venezuela, and East Timor.

GAIL bought its first U.S. shale gas asset, a stake in Houston-based Carrizo Oil & Gas's Eagle Ford shale tenement in late 2011. It will spend about $300 million with Carrizo over five years, and said it was prepared to spend another $1 billion for more such assets in North America.

Reliance Industries, controlled by India's richest man, Mukesh Ambani, has its primary oil-sector focus on exploration and production off the coast of India, mainly in the Krishna Godavari Basin in the Bay of Bengal where it began producing oil and gas in 2009. But it has also made some important acquisitions overseas, including a $1.7 billion deal to buy 40 percent of Atlas Energy's Marcellus Shale project in Pennsylvania, 60 percent of another adjoining shale prospect from Carrizo Oil & Gas, and a $1.8 billion deal with Pioneer Natural Resources for a 45 percent stake in its Eagle Ford shale gas field in Texas. It has other blocks in Peru, Yemen, Oman, Iraq, Colombia, Australia, and East Timor. In February 2011, Reliance struck a landmark deal with BP in which the UK-based oil major is paying $7.2 billion to partner it in 23 oil and gas production blocks in Indian waters.

Essar Oil, controlled by the Mumbai billionaire brothers Shashi and Ravi Ruia, has interests in African, Asian, and Australian exploration blocks, while London-listed Essar Energy has refinery interests in the United Kingdom and Kenya. Another UK-listed company, Anil Agarwal's Vedanta Resources, completed the $8.7 billion purchase of a controlling stake in oil and gas producer Cairn India from its UK parent Cairn Plc in December 2011. The deal gives Vedanta oilfields in Rajasthan state and a large gas discovery in Sri Lanka.

Like China, India is looking at transnational pipeline opportunities. In addition to the Oman-India sub-sea pipeline, India is keen to be involved in other projects that bring hydrocarbons from the Middle East, Central Asia, or even neighbouring Myanmar and Bangladesh. But little progress is being made because of the political tensions and security risks in these deals. A pipeline from Iran through Pakistan to India has been mooted for years, while other proposed projects suggest bringing gas from Kazakhstan through Uzbekistan, Tajikistan, or Turkmenistan and on through Afghanistan and Pakistan to India. The project that looks to have the greatest chance of coming to fruition is the 1,050-km (650-mile) TAPI (Turkmenistan-Afghanistan-Pakistan-India) gas pipeline, which would ship gas from Turkmenistan's South Yolotan field. In December 2010, the four countries signed an initial agreement that could lead to its construction—with funding from the Asian Development Bank—by 2014–2015.

Refining Shifts out of Europe

About 40 percent of the world's seaborne crude oil passes through the Strait of Hormuz, a 50-km (30-mile) opening at the entrance to the Persian Gulf that has immense strategic significance for the global energy trade. Massive 300,000-tonne oil tankers known as VLCCs (very large crude carriers) steam down from loading terminals in Iran, Iraq, Saudi Arabia, Kuwait, and the United Arab Emirates through the Strait, bound for refineries in Asia, Africa, Europe, and Australia. In most cases it will take weeks to reach their destinations. But some of those carriers have a much shorter journey to make. Just two days of sailing time eastward across the Arabian Sea to the west coast of India stands the vast Jamnagar refinery and petrochemical complex of Reliance Industries. In 2008, Reliance executive chairman Mukesh Ambani spent $6 billion to double the size of the refinery, first opened by his late father Dhirubhai Ambani in 1999, lifting its processing capacity to 1.24 million barrels of crude a day. That equates to 1.6 percent of global refining capacity—and more than 30 percent of India's capacity—making Jamnagar the single largest refinery complex in the world. It is also highly vulnerable if things get ugly between India and its fractious neighbour Pakistan. Less than 20 minutes' flying time from an air base near Karachi could put Pakistani F-16 jets over the Gulf of Kutch, potentially threatening Jamnagar and the surrounding complex of ports, pipelines, and petrochemical plants that constitute a good part of India's industrial capacity.

The first Gulf War in 1990–1991 showed the sort of damage that could be visited on the global oil sector by a determined adversary;

Saddam Hussein's scorched-earth policy as his troops retreated from Kuwait left 700 oil wells alight. It would take nine months before the last fire was extinguished in November 1991.

Despite its regional vulnerability, Jamnagar is just one example of how complex refining capacity is moving away from Europe to the Middle East, Asia, Africa, and Latin America. The four biggest refineries in the world now under construction are in Saudi Arabia and India. State-owned Saudi Aramco, which already has a 650,000 b/d refinery at Ras Tanura, aims to complete three new plants, each of 400,000 b/d capacity, between now and 2017—one on its own at Jazan, one with French partner Total at the industrial city of Jubail, and the other—the Red Sea refinery at Yanbu—with Chinese partner Sinopec. All told, Saudi Arabia plans to spend $125 billion between 2011 and 2016 on oil and gas output and down-stream projects such as refining and petrochemical plants. One of these is likely to be the $6 billion Rabigh expansion venture, where Aramco's partner is the Japanese company Sumitomo Chemicals.

In India, state-owned Indian Oil Corp. aims to have its 300,000 b/d refinery at Paradip in Odisha state (formerly known as Orissa) open by late 2012, and another four Indian refineries are either under construction or in the planning stage. Essar Oil aims to expand its existing 300,000 b/d refinery at Vadinar in Gujarat state to 415,000 b/d by late 2012.

Like India, China is keen to boost its refining capacity and global reach. It has eight or nine domestic refinery projects on its books, mainly in the 200,000 b/d range. One of these is the $5 billion Oriental Refinery joint venture between PetroChina and Russian oil major Rosneft, involving a 13 million mtpa (260,000 b/d) plant in the northern industrial city of Tianjin. Sinopec already operates a 200,000 b/d refinery in Tianjin, which is the main port for Beijing.

As well, China is eager to advance refinery partnerships in the Middle East such as those it already has with Saudi Arabia and Iran. Apart from these, it is also involved in two African refineries: Chad's N'Djamena project and Niger's Zinder project.

In Algeria, state-owned Sonatrach is upgrading its Skikida refinery to 330,000 b/d with help from Samsung Engineering, while Iran hopes to have the first stage of its 360,000 b/d Persian Gulf Star greenfields refinery at Assalouyeh operating by the end of 2013. Iran is looking to build seven new refineries, costing $26 billion, over the next few years to cut down on its imports of refined petroleum products such as gasoline. Aside from Assalouyeh, the other plants include the 300,000 b/d projects at Hormuz and Caspian, and smaller units at Pars, Anahita, Khuzestan, and Shahriyar.

Iraq has started work on a 300,000 b/d plant at Nassiriyah as part of the country's plans to lift refining capacity to 1.6 million b/d by 2017 and double that by 2030. All told, Iraq plans to spend $20 billion on Nassiriyah and three smaller plants at Karbala, Kirkuk, and Maysan.

South Korea stands near the top of the tree when it comes to refining capacity. It has three of the world's top-ten refineries: the 817,000 b/d Ulsan plant operated by SK Group; the 750,000 b/d Yeosu plant operated by GS Caltex, and the 565,000 b/d Onsan plant run by S-Oil.

The other significant project in Asia is Vietnam's 200,000 b/d Nghi Son refinery, a $6 billion plant due for completion in 2014. Nghi Son, which has the potential to double in size, brings together Vietnam Oil & Gas Co. with partners Kuwait Petroleum Corp. and Japan's Idemitsu Kosan and Mitsui Chemicals.

In Brazil, the 230,000 b/d Abreu e Lima Pernambuco refinery project is due for completion by 2013. South America is already home to the massive Paraguana refinery centre in Venezuela, controlled by the state oil company Petroleos de Venezuela (PDVSA). Until the completion of Jamnagar, it was the world's largest refinery complex with capacity of 940,000 b/d. It is located in Falcon state, and brings together three refineries: Amuay, Bajo Grande, and Cardon.

ExxonMobil has two of the world's largest refineries: its 605,000 b/d Jurong-Pulau Ayer-Chawan complex in Singapore and its 560,000 b/d Baytown plant in Texas, United States.

There are several reasons why European refineries are declining in the global picture. Apart from the massive demand that is starting to build in Asia, many of the European plants are outdated, difficult to modernise and lack the complexity of modern Asian counterparts. The momentum is with Asia: many of the refineries built there have been set up for export while they wait for domestic demand to grow. According to the International Energy Agency, the world's petrochemical sector will see significant growth over the next five years, with feedstock demand rising by 1.7 million b/d between 2010 and 2016. The IEA says that much of the new capacity in Asia and the Middle East will run on cheap ethane and LPG. That will put older refineries in the OECD group of countries under "intense competitive pressure."[6]

In June 2011, the International Energy Agency chose the Russian city of St. Petersburg on the Volga River as the venue for the launch of its 2011–2016 energy outlook, covering demand predictions for oil and natural gas.[7] IEA then-executive director Nobuo Tanaka said the report shows that oil's role is becoming "ever more concentrated in the transport and petrochemical sectors." By contrast, gas continues to make gains in power generation as well as industry and space heating. But while oil is a genuinely global commodity in terms of markets and pricing, Tanaka noted that gas is bound by some regional constraints, including transport. Neither of them is about to knock "old king coal" off its perch as the world's most widely used energy source, and its position as the world's biggest emitter of greenhouse gases.

Notes

1. International Energy Agency, "World Energy Outlook" (9 November 2011). www.worldenergyoutlook.org/.
2. Ibid.
3. Quoted in Reuters, "Transneft Sees Russian Oil Output Growth until 2012," at Reuters Russia Investment Summit, Moscow, 10 September 2008.
4. Information Office, State Council of China, "China's Energy Conditions and Policies" (December 2007), http://en.ndrc.gov.cn/policyrelease/P020071227502260511798.pdf.
5. Julie Jang and Jonathan Sinton, *Overseas Investments by Chinese National Oil Companies*, International Energy Agency, Information Paper (February 2011). www.iea.org/papers/2011/overseas_china.pdf.
6. International Energy Agency, "World Energy Outlook."
7. International Energy Agency, *Medium-Term Oil and Gas Markets 2011*, (St. Petersburg, Russia: International Energy Agency, 16 June 2011).

C H A P T E R

Old Coal Still Burning Brightly

Steam is no stronger now than it was a hundred years ago, but it is put to better use.

—Nineteenth-century American essayist
Ralph Waldo Emerson

For the Panama-flagged coal ship *Pasha Bulker*, there was nowhere to hide from the violent storm known as an "east coast low," that overwhelmed it one winter's morning in June 2007. The 77,000-dwt Panamax-class ship, which had been launched in Japan only a year earlier, had spent the previous two weeks in the coal queue that forms off the Port of Newcastle on the Australian east coast. As the first storm warnings went out from the local weather bureau, the master of the *Pasha Bulker* made an ill-judged call to stay put—he was there to load 58,000 tonnes of coal. By early morning on June 8, with his anchor dragging and the waves growing ever larger, the situation had changed enough for the captain to decide he had to make a run for deeper water. But with no heavy ballast in the tanks of his unladen vessel and little room to manoeuver, he'd left it too late. The *Pasha Bulker* was making little headway to the north, so the captain began a looping change of course to the south. But the wind and wild waves were too much to overcome. The stern of the 225-metre vessel was lifted clear of the water and it was quickly propelled, like a massive steel surfboard, toward the little beach known as Nobbys that lies south of the Newcastle breakwall, there to lodge hard and fast on a rock shelf a few metres offshore. The 22 crew members on board the stricken vessel were winched to safety by a helicopter over the next few hours, but it would be another three weeks before tugboats could finally free the massive ship. With its hull buckled, the *Pasha Bulker* was towed into Newcastle harbour for a damage assessment and a few weeks later was sent to Vietnam for repairs. It resumed service in 2008 under a new name, the *Drake*.

On the calmer, sunnier days than usually prevail in this part of the world, a panorama of coal-driven commerce unfolds from the clifftops that overlook Newcastle port. Out to sea, row upon row of bulk carriers ride the Tasman Sea swell, waiting for their turn to be loaded with Hunter Valley steaming coal or coking coal, bound for markets in China, India, Japan, and Korea. At the entrance to the port stands Fort Scratchley, once a coastal defence battery built in the 1880s against a possible Russian attack, but now a museum. The fort fired its guns in anger only once, after a Japanese submarine surfaced and shelled the city in 1942. Now the only battles being fought around here are between antimining groups and the energy companies that want to further develop the mineral resources of the Hunter, a lush valley that is known as much for its wine and thorough-bred stud farms as for its coal. The first coal exported from the region was shipped to Bengal, India, in 1799. Now, from a string of underground and open-cut mines that extend deep into the valley, a constant procession of heavily laden coal trains trundle into Newcastle port's storage areas to dump their 8,000-tonne loads. Like giant mechanical insects, an expensive and highly complex array of coal stackers, reclaimers, and loaders swarm across the stockpiles of coal, scooping it up and onto the conveyor belts that shuttle the load to shipside and fill a typical 90,000-tonne coal carrier in eight hours. Once Newcastle was known as Australia's "Steel City" for the BHP steel mill that dominated the city's industrial base. But the mill is long gone—closed in 1999 in the face of cheaper competition from steel producers in Asia.

Busiest Coal Port

BHP is still a big name in Newcastle, but now it has morphed into BHP Billiton, the world's largest mining and energy company (see Exhibit 6.1). Here it jostles with Xstrata, Vale, Rio Tinto, Peabody Energy, Anglo American, and the Chinese miners Yanzhou and Shenhua for the right to explore, extract, and export coal from the rich seams of the Hunter Valley and, more recently, from the Gunnedah Basin another 200 km (120 miles) to the northwest. Newcastle is now the world's busiest coal port, shipping out 125 million tonnes a year, with plans to expand capacity to 200 million tonnes by 2014. Forty coal mines split among 13 producers, three large train haulage operators handling 16,000 rail movements a year, and three coal loading terminals at the port handling 1,200 vessels a year between them, keep the coal chain running. China Shenhua Group, the world's No. 2 coal producer with annual output above 325 million tonnes, has snapped up rich farming land in the Gunnedah Basin so that it can mine the coal beneath the black-soil plains, sparking debate about the need to preserve food-producing land versus the value of mineral resources.

Two thousand kilometres (1,240 miles) to the north, something similar is going on in the Queensland coal basins of Surat, Bowen, and Galilee, where much of the prized black coking coal is bound for the blast furnaces of Asian steel mills. In the Bowen Basin, for example, Macarthur Coal, which produces a sought-after pulverized low-volatile coal for injection into blast furnaces, is owned by a U.S. miner Peabody Energy after a 2011 buyout of shareholders that included China's CITIC, global steel-maker ArcelorMittal, and Korean steel giant POSCO. Yanzhou has bought a thermal coal mine in the Surat Basin (and another across the continent in Western Australia), while Shanxi Meijin Energy, controlled by young Chinese entrepreneur Yao Jinlong and his family, has its "China Stone" project in the works in the Galilee Basin. There, its MacMines AustAsia operation is planning

1. Coal India Ltd. 431	**6.** Datong Coal 120
2. China Shenhua Group 328 (2010)	**7.** Arch Coal 114
3. Peabody Energy 221	**8.** BHP Billiton 105
4. Rio Tinto 140	**9.** RWE Power 100
5. China Coal 125	**10.** Anglo American 96

Exhibit 6.1   World's leading coal-producing companies (millions of tonnes, 2009)

Source: IEA World Energy Outlook 2010

to export 30 million tonnes a year from 2014 to 2015—provided it can get access to rail and port infrastructure.[1] Other thermal coal assets in the region have been snapped up by Brazil's Vale and Indian power and infrastructure companies such as the GVK Group and the Adani Group, which have both bought Galilee Basin tenements. The Adani Group's billionaire founder, Gautam Adani, has set a clear goal for 2020: He wants to mine 200 million tonnes of coal a year from around the world, to trade another 50 million tonnes of coal a year, and to have a power generation capacity in India of 20,000 MW.

The world consumes about 7 billion tonnes of hard coal a year, and another 1 billion tonne of brown coal or lignite. With coal accounting for 40 percent of global power generation (and almost 70 percent in the case of China and 52 percent for India), it is no surprise that demand for coal keeps rising, and that Chinese and Indian state-controlled coal companies are competing with the big private enterprise players for the right to develop new mines, ports, railways, and other infrastructure from Australia to Indonesia, Africa, Latin America, and beyond. There are 24,000 coal mines around the world, including more than 18,000 in China alone, and another 2,000-plus shared by the United States and India. They supply thermal coal to 2,300 power stations worldwide—again with China hosting the lion's share, at 600-plus plants. China is building the equivalent of two new coal-fired power stations every month, and India is not too far behind. These twenty-first-century power plants are far cleaner than ones built decades ago—by as much as 40 percent, according to the World Coal Association—but even so they rank as the most significant contributors to global CO_2 emissions.[2] Clean or not, coal is set to dominate electricity generation for the next 20 years at least, and that fact underpins the search for new thermal coal mines. According to an energy outlook prepared by U.S. oil producer ExxonMobil in early 2011, global electricity demand in 2030 will be 80 percent higher than 2005 levels, with most of the new demand coming from outside the OECD group of advanced nations.[3] China, India, and other non-OECD countries—where more than 5.8 billion people live compared to 1.2 billion in the OECD—will see power demand soar 150 percent. According to the International Energy Agency, China will account for a quarter of all global energy usage in 2035, while the U.S. share will drop to 15.5 percent and India will rise to just over 5 percent.[4] India's relatively modest share reflects the fact that despite a population size likely to overtake China within a decade, India's per capita usage of energy is still very low by world standards. In 2005, its energy usage was just 531 kg of oil equivalent a year, compared with 1,242 kg for China, 4,176 kg for Japan, and 7,913 kg for the United States.

China's Energy Plan

One of China's economic imperatives, as set out in its twelfth five-year plan covering 2011 to 2015, is to sharply reduce the proportion of fossil fuels (such as coal) that make up its primary energy consumption. To do that, it must dramatically increase the contribution of non–fossil fuels, such as wind and solar. Trevor Houser, a partner at U.S.-based Rhodium Group, told the Brookings Institution in May 2011 that while China was proposing to add 320 to 480 gigawatts (GW) of low-carbon technology, it would also be adding 400 to 500 GW of coal-fired power capacity. China, he said, was "unique in its ability to be the price setter of both of those technologies at exactly the same time."[5]

China is by far the world's biggest coal producer, (see Exhibit 6.2), mining more than 3 billion tonnes a year, of which China Shenhua Group contributes around 325 million tonnes from its 60 mines. Another state-owned miner, China National Coal Group, is the No. 2 producer, with output of about 125 million tonnes a year. Its listed arm is China Coal Energy Co. Third-ranked Datong Coal Group (also state-owned) produces about 120 million tonnes and exports some of this to Japan, South Korea, and India. Other significant producers are Xishan Coal, which specializes in coking coal, and Yanzhou Coal Mining, which is majority owned by the diversified state-owned Yankuang Group.

1. China 3250		**6.** Indonesia 320	
2. United States 986		**7.** South Africa 254	
3. India 570		**8.** Germany 182	
4. Australia 430		**9.** Poland 133	
5. Russia 317		**10.** Kazakhstan 110	

Exhibit 6.2   World's biggest coal-producing nations (millions of tonnes, 2010)

Source: World Coal Association

The United States mines about 1 billion tonne, mainly from the Powder River Basin that runs through Montana and Wyoming, where two huge open-cuts—Arch Coal's Black Thunder mine and Peabody Energy's North Antelope Rochelle mine—between them account for 180 million tonnes; another seven Wyoming mines are in the range of 20 to 40 million tonnes each. West Virginia and part of the Appalachian Mountains in northeastern Pennsylvania are also significant coal regions. The United States exported 75 million tonnes in 2010 but is regarded as more of a "swing" supplier than a major exporter. Most of the coal it sends abroad goes to the Atlantic markets of Europe and Canada, rather than the Pacific-based markets of Asia. That could change if there were better coal-handling facilities on the U.S. west coast. But the U.S. experience has not been particularly fruitful—the Los Angeles Export Terminal was upgraded to support coal exports in the late 1990s but closed in 2003 for lack of demand. There is a proposal to build a coal terminal in Washington state that would ship coal from Montana and Wyoming to China, but it faces environmental opposition. North America's busiest coal terminal currently is the Westshore facility south of Vancouver, Canada, which ships about 20 million tonnes a year.

India ranks third among global coal producers, with about 570 million tonnes, of which about 80 percent comes from mines operated by Coal India Ltd., the world's single largest coal producer. Coal India runs more than 470 mines across 21 major Indian coalfields, with most of its output coming from about 160 open-cuts. By 2013 it aims to lift domestic production to around 480 million tonnes. Singareni Collieries, which is owned jointly by the state of Andhra Pradesh and the Indian central government, is a major producer in the south, with output of about 50 million tonnes a year. Another state-owned entity, Chennai-based Neyveli Lignite Corp., mines about 26 million tonnes a year to feed four thermal power stations.

The three big producing nations of China, the United States, and India consume virtually all the coal they produce, and in the case of China and India, still need to import more coal—though China also exports an amount equal to about 1 percent of its output. India's imports, sourced largely from Australia, Indonesia, South Africa, and more recently from Russia, go to the many new coal-fired power plants either built or planned along the coast. While some of these power plants are built with "captive" coalfields nearby, inadequate port infrastructure remains a big issue.

Australia, the fourth-ranked producer at 430 million tonnes, exports most of its output and is the world's biggest exporter, ahead of Indonesia and Russia (see Exhibit 6.3). Apart from their stakes in the Hunter Valley, Gunnedah Basin, and the Central Queensland basins, Chinese and Indian companies have also taken interest in thermal-coal deposits in Western Australia and in the eastern state of Victoria, where there are large reserves of brown coal. India's Lanco Infratech paid about $800 million for the Griffin Coal mines south of Perth in 2010. China's Yanzhou Coal paid $300 million for the nearby Premier mine in 2011, while Hong Kong-based China Light & Power's subsidiary TRUenergy controls the Yallourn power station in Victoria—one of the brown-coal-fired plants earmarked for eventual closure (and financial compensation) under Australia's carbon policy.

Russia's Massive Reserves

Fifth-ranked Russia has massive coal reserves, but much of it is in regions a long way from export terminals. Russia's main coal-producing region is the Kuznetsk Basin, usually shortened to Kuzbass, in Western Siberia, which accounts for more than half of all coal produced. But it carries a heavy transport cost: its capital Kemerovo lies 3,500 km (2,170 miles) from Moscow, 5,000 km (3,100 miles) from Russian Far East ports, and up to 6,000 km (3,700 miles) from Murmansk and Baltic ports. For many years before the emergence of Kuzbass, Russia's most productive basin was the Donetskii, which lies between Russia and the Ukraine. Most of Russia's exports from Rostov in this region go to European markets. There are several other high-value basins in Siberia and Russian Far East, including Kansk-Achinsk, Irkutsk, Chita, and South Yakutsk. A highly prospective

1. Australia 289	**6.** United States 60
2. Indonesia 261	**7.** China 38
3. Russia 130	**8.** Canada 32
4. Colombia 75	**9.** Vietnam 28
5. South Africa 74	**10.** Kazakhstan 26

Exhibit 6.3   World's biggest coal-exporting nations (millions of tonnes, 2009)

Source: World Coal Association

coal basin for the future is Tunguska, in a remote part of Western Siberia. Tunguska, which may hold more than 2 trillion tonnes of coal, is the site of the 1908 meteoroid or comet airburst explosion that leveled several thousand square kilometers of forest.

Like Russia's oil, media, steel, metals, and banking sectors, coal has proven to be a profitable hunting ground for its wealthiest tycoons. Russia's biggest coal producer is Siberian Coal Energy Co. (SUEK), headquartered in Moscow and controlled by Russian billionaires Andrey Melnichenko and Sergey Popov. Melnichenko is SUEK's board chairman, while a key associate and director is long-time adviser to the Russian government, Martin Andersson. SUEK, which produced 90 million tonnes of coal in 2010, including 29 million tonnes for export, has 10 major mining operations in Kemerovo, Krasnoyarsk, Primorsky, Buryatia, Khakassia, Khabarovsk, and Zebaikalye.

Another of Russia's ubiquitous oligarchs, Uzbek-born Iskander Makhmudov, controls the No. 2 coal producer, Kuzbassrazrezugol (50 million tonnes) and a smaller company, Prokopyevskugol (5 million tonnes). Between them, SUEK and Makhmudov's two companies account for 40 percent of Russian coal production. The next three biggest producers are South Kuzbass Coal (controlled by Igor Zyuzin's Mechel Group), Alexei Mordashov's Severstal Group, and state-owned Russky Ugol (Russian Coal). All three have output of about 15 million tonnes. Severstal also has a U.S.-based company PBS Coals, which operates in the northern Appalachian coalfields in Pennsylvania. Other significant Russian producers are coking-coal specialists Raspadskaya and Yuzhkuzbassugol, both of which are under the Evraz Group founded by Alexander Abramov and Alexander Frolov. Roman Abramovich and Eugene Shvidler are also shareholders in Evraz. Raspadskaya's output was cut after a bad accident at its main mine in 2010, prompting Evraz to consider its sale. Most of Russia's coking coal goes to domestic steel producers Evraz, Severstal, MMK, and NLMK, while the main thermal coal buyers are the various regional successor companies to former state-owned power utility Russian Unified Electrical System (RAO UES), which was dismantled in 2008.

Kazakhstan's Resource Scramble

For decades since the Soviet era, Kazakhstan's coal mines have supplied steaming coal to its domestic power plants and to other plants in southern Russia. Most thermal coal comes from the Ekibastuz field in the northeast of the country, where the largest producer is Bogatyr Access Komir, initially set up by Len Blavatnik's U.S.-based Access Industries but now a joint venture between Oleg Deripaska's Rusal and Kazakhstan's state-owned energy arm, Samruk Energo. The two key mines operated by the joint venture are Bogatyr and Severnyi, which produce about 45 million tonnes a year and account for 40 percent of Kazakhstan's total coal output. The second largest thermal-coal miner is Eurasian Energy Corp.—part of London-listed Eurasian National Resources Corp.—which has a large open pit at Ekibastuz. Lakshmi Mittal's global steelmaker ArcelorMittal mines coking coal in the Karaganda basin about 200 km southwest of Ekibastuz for its own use at its Timertau steel mill in Karaganda. Kazakhstan has Central Asia's largest coal reserves, but lack of rail infrastructure has hampered exports in the past. That is likely to change as Kazakhstan pushes ahead with transport upgrades, aided by Chinese investment in the energy and mining sectors. Although China's influence is on the rise, Kazakhstan is seeking to balance that against Russian and Western investors also eager to take part in the country's resources scramble.

Colombia a New Exporter

Colombia in South America is emerging as a significant producer for the export market, with the government targeting annual output of 160 million tonnes by 2019. That has attracted the attention of India, with a consortium of Indian steel producers and thermal and coking-coal buyers looking at acquisitions there. According to an outlook prepared by the U.S. Energy Information Agency, transport infrastructure will be an issue, requiring heavy investment in rail lines, ports, and mine capacity.[6] Work on the 8.6-km La Linea tunnel under part of the Andes mountains should be completed by 2013, enabling coal to be trucked to the Pacific Ocean port of Buenaventura for export to Asia. Most of Colombia's port expansion projects are on the Caribbean coast near the eastern entrance of the Panama Canal, which is being widened. The likely completion of the canal's upgrade in 2014–2015 should also mean greater access to Asia-Pacific markets for Colombia-based producers such as Cerrejon—a joint venture between international miners BHP Billiton, Anglo American, and Xstrata—which sent

15 percent of its 32 million tonnes of exports in 2010 to Asia. U.S. miner Drummond, the No. 2 producer behind Cerrejon, expects to lift output at its El Descanso mine in the north of the country to 40 million tonnes over the next 20 years. Japanese trading house ITOCHU has taken a 20 percent stake in Drummond's Colombian coal business. Prodeco, a high-grade open-cut operation with its own jetty at Puerto Zuniga and part share of a rail link, is the third-largest producer with output of 14 million tonnes a year of export thermal coal for European and U.S. power generators. Global commodities trader Glencore, which bought back Prodeco from Xstrata in 2010, says it aims to lift Prodeco's output to 20 million tonnes by 2013, at which time it will shift exports to a new coal terminal being built in Cienaga. Brazilian energy company MPX, controlled by billionaire industrialist Eike Batista, is planning a coal export terminal along Colombia's Atlantic coast with annual capacity of 20 million tonnes.

In Asia, Mongolia is shaping to join Kazakhstan as a big producer and supplier, and has drawn the attention of major players, while Mozambique in Africa has high potential further into the future. Typical of the way deals are being done in these emerging zones was the announcement in July 2011 by the Mongolian government that bidders from China, Russia, and the United States would share in developing part of the riches of Tavan Tolgoi, a massive coking-coal deposit in the land-locked country's South Gobi Desert, close to the Chinese border. China Shenhua Group will have the largest stake in the venture at 40 percent, followed by a Russian-Mongolian consortium with 36 percent and U.S. bidder Peabody Energy— the world's largest private-enterprise coal miner—with 34 percent. Unsuccessful bidders included three of the world's top resources companies, Vale of Brazil, Anglo-Swiss miner Xstrata, and top steelmaker ArcelorMittal, while South Korean and Japanese companies that sought to partner with Russian and Chinese interests also were excluded. Tavan Tolgoi contains 6.5 billion tonnes of coal, including high-quality coking coal, making it potentially the richest untapped reserve in the world. Mongolia will use foreign companies to develop the western half of Tavan Tolgoi, while state-owned Erdenes-Tavan Tolgoi Ltd. will develop the eastern part. Another big play in the coking-coal sector is Rio Tinto's $4 billion takeover of Mozambique-focused Riversdale Mining after India's Tata Steel decided to sell its 26 percent stake in mid-2011. Riversdale's two big projects in Mozambique have a long-term potential of 30 million tonnes a year, which could lift the African state to the No. 2 position among the world's coking-coal exporters in the next 10 to 15 years. Coal India Ltd. is also exploring for coal in the northwest of Mozambique as part of its supply diversification strategy.

Indonesia's Contribution on the Rise

In the thermal-coal sector, the world can expect to see a major contribution to supply coming from Indonesian exporters such as Bumi Resources and Adaro Energy. Energy research house Wood Mackenzie says Indonesia will contribute the biggest share of export growth in this sector over the next decade, and the two Indonesian companies will be among the world's top three exporters of thermal coal by 2015 (see Exhibit 6.4). Most of its exports now go to India, China, South Korea, Japan, and Taiwan. Wood Mackenzie expects Indonesian coal production to jump from 320 million tonnes in 2010 to 500 million tonnes by 2020, including 130 million tonnes from greenfield sites. But the U.S. Energy Information Administration strikes a cautionary note on Indonesian exports and the development of new mines there, citing infrastructure and environmental concerns and whether domestic coal consumption might be given preference over exports. Indonesia is one of the *Next-11* economies identified by investment bank Goldman Sachs as likely to follow the high-growth path set by Brazil, Russia, India, and China.

1. United States 238.3	**6.** Germany 40.7*
2. Russia 157	**7.** Ukraine 33.9
3. China 114.5	**8.** Kazakhstan 31.3
4. Australia 76.2	**9.** South Africa 30.4
5. India 58.6	**10.** Serbia 13.7*

Colombia, Canada, Poland, Indonesia, and Brazil also have significant reserves in the range of 4.5 to 7.0 billion tonnes each.

Exhibit 6.4   Countries with biggest coal reserves, proven reserves at end of 2009 (billions of tonnes)

*primarily lignite (brown coal)

Source: World Coal Association

Coal's Technological Response

Although there is no doubt coal and other fossil fuels such as oil and gas will remain a key part of the world's energy supply over the next 20 years, coal's contribution to global warming has evoked a technological response. For example, Japan, China, India, Germany, and other countries that must rely on coal for a large part of their energy needs are investing in supercritical and ultrasupercritical thermal power stations that use *clean-coal* technology—a grab-bag of processes that all have the objective of reducing greenhouse gas emissions. Generally, clean-coal technology can include carbon capture and storage (also called sequestration), the steam-cleaning of flue gases to remove sulphur dioxide, the prewashing of coal with chemicals that remove impurities, and the dewatering of low-value brown coal to increase its calorific value. According to the World Coal Association, the average efficiency of coal-fired power stations worldwide is just 28 percent, rising to 45 percent or more for the newest ones that use supercritical or ultrasupercritical thermodynamic processes—defined as temperature of 566°C and pressure of 24.1MPa for supercritical, and temperature above 593°C and pressure above 24.1MPa for ultrasupercritical. The association claims that repowering the world's oldest power plants—in its view, anything older than 25 years—with the new technology could cut coal CO_2 emissions by 25 percent, representing a 6 percent reduction in global CO_2 emissions.[7]

The association says research in Denmark, Germany, and Japan on ultrasupercritical units offers potential efficiency of 50 percent, with the focus on the development of new steels for boiler tubes and on high-alloy steels that minimise corrosion. What is regarded as the world's first clean-coal power plant was commissioned in September 2008 by Swedish energy company Vattenfall in the Germany city of Spremberg. There, the 30 MW Schwarze Pumpe pilot plant is seen as an engineering test-bed for a future 350 MW demonstration plant. Vattenfall says the pilot plant will help it better understand the dynamics of "Oxyfuel combustion" (a process that separates, purifies, compresses, and captures carbon dioxide), and to show how the carbon capture technology works. Although Vattenfall's plant and other clean coal projects underway around the world may well reduce individual plant emissions, the sheer growth in the number of coal-fired power plants expected to be operating in China and

1. China 6502	**6.** Germany 803
2. United States 5596	**7.** Canada 551
3. Russian Federation 1594	**8.** United Kingdom 511
4. India 1428	**9.** Iran 505
5. Japan 1151	**10.** South Korea 501

Exhibit 6.5   World's biggest emitters of CO_2 from fuel combustion (in millions of tonnes, 2008)

Source: International Energy Agency report, CO_2 Emissions from Fuel Combustion, December 2010

India by 2035 will see global CO_2 emissions continue to rise from 30 billion tonnes in 2010 to 42 billion tonnes, including 35 billion tonnes from power generation (see Exhibit 6.5). About 60 percent of those emissions are already "locked in" because of fossil fuel-fired power stations that are already built or under construction. Between now and 2035, China is likely to add 600 GW of coal-fired power; for India, the figure is likely to be 51 GW. In a report in December 2010, the International Energy Agency found that CO_2 emissions from China (6.5 billion tonnes) and the United States (5.6 billion tonnes) between them accounted for 41 percent of the world's total emissions of 29.4 billion tonnes in 2008. Adding Russia, India, and Japan took the top five figure to 16.27 billion tonnes, or 55 percent, while the top 10 accounted for 19.1 billion tonnes, or 65 percent of the world total.[8]

The way power is likely to be generated in the future is changing, but not quickly enough to cut emissions that would limit warming to less than 2°C above preindustrial levels, a position agreed to by governments in 2010. In its central scenario for 2035, the IEA projects that the role of renewables (including wind, solar, marine, geothermal, hydropower, and modern biomass) in electricity generation will grow from 19 percent in 2008 to 32 percent. That still leaves a share of 32 percent for coal and 23 percent for oil and gas, with the remainder from nuclear and other sources. Coal will be king for many years to come in the power sector.

Notes

1. Press release, "Macmines signed a long-term Coal Sales Cooperation Agreement with China Huaneng Group Fuel Co. Ltd.," 12 July, 2011.

2. World Coal Association, information page, "Carbon Capture and Storage." www.worldcoal.org/carbon-capture-storage/.
3. ExxonMobil report, "Outlook for Energy: A View to 2030" (27 January 2011), www.exxonmobil.com/Corporate/Files/news_pub_eo_2009.pdf.
4. International Energy Agency, "World Energy Outlook" (9 November 2011), www.worldenergyoutlook.org/.
5. Trevor Houser, Rhodium Group, presentation to Brookings Institution, Washington, DC, 31 May 2011.
6. U.S. Energy Information Administration, "Colombia Country Analysis Brief," June 2011, www.eia.gov/countries/country-data.cfm?fips=CO.
7. World Coal Association, information page, "Coal Use & the Environment: Improving Efficiencies." www.worldcoal.org/coal-the-environ ment/coal-use-the-environment/improving-efficiencies/.
8. International Energy Agency, "CO_2 Emissions from Fuel Combustion," December 2010, www.iea.org/co2highlights/co2highlights.pdf.

CHAPTER

Going Nuclear in a Post-Fukushima World

This is Japan's most severe crisis since the war ended over 65 years ago.

—Naoto Kan, then Japanese prime minister,
13 March 2011

It began with a series of "foreshock" tremors off the northeast coast of Japan. Two tectonic plates—the North American plate and the Pacific plate—were grinding, shifting, and thrusting away at each other on the sub-sea boundary line known as the subduction zone, about 100 km (62 miles) east of the Japanese city of Sendai. When the inevitable rupture happened 30 km (18 miles) below the ocean floor on the afternoon of Friday, March 11, 2011, life in Japan changed forever. More than 20,000 people died in the massive 9.0 magnitude earthquake that struck Japan at 2.46 PM local time, triggering a terrifying tsunami that crashed onto the east coast of the main island Honshu less than 20 minutes later. The deadly black wave, 10 metres (33 feet) high in some locations, overwhelmed coastal villages, splintering houses, tossing boats and cars around like corks, setting off fires from ruptured oil and gas tanks, and leaving a mangled mess of debris, bodies, sodden crops, and broken buildings.

As horrifying as the tsunami was, it was the aftermath of the earthquake's impact on the Fukushima No. 1 nuclear power plant that captured the world's attention in the following days. As heavy snow and freezing conditions hampered the rescue and recovery effort centred on the major city of Sendai and a string of seaside villages to the north, a series of equipment failures and explosions meant that the spectre of a nuclear catastrophe was beginning to darken the sky over the Fukushima plant, about 65 km to the southeast. What followed was a weeks-long battle by a small band of plant workers, as they sought to cool and contain the plant's reactors and stem the release of radioactive material. It was a tense edge-of-the-seat affair not just for the Japanese rescue workers and the people living near the nuclear plant, but for a global audience that had the 1986 Chernobyl accident in the Ukraine as its only point of reference. Would the reactor cores melt, and would the world once again live under the cloud of potential nuclear contamination? It was not until May that the plant's operator, the Tokyo Electric Power Company (Tepco), could safely assert that the reactors at Fukushima No. 1 were back under some semblance of control. By then, the reputation and market value of Tepco, the world's fourth largest electricity producer, had been trashed over its clumsy handling of the disaster. Tepco had built and operated the Fukushima plant and others like it since the 1970s, but seemed incapable of telling the world just exactly what was going on inside the stricken plant. Eight weeks after the big quake, and with the Japanese public apprehensive about more tremors, then-Prime Minister Naoto Kan on May 6 ordered the shutdown of another nuclear plant, at Hamaoka on the coast 200 km southwest of Tokyo, because of its precarious position should a long-anticipated severe Tokai (literally "East Sea") earthquake hit the area.

In the meantime, the rest of the world had an opportunity to rethink the nuclear option, and for some countries the answer clearly was "no thanks." Germany's Chancellor Angela Merkel swiftly decided that she wanted 7 of Germany's 17 nuclear power stations to be idled, and the other 10 would be phased out by 2022—far earlier than an original 2036 timetable. Switzerland also put the brakes on and Italy deferred plans to resume nuclear power generation after a long post-Chernobyl hiatus. China, too, called for a "safety check" time-out on its ambitious nuclear power expansion program, a decision that had uranium miners around the world checking their cash flow projections.

Long History on the Nuclear Road

Japan had been travelling the nuclear road for 40 years, having opened the Fukushima plant in March 1971 in response to environmental concerns and the 1967 oil export embargo imposed by some Arab producers following the Six-Day War between Israel and its Arab neighbours. That brief embargo was followed by the much more severe "oil shock" of 1973–1974, when Arab producers within the Organization of Petroleum Exporting Countries (OPEC) declared sharp price rises, production cuts, and an oil embargo targeting the United States and some other Western nations over their support for Israel in its October 1973 Yom Kippur War with Syria and Egypt. This second oil shock encouraged Japan and other advanced economies to further embrace the nuclear option. A third oil shock came in 1979, when the Iranian Revolution disrupted production there, sending global oil prices higher. That spurred increased oil production from a variety of new, non-OPEC sources in the 1980s, which, combined with energy conservation and slower economic growth, meant oil prices declined sharply from the mid-1980s. But by this time, Japan was well advanced with its nuclear power program.

Japan's first commercial nuclear power plant began operating at Tokai in Ibaraki prefecture in 1966, so that by the time of the March 2011 earthquake, Japan had 45 years of active operational experience. Its 54 reactors were producing close to 50 GW, meaning that nuclear power was supplying about a third of the country's needs. In a heavily populated advanced economy that relied on imported oil, gas, and coal for much of its power generation, nuclear was the fourth leg of support. After Kan ordered the Hamaoka reactor shut down, the chairman of Japan's Federation of Electric Power Companies (FEPC), Makoto Yagi, noted: "Nuclear power generation is and will continue to be a crucial source of electricity for Japan, a resource-poor country, in order to secure a stable supply of energy. Especially in the summer when electricity demand reaches the peak, nuclear power will have a significant role to play." Yagi said Japan would "continue to develop nuclear power as a mainstay of non–fossil energy, while placing the highest priority on safety."[1] Three months after the Fukushima disaster, the Japan Centre for Economic Research released its sobering projections for the total cost of the nuclear meltdown. Including decommissioning the reactors and supporting the communities evacuated from within

20 km of the reactor site, it said the cost could range from 5.7 trillion yen to as much as 20 trillion yen ($70 billion to $245 billion).[2] At the political level, Japan continued its pattern of a revolving door of Japanese prime ministers that had prevailed since Junichiro Koizumi's five-year administration ended in 2006. Kan was out the door by August 2011, replaced by his finance minister Yoshihiko Noda. In his January 2012 New Year's address, Noda pledged to bring "rebirth" to the Fukushima area and said the crippled nuclear plant's reactors were in a state of "cold shutdown." By the end of the month, only five of Japan's 54 reactors were operating.

There are about 432 commercial nuclear reactors in service around the world, generating about 370 GW of power at October 2011.[3] The majority of them are in the United States, with 104 reactors, and France (58). Russia (32), South Korea (21), United Kingdom (18), Canada (17), and the Ukraine (15) also are significant users. That 2011 snapshot is changing rapidly, as China and India are the two big movers in the nuclear field. China, which has 14 reactors now, has approved plans to build 50 new reactors in the next decade, and a further 110 have been proposed. By 2020, as much as 70 GW of China's energy could come from nuclear plants. India has 20 reactors, with another 20 approved and 40 more proposed to be built between now and 2025. If all of its plans proceed, India could be generating 64 GW of nuclear power by 2032 (see Exhibit 7.1).

Most of the world's new generation-3 reactors—which are designed to be simpler, more rugged, and more efficient than the decades-old reactors found in plants like Fukushima—come from alliances between European, U.S., and Japanese companies. These are the French state-owned nuclear power company Areva with Mitsubishi Heavy Industries; General Electric with Hitachi; and Westinghouse with Toshiba, which now owns 67 percent of the

1. United States 800	**6.** Germany 120
2. France 400	**7.** Canada 80
3. Japan 250	**8.** Ukraine 75
4. Russia 150	**9.** China 60
5. South Korea 140	**10.** United Kingdom 60

Exhibit 7.1   Top 10 nuclear electricity generators (in net TWh, 2009)

Source: International Atomic Energy Agency

U.S. company. Designs from Canada (Atomic Energy of Canada Ltd.) and Russia (OKB Gidropress, which is a subsidiary of state-owned Rosatom) are also in use, along with Chinese, Indian, and South Korean reactors.

Efficient, Low-Cost Fuel

Irrespective of how the Fukushima disaster changes Japan's energy policy, nuclear power is not going to go away soon for its major proponents—the United States, Russia, and France—and big emerging economies such as China and India, primarily because it is the most efficient fuel. One tonne of uranium oxide generates the same amount of energy as 20,000 tonnes of black coal. And while upfront costs for a nuclear plant are high, total running costs over a plant's lifetime result in kilowatt-hour costs that are less than half that of fossil fuels. Plus it is a low-carbon technology, albeit with a waste-disposal problem and a safety image problem.

There are widely varying predictions about the size of nuclear's role in the world's future energy mix, with coal and LNG seen as the fuel sources most likely to gain ground at nuclear's expense, and some critics seeing Fukushima as the trigger for its decline. An example is the EU-27 group of countries, where nuclear's share will fall in the face of a growing switch to renewables, but will still constitute 24.1 percent of supply in 2015. According to the Centre for Global Energy Studies, a London-based think-tank founded by former Saudi Oil Minister Sheikh Ahmed Z. Yamani, coal will have a 25.2 percent share of EU-27 electricity production in 2015, gas will rise to 22.9 percent and oil will be at 3.1 percent. Hydropower will provide 9.9 percent of the renewable sector's share of 24.7 percent, and other renewable sources such as wind, solar, geothermal, and bioenergy will cover the remaining 14.8 percent.[4]

The WorldWatch Institute says in its 2010–2011 nuclear industry status report that nuclear accounts for only 11 percent of electricity generation globally. The Washington, DC-based institute, which promotes renewable energy and an environmentally sustainable society, is no supporter of the "nuclear renaissance" theory that was gaining ground before Fukushima; it claims the industry is in "clear decline" and unable to keep up with its renewable energy competitors.[5] The World Nuclear Association, which promotes the industry, gives a global figure of 13.8 percent and says that nuclear's share of electricity generation is highest in France (about 74 percent) and in several other European nations such as Lithuania, Slovakia, and Ukraine. In the world's biggest nuclear-using country, the United States, the figure is just under 20 percent.[6]

Uranium's Many Supply Sources

The amount of uranium required in 2011 to fuel the world's reactors is just under 69,000 tonnes, according to the World Nuclear Association. For now, much of that comes from producers such as Kazakhstan, Canada, and Australia, which between them supply about two-thirds of the world's needs. The United States, the biggest uranium user at just over 22,000 tonnes a year, bought about 37 percent of its 2010 imports of 20,400 tonnes from Canada and Australia, and 41 percent from Russia, Kazakhstan, and Uzbekistan. The Russian material is mostly weapons-grade highly enriched uranium (HEU) that has been down-blended to low enriched uranium in Russia. The remaining 14 percent came from a variety of suppliers in Europe, Brazil, and African nations such as Malawi, Namibia, Niger, and South Africa. The United States, which has about 4 percent of the world's known recoverable uranium reserves, was a significant uranium miner from the 1950s onward, and reached peak production of 16,800 tonnes of uranium oxide in 1980. But this gradually declined until now only about 8 percent of its annual usage comes from domestic U.S. mines (see Exhibit 7.2).

Globally, China, India, and France lead the search for strategic supplies of uranium that are economically feasible to recover, ahead of a possible supply shortage after 2014. Africa, Mongolia, Central Asia, and parts of South America all have promising sites, but the best deposits are in Australia, Canada, and Kazakhstan. Usually, raw uranium ore is crushed and processed through a leaching

1. Kazakhstan 17803	6. Russia 3562
2. Canada 9783	7. Uzbekistan 2400
3. Australia 5900	8. United States 1660
4. Namibia 4496	9. Ukraine 850
5. Niger 4198	10. China 827

Exhibit 7.2   Major uranium producing countries (Tonnes U, 2010)

Source: World Nuclear Association

solution to create the material known as yellowcake, the dried uranium concentrate powder which these days is actually brown or black. Yellowcake is then smelted into uranium dioxide as part of the process of creating fuel for a nuclear reactor, depending on what type the reactor is.

India's Complicated Outlook

Australia has about 40 percent of the world's low-cost uranium deposits, including BHP Billiton's massive Olympic Dam mine that could be producing close to 20,000 tonnes a year by 2030, when the company believes global uranium demand will be 92,000 tonnes. Australia already sells to the United States, the European Union, Japan, China, South Korea, Canada, and Russia. It is yet to sell to nuclear-armed India because India is not a signatory to the nuclear Non-Proliferation Treaty (NPT), though that restriction could be relaxed by end-2012. Other nations that are not in the NPT are Pakistan, North Korea, and Israel. That means India, which buys its nuclear technology from Russia and France—and got its first reactors from Canada in the 1960s—sources its uranium from its limited domestic supplies and from producers such as Kazakhstan, Russia, and France. It also has supply agreements with Canada and Namibia, and there are other potential sources in Africa and Asia. If India maintains its nuclear expansion program, it is likely to need 8,000 tonnes of uranium a year over the next decade.

India also can't gain access to Japanese nuclear technology because it has not signed the Comprehensive Nuclear Test Ban Treaty (CTBT). That flows through to some limitations for U.S. suppliers such as General Electric and Westinghouse, although that might change. After a long period on the outer for New Delhi following its first nuclear test in May 1974, India and the United States finalised a civilian nuclear agreement when then-U.S. President George W. Bush visited India in 2006. His successor Barack Obama gave another push for India's entry into the wider nuclear community when in November 2010 he promised to support India's full membership of the Nuclear Suppliers Group (NSG). This was a group set up in 1974 specifically as a response to India's nuclear test, which was the first by a nation outside the "Big Five" of the United States, United Kingdom, France, Russia, and China. Obama's support is "phased" and predicated on India moving to full adoption of the NSG's export control requirements.

There is another issue for potential suppliers of civilian nuclear technology to India—legal liability. A new law passed by the Indian parliament in August 2010 was supposed to clarify the situation, but has not done so. Without clarity on compensation procedures for nuclear damage, it is difficult for suppliers such as France's Areva and Russia's Atomstroyexport to go ahead with their reactor construction plans. Under a deal struck in December 2010, Areva is to build two 1,650 MW pressurised water reactors at Jaitapur in Maharashtra state for the Nuclear Power Corporation of India (NPCIL) by 2017–2018, with France guaranteeing a fuel supply for 25 years. Another four reactors are due to follow at the same site— which is in a seismically sensitive area—giving an eventual combined output of just under 10 GW. Something similar is happening at Kudankulam in Tamil Nadu state, where two Russian 1,000 MW lightwater reactors are being built by Atomstroyexport and four more are in the cards. The first unit is due for commissioning in May 2012, followed by the second a year later, though antinuclear protests near the site may derail this timetable. But if legal ambiguity means France and Russia are reluctant to proceed, where will India go for technology in future? Germany, the United States, Canada, and Japan would all face the same liability hurdles, which leaves China as a potential technology supplier. But China already supplies technology to India's archenemy Pakistan, making this an unlikely scenario.

India's first nuclear test was made possible by the nuclear reactor sent from Canada, which subsequently cut off the supply of further nuclear material and technology. Since then, Pakistan and North Korea have joined the nuclear club, and there has long been speculation about the nuclear capabilities of Israel and South Africa. A 1979 event known as the "Vela Incident" in the southern Indian Ocean near a French territory known as the Crozet Islands might have been a nuclear test involving Israel and/or South Africa, though other explanations such as a meteor strike, lightning superbolt, or faulty instruments aboard the U.S. satellite Vela Hotel 6991 have been put forward.

China's 70 GW Goal

Undoubtedly, India is a big customer for uranium and nuclear technology, but as with all things energy and resource-related, China is the dominant presence. According to the World Nuclear Association, even after a Fukushima-induced slowdown, China has 25 new nuclear plants under construction and should meet its target of 70 GW of new nuclear power in operation by 2020, with another 30 GW probably under construction at the same date. State-owned China National Nuclear Corporation (CNNC) said in September 2010 that it would invest about $120 billion over the ensuing decade in nuclear energy projects. Another big state-owned player, China Guangdong Nuclear Power Group (CGNPG), is active in southern China, where its main Daya Bay plant already supplies nuclear power to neighbouring Hong Kong. Guangdong Nuclear Power alone says it will need 10,000 tonnes of uranium a year by 2020, up from 2,000 tonnes in 2009.

China's overall goal is to lift nuclear's share of energy production from 2 percent now to 5 percent by 2020. The State Council Research Office, a government advisory body, struck a general cautionary note in January 2011 about not being too ambitious in case quality control issues arise in the rush to build, but that is a situation that applies to all of China's new power projects, be they nuclear, solar, or wind.

China already has its own nuclear technology, based on Russian, European, and North American designs. In mid-2011 it connected its newest (and fourteenth) reactor, the Lingao II-2, to the grid in Guangdong province. Work on this 1,080 MW unit, known as the CPR-1000 type and based on Areva's pressurised water reactor, began in May 2006. This shows remarkable speed, given that most nuclear plants take 10 years from breaking ground to generating power. Guangdong Nuclear Power is building another 12 units using the CPR-1000, and China National Nuclear Corp. is building five. China is also working on designs based on the Westinghouse third-generation AP1000 pressurised water reactor, and has the goal of exporting this technology in its own right. Westinghouse, now owned by Japan's Toshiba, claims that the AP1000's simplified design allows for even greater construction speed, with a time of 36 months from pouring first concrete to loading of fuel. As China develops its reactor expertise, it is likely to have a significant cost advantage over Western rivals in making and exporting nuclear components.

Along with construction speed and the ability to develop and export its own technology, uranium supply diversity is one of China's goals for its nuclear industry. In 2010 it tripled its uranium imports, taking more than 17,000 tonnes from suppliers in Kazakhstan, Australia, Russia, Uzbekistan, and Namibia. Since then, it has signed additional supply agreements with Canadian producer Cameco. But China also wants to own mines overseas and has sought to buy into a variety of ventures in Africa and Australia. One such project is the Azelik mine in Niger, where China National Nuclear Corp. announced in December 2010 that it had produced its first barrel of overseas uranium. Niger, a former French colony, has been mining uranium since the 1950s but is only now reaching global scale as private and state-owned entities from China, Russia, India, France, Canada, and Australia pursue a variety of exploration deals.

So far, world supply has been dominated at the commercial level by global miners such as Rio Tinto and BHP Billiton, operating mainly in Canada and Australia. The world's largest-producing mines are McArthur River in Canada operated by Cameco, BHP Billiton's Olympic Dam in Australia, Krasnokamensk in Russia near the Chinese border, and Rio Tinto's Ranger (Australia) and Rossing (Namibia) mines.

Niger and other African states all have large potential uranium mine sites on their books, but when the world goes looking for uranium it is Central Asia's Kazakhstan that is the country of most allure to investors because of its enthusiasm for joint ventures and for the creation of a substantial uranium processing industry. State-owned Kazatomprom controls all uranium exploration, mining, and trading, and has struck deals with Russia, Japan, China, India, Canada, and South Korea covering a variety of nuclear-related activities. It also has a 10 percent stake in Westinghouse Electric, which it bought from Toshiba in 2007 after the Japanese company took over Westinghouse in 2006. U.S. engineering and construction group Shaw held 20 percent of Westinghouse from 2006 to 2011, before selling it back to Toshiba. Uranium has been mined in Kazakhstan since the 1950s, and in 2009 it overtook Canada as the world's largest uranium producer. In 2010, it produced about 17,800 tonnes of uranium (28 percent of global production) and has a target of 30,000 tonnes by 2018. President Nursultan Nazarbayev, who has led the country since 1989 and won his last election in April 2011 with 95.6 percent of the vote, runs an investment-friendly government that seeks to woo big miners.

Worrying Past

But Kazakhstan has a worrying nuclear past. During the Soviet era, when it was part of a far-flung empire ruled from Moscow, Kazakhstan's remote northeastern region was the site of hundreds of above-ground and underground nuclear tests conducted between 1949 and 1990. Few people were aware of the tests until 1985, when a Kazakh television program revealed what was happening. After above-ground tests ended in 1963, the Soviet Union detonated 295 nuclear devices in a network of tunnels built under the Degelen Mountains at the remote Semipalatinsk Test Site. The fissile material left behind in the tunnels is a security nightmare for Kazakhstan, Russia, and the United States, which has been helping to try to make the site safe and secure against scavengers or more malignant intruders.

In terms of nuclear tests, a similar link to the past prevails in Australia, where what is destined to be the world's biggest uranium mine, BHP Billiton's Olympic Dam, lies just outside the eastern boundary of the Woomera Prohibited Area, a vast weapons-testing range in South Australia state. Woomera is the largest defence area in the world—larger than some European countries such as Switzerland, Denmark, or the Netherlands. Between 1955 and 1963, Britain conducted seven major nuclear tests and hundreds of smaller trials at Maralinga, on the western edge of the Woomera area.

Uranium, along with copper and silver, has been mined underground at Olympic Dam since 1988. It is one of only three uranium mines fully operating in Australia; the others are Beverley mine (also in South Australia), which is owned by Heathgate Resources, a subsidiary of U.S. company General Atomics, and the Ranger mine in the Northern Territory, owned by Energy Resources Australia, which is majority owned by Rio Tinto. A fourth mine, Honeymoon, owned by Canada's Uranium One (which is majority owned by Russia's Atomredmetzoloto), is in trial production in South Australia. Unlike Canada, all of Australia's annual uranium production of 10,500 tonnes is exported.

BHP Billiton has big plans for Olympic Dam, which sits about 550 km (340 miles) north of Adelaide in a hot, arid, and flat landscape of saltpans and red plains. It will spend $30 billion over the next decade on mineworks and associated infrastructure that includes a desalination plant 320 km (200 miles) away on the coast, an extra power transmission line or a pipeline to a gas-fired power station at the site, a 105 km (65 miles) rail line to connect to the national rail network, a new airport, new port facilities at Adelaide and Darwin to handle exports and import supplies, and an expansion of the Roxby Downs township, 14 km (9 miles) south of the mine, where most of the workforce live. Creating the vast "open pit" mine also means removing a layer of overburden that is 350 m (1,100 feet) thick—a process that will take six years. Copper will be Olympic Dam's biggest income earner in the early years, but the BHP executive in charge of the project believes that over the 40-year life of the project—which may extend to 100 years—uranium will come into its own. At full stretch, the combined underground and open pit mines will see a sixfold increase in output to 72 million tonnes of ore a year, from which BHP aims to produce 750,000 tonnes of refined copper, 800,000 ounces of gold, 2.9 million ounces of silver, and 19,000 tonnes of uranium.

Canada's Productive Mines

Across the Pacific in Canada—which ranks roughly level with Australia as a producer—the world's single most productive uranium mine, Cameco's McArthur River site in northern Saskatchewan province, provides a sharp contrast to Olympic Dam. Part of the uranium-rich Athabasca Basin, McArthur River lies amid lakes and forests in the subarctic zone that can be hot in summer but where winter temperatures can drop below –50°C. Its remote location, 600 km (370 miles) north of the city of Saskatoon, makes for logistical challenges, but all-weather roads now link most of the mine sites in northern Saskatchewan. The McArthur River mine (in which Areva has a 30 percent stake) produces about 7,800 tonnes a year out of Canada's total 10,000 tonnes, of which 1,675 tonnes is used domestically and the rest exported. About 60 percent of exports go to the United States. Areva's McLean Lake further to the northeast is the other major producer. Areva also has a 70 percent stake in the nearby Midwest deposit, which may be brought into production later this decade. The other big project in northern Saskatchewan is Cameco's massive Cigar Lake mine (where Areva is a 37 percent stakeholder), which is expected to boost Canadian production from 2012 onward. Cigar Lake's output is likely to reach 8,200 tonnes.

Africa, the Next Big Player?

Africa is potentially a big source of uranium, and has attracted interest from a host of outside mining companies. China, India, Russia, France, South Korea, and Australia are all active there. The main producing countries are Niger, which provides about 7.5 percent of world output from two high-grade mines at Azelik and Arlit/Arlette; Namibia, which hosts one of the world's largest mines at Rossing; and South Africa, which has its own nuclear power industry and gets about 5 percent of its electricity from nuclear power plants. Between them, these three African nations account for about 18 percent of world uranium output. Tanzania also has large reserves and could become a significant producer in the future. Botswana, Malawi, the Democratic Republic of Congo, Guinea, Gabon, and Nigeria are the focus of other uranium-related mining exploration and activity.

South Korea's Plant Expertise

Aside from Japan, China, and India, South Korea is the other major Asian nation with a substantial nuclear power industry, and is one of just six nations that exports peaceful nuclear technology. South Korea gets about 40 percent of its power from 21 nuclear reactors, and plans a 50 percent-plus increase in nuclear plant capacity to 27 GW by 2020. That will involve building up to 11 more reactors.

South Korea has no domestic uranium mines operating, so it buys its yellowcake mainly from Canada and Australia. But it is keen to diversify its sources of supply. Korea Electric Power Corporation (Kepco), which is majority-owned by the government, is an investor with France's Areva in the Imouraren uranium project in Niger, which is due to begin production in 2013–2014 with a likely output of 5,000 tonnes a year. State-owned Korea Resources Corp. also is on the lookout for potential uranium investments in Africa and Asia. A consortium led by Kepco, Japan's Toshiba Power Systems, and its subsidiary Westinghouse Nuclear Power Plants, has begun work on a project to build four nuclear power plants of 1,400 MW each at Braka in the United Arab Emirates, using the Korea Hydro & Nuclear Power Co.'s APR1400 reactor type, which is an evolution of the U.S.-designed System 80+ type. The UAE's first reactor is expected to come on line in 2017. South Korea also expects to supply Turkey with a nuclear reactor in the coming decade.

Russia, a Strong Proponent

Russia was the first country to produce electricity from nuclear power when its Obninsk reactor started in 1954. Today it is one of the strongest proponents of nuclear energy, and government policy is to aggressively look for commercial opportunities around the world for the nuclear expertise contained within state-owned atomic energy company Rosatom. For example, Iran's first nuclear power plant is a 915 MW Russian-built design that began operating at Bushehr in the first half of 2011. Other Russian-sourced plants are being built or proposed in India, Vietnam, Turkey, and Argentina. Domestically, Russia operates 32 reactors with a capacity of 23 GW. According to the World Nuclear Association, it aims to almost double nuclear output by 2020 to 43 GW. Rosatom plans to build up to eight floating nuclear plants by 2015 to use as electricity-generating bases in remote Arctic locations and on the Kamchatka peninsula, and Russia also uses nuclear power for its ice-breaking fleet that keeps its northern seaways open for cargo vessels.

Russia produces about 3,600 tonnes of uranium a year, but has the goal of becoming the No. 2 producer globally by 2020, behind Kazakhstan. It has about 10 percent of the world's known recoverable uranium deposits, which ranks it No. 3 behind Australia (23 percent) and Kazakhstan (15 percent). Atomredmetzoloto (ARMZ), Rosatom's uranium mining arm, operates the world's fourth-largest mine at Kraznokamensk in Russia's Far East, near the Chinese border. Kraznokamensk produced almost 3,000 tonnes in 2010. ARMZ has new uranium projects in Armenia, Mongolia, and Namibia. As part of its aggressive overseas expansion drive, in December 2010 ARMZ bought a 51.4 percent stake in Canadian producer Uranium One, which has mines in Kazakhstan and the United States, and another near production in Australia. Uranium One's 2012 production target is about 5,350 tonnes. In mid-2011, ARMZ completed a deal to pay about $1.1 billion for 100 percent of Australian company Mantra Resources, which held the rights to the low-production cost Mkuju River project in Tanzania. This project, with reserves of 39,000 tonnes of uranium, is designed to produce 1,400 tonnes a year, with potential to go to 2,500 tonnes, at a cost of less than $80/kg.

France, the Nuclear Champion

France is unique in the nuclear power world. Its 58 reactors, operated by state majority-owned nuclear power utility Electricite de

France (EDF), produce 75 percent of its electricity, and the country has so much spare capacity that EDF exports more than 10 percent of its output to neighbours such as Germany, Italy, Spain, Switzerland, Belgium, and the United Kingdom. Energy independence, a policy pursued by France since the oil shocks of the 1970s, is at the heart of nuclear power's prominence in France, and even with the inroads made by renewable energy sources and cheaper gas, nuclear is unlikely to lose much ground. France actively champions its nuclear capabilities. Areva, another state-owned (90 percent) entity, is the world's largest nuclear company, and has multiple agreements and joint ventures around the world aimed at securing uranium supplies, processing deals, technology development—such as with Siemens in Germany—and customers for its nuclear reactors. French reactor technology is used in China, South Korea, South Africa, and Belgium.

France uses about 10,500 tonnes of uranium a year, sourced mainly from Areva's mines in Canada (McLean Lake, a stake in McArthur River and the forthcoming Cigar Lake) and Niger, and from suppliers in Australia, Russia, and Kazakhstan. Areva bought Canada's UraMin in 2007 to gain access to deposits in South Africa, Namibia, and the Central African Republic.

UK Momentum Shifts

The United Kingdom has 19 reactors, generating 63 GW, or about 19 percent of the country's energy needs. But the energy momentum is swinging more to gas and renewable sources such as wind power. British policy is that more than half the 60 GW of total new power capacity required by 2025 should come from renewable sources. Almost all of the United Kingdom's existing nuclear plants will be closed by 2023, supplanted by about 19 GW of new nuclear capacity that should start to come on line around 2018. French utility EDF, which bought British Energy in 2009 and now runs it as part of EDF Energy, plans to build four nuclear power stations with the first operating between 2017 and 2018. Two other groups, Horizon and NuGeneration, which are combinations of German, Spanish, French, and United Kingdom power companies, also plan to build nuclear power stations in the United Kingdom. About 2,300 tonnes of annual uranium supply is sourced mainly from Canada and undergoes conversion, enrichment, and fuel fabrication in the United Kingdom.

Brazil's Enrichment Role

South America's biggest economy, Brazil, is so rich in hydro resources that this form of power generation dominates the energy sector with a share of 84 percent. Nuclear's share is just 3 percent, produced by two pressurised water reactors with a combined size of 1,900 MW. A third reactor is under construction and four more are due to come on line between 2018 and 2025. Coal, oil, gas, and biomass make up the remaining 13 percent of Brazil's energy mix.

Brazil has about 5 percent of the world's known uranium reserves, and all output is used domestically after enrichment overseas. State-owned Industrias Nucleares do Brazil (INB) operates the Lagoa Real/Caetite mine in Bahia state, and a second mine Itataia/Santa Quiteria in Ceara state. Brazil has a significant capability in uranium enrichment and fuel fabrication at Resende in Rio de Janeiro state, and is also working on the development of advanced reactor designs and systems. No private investment in nuclear power is allowed. A secret nuclear weapons program embarked on by Brazil's military government in the 1970s was abandoned by the civilian administration in the 1980s, and Brazil subsequently renounced any interest in developing nuclear weapons. Brazil's neighbour Argentina, which briefly pursued a nuclear weapons program in the 1980s, operates three nuclear reactors that use Canadian and German designs. It plans to build a fourth, possibly in cooperation with Russia's Rosatom.

In the Middle East, Saudi Arabia has the most aggressive nuclear power program, announcing plans in mid-2011 to have 16 reactors by 2030 to help meet its fast-growing energy demands. The first two plants are expected to be operating by the early 2020s. Egypt and Jordan also have looked at building plants, but the UAE's first reactor should be the first running in the region, in 2017.

New Reactor Technology

For the longer term, companies around the world are working on new reactor technology that will use the raw material thorium, which is more abundant than uranium and has less radioactive waste. The biggest known economically recoverable deposits of thorium are in Australia, the United States, Turkey, India, Venezuela, and Brazil. China, India, and Russia are all pursuing thorium-based reactor development. State-owned Nuclear Power Corporation of

India Ltd. (NPCIL) announced in March 2011 that it had developed a 300 MW prototype of a thorium-based advanced heavy-water reactor, and this design was being reviewed by the national regulator, the Atomic Energy Regulatory Board. NPCIL said it was looking for a suitable reactor site and aimed to start work in India's twelfth five-year plan (2012–2017). China is working on its own thorium molten-salt reactor project.

The companies to watch in the nuclear space in the years ahead include Areva and EDF of France, Siemens of Germany, Russia's Rosatom and its mining arm ARMZ, and reactor subsidiary OKB Gidropress, China National Nuclear Corp., and China Guangdong Nuclear Power Corp., Japan's Toshiba, Hitachi, and Mitsubishi Heavy Industries, U.S. names such as General Electric and Westinghouse, Canada's AECL and Cameco, Kazakhstan's Kazatomprom, Brazil's INB, India's NPCIL, and Anglo-Australian mining groups Rio Tinto and BHP Billiton.

As always, a key issue now and for the future is how to store the high-level radioactive waste that is the by-product of nuclear power stations. Deep underground caverns, synthetic rock (where waste is mixed and dried into a powder that is then compressed into a dense rock) and concrete-encased storage containers in remote locations are some of the proposed solutions. Waste, of course, is not the only issue. How nuclear-armed North Korea and Pakistan—and possibly Iran—conduct their nuclear energy programs, and the reactions they provoke, may well determine the fate of much of the world's population.

Notes

1. Statement by Makoto Yagi, chairman, Japan Federation of Electric Power Companies, "Comments about Suspension of Operation of Hamaoka Nuclear Power Station of Chubu Electric Power Company," 9 May 2011.
2. Projection by Japan Centre for Economic Research, "Update of 37th Medium Term Forecast for the Japanese Economy 2011–2020: Economic Losses Could Hit ¥7 Trillion if All Nuclear Plants Cease," 14 June 2011.
3. World Nuclear Association, "World Nuclear Power Reactors & Uranium Requirements" (21 October 2011), www.world-nuclear.org/info/reactors .html.

4. Centre for Global Energy Studies, "Renewable Energy Outlook—Will the EU Reach Its Targets?" *Quarterly Oil Demand*, London, (May 2011), www.cges.co.uk/resources/articles/2011/05/19/renewable- energy-outlook-% E2%80%93-will-the-eu-reach-its-targets.

5. Mycle Schneider, Antony Froggatt, and Steve Thomas, *World Nuclear Industry Status Report 2010–2011: Nuclear Power in a Post-Fukushima World* (Washington, DC: WorldWatch Institute, April 2011).

6. World Nuclear Association, "World Nuclear Power Reactors & Uranium Requirements."

New Energy—Clean, Green, and Expensive

In the 1980s, America was home to more than 80 percent of the world's wind capacity, and 90 percent of its solar capacity. We owned the clean energy economy. But today, China has the most wind capacity. Germany has the most solar. Both invest more than we do in clean energy. Other countries are exporting technology we pioneered and chasing the jobs that come with it because they know that the countries that lead the 21st century clean energy economy will be the countries that lead the 21st century global economy. I want America to be that nation. I want America to win the future.
—U.S. President Barack Obama, 30 March 2011
(energy policy speech, Georgetown University,
Washington, DC)

The resource-based Earth wars have their parallel in the sun, wind, and water wars that are at the heart of the quest for cleaner energy. Even Saudi Arabia, the world's most cost-effective oil producer, is looking at solar power and other renewables in what Khalid Al-Falih, chief executive of state-owned oil major Saudi Aramco, calls his company's "hydrocarbons-plus" diversification strategy.[1] Chinese state company SinoHydro builds the world's biggest hydropower dams not just at home, but in locations scattered across Southeast Asia, Africa, and South America. Brazilian sugar producer Cosan, controlled by billionaire Rubens Ometto Silveira Mello, has linked with oil major Shell to set up Raizen, a joint venture that aims to be the world's biggest biofuel maker and marketer. Icelandic firm Enex uses its geothermal expertise in projects that stretch from China to Europe and the Americas. In post-Fukushima Japan, researchers at Tohoku University are working on solar cells that lift energy conversion rates to 45 percent. In North Africa, the Desertec Foundation has water desalination as one objective for its solar energy projects.

In these and thousands of other locations around the globe, scientists, inventors, and entrepreneurs are researching, competing, and working on new ways to meet specific clean energy needs. And as Barack Obama noted in his call to arms for America's green economy, some of the key technologies developed in the United States have been refined and advanced by innovative and/or low-cost producers in China, India, Japan, Germany, Denmark, South Korea, and Taiwan. Today's market leaders in solar cells, wind turbines, biomass, compact hydro, geothermal, and wave-generating energy include companies such as Voith Hydro in Germany, Vestas in Denmark, Suzlon Energy in India, and Sinovel, LDK Solar, Suntech, and DP CleanTech in China.

About 10 km (6 miles) west of the Nevada border in southern California's Mojave Desert, the beginnings of Obama's sought-after technological energy fightback are taking shape. Here, in a hot and dry part of the world where the sun shines 340 days a year, BrightSource Energy's Ivanpah concentrated solar thermal power plant is being built, with a goal of full operation by mid-2013. The utility-scale 392 MW facility, the world's largest of its type, carries $1.6 billion of U.S. government loan guarantees, a $300 million investment from NRG Solar (part of New Jersey-based NRG Energy), $168 million from equity investor Google, and long-term power contracts with Pacific Gas & Electric and Southern California Edison. Depending on how you view renewable energy, it is either one of several technological game changers that the world has been waiting for or simply the latest expensive folly in the vastly subsidized business of "going green." Ivanpah is made up of three separate solar thermal plants that use mirrors to concentrate the sun's heat onto water-filled boilers sitting atop steel towers. High-temperature steam from the boilers is piped to conventional turbines, which generate electricity. The mirrors are mounted on individual pylons—rather than in banks on a concrete pad—to allow the solar field to be built around the site's natural contours. The project also uses air cooling to convert steam back into water in a closed-loop cycle, thereby cutting water usage by 95 percent.

Ivanpah's founder and solar industry veteran Arnold Goldman knows this part of California well. Back in the 1980s and early 1990s, when he was founder and CEO of Luz Industries, Goldman set up what was then the world's largest collection of commercially viable solar power plants—nine in all—in three separate locations of the Mojave Desert. This was the 354 MW Solar Electric Generating Systems (SEGS), a project still producing power today. Using more than 900,000 mirrors, the plants employ parabolic trough solar thermal technology, supported by natural gas, to generate electricity. The split is about 90 percent solar and 10 percent gas, and SEGS—now run mainly by NextEra Energy—is a major supplier to Southern California Edison.

While BrightSource pushes ahead with Ivanpah, the world's biggest thin-film solar company, First Solar Inc., founded by executive chairman Michael Ahearn in 2000 with backing from the late John Walton (son of Wal-Mart founder Sam Walton), has sold three other solar projects in California that it is building based on its thin-film photovoltaic (PV) modules: the 230 MW Antelope Valley Solar Ranch 1 plant in the western Mojave Desert (bought by Exelon Corp in September 2011); the $1.4 billion two-phase 550 MW Desert Sunlight project in Riverside County (bought by NextEra Energy and GE Energy, also in September 2011); and the $2 billion 550 MW Topaz Solar project in eastern San Luis Obispo county. Iowa-based MidAmerican Energy, a unit of Warren Buffett's Berkshire Hathaway, agreed in December 2011 to buy the Topaz project, which is due for completion by 2015. In the same month, MidAmerican also agreed to buy 49 percent of another First Solar PV project, the $1.8 billion 290 MW Agua Caliente plant in Arizona, from NRG Energy. The price of PV panels has come down so much since 2008—driven in part by low-cost Chinese production—that PV is seen as a cheaper, quicker way to get a solar plant up and running in the United States, where PV power generation costs are about 13 cents a kilowatt-hour, compared with 16 cents for concentrated solar thermal. Solar Trust of America, a venture begun by Germany's Solar Millenium and later bought by Solarhybrid, plans to have a 1,000-MW complex known as the Blythe solar project operating between 2013 and 2018 in Riverside County, California, using PV in the first 500 MW phase.

Power Storage Ability

PV may be cheaper, but along with cost, a key factor for solar power plants—and other renewable sources—is whether they have the ability to store power for later use. An example of where the technology is headed comes from the $2 billion 280 MW Solana concentrated solar power (CSP, sometimes known as CST for concentrated solar thermal) plant being built—also with a U.S. government loan guarantee—near Gila Bend in the Arizona desert by Abengoa Solar, a unit of the Spanish utility Abengoa. As a typical CSP project, Solana employs parabolic trough technology to heat a liquid used to boil water to drive a steam turbine generator. But Solana has an X-factor: a system called molten salt storage, made up of two large insulated hot and cold salt tanks. These can store 40 percent of the heat generated by the plant, allowing it to send power to the grid at peak periods such as early evening, and providing an extra six hours a day of capacity. California-based energy developer Solar Reserve also has won a U.S. government loan guarantee for a similar project at Tonopah in Nevada that it claims will be the world's largest molten salt power tower on completion in late 2013. The 110 MW project, named Crescent Dunes, will be able to run as much as 12 hours without sunlight. Rather than a parabolic trough, it uses the newer technology of a bank of mirrors focused on a solar collector at the top of the tower. The first example of this technology, the Gemasolar plant near Seville in Spain, was commissioned in June 2011 as a joint venture between the Abu Dhabi energy investment fund Masdar, and Spanish engineering group SENER.

These large-scale solar projects in the United States and elsewhere are typical of the way renewable energy is winning the support of governments and big corporates around the world. Ivanpah backer Google, for example, is also a big investor in two massive U.S. wind farms: Caithness Energy's 845 MW Shepherds Flat facility in Oregon, and TerraGen's Alta Wind Energy Centre in California that aims to generate 1,020 MW by 2012 and 1,550 MW on full completion. Another of Google's investments is in a 360 km sub-sea transmission line designed to serve offshore wind farms along the

U.S. east coast. All told, in the last few years, the U.S. Department of Energy has issued loans, guarantees, or conditional commitments totaling $38 billion to clean energy projects. But it has not been plain sailing: high-profile Solyndra, recipient of a $535 million government loan guarantee in 2009 on a promise that it would create 4,000 "clean energy" jobs, was one of three U.S. solar companies to file for bankruptcy in 2011 as Chinese competition squeezed PV panel prices.

Half a world away in Europe, funding support for renewable energy has been in place for years through rebates and generous feed-in tariffs, but may now be coming to an end as economic conditions prompt legislators to review the situation. Countries such as Spain, Germany, and Italy have spent billions to support the take-up of wind and solar power over the past decade. Now the clean industry is being asked if it can sustain itself without subsidies.

Perhaps one part of the answer can be discerned in England among the chalky-white cliffs, sandy beaches, and ancient religious buildings that are the hallmarks of the Viking Coastal Trail, the 43 km mix of walking and cycling paths that runs along the Kentish coast and inland through a series of quiet villages. It was here in the ninth century that Viking marauders from Denmark sailed their longships across the English Channel and into the bays around the modern-day coastal town of Ramsgate. The same winds that propelled the Vikings now turn the blades of one of the world's biggest offshore wind farms, the 300 MW Thanet field, which rises out of the channel waters a short distance off the coast. For the strollers along the trail between Ramsgate and the little town of Broadstairs to the north, the slowly spinning blades of Thanet's 100 Vestas wind turbines make an incongruous backdrop to the weekend yacht races. Thanet, which is owned by the Swedish state energy group Vattenfall, has been delivering power into the UK grid since late 2010, and by late 2012 will be joined by two bigger wind farms nearby, the 140-turbine 504 MW Greater Gabbard field and the spectacular 630 MW London Array, a 175-turbine farm spreading across 245 square kilometres of the Thames Estuary between the coasts of Kent and Essex.

If all goes well in stage one of the London Array, the consortium behind it—made up of DONG Energy of Denmark, German power company E.ON, and the Abu Dhabi energy fund Masdar—may expand it to 1,000 MW. E.ON already owns and operates three large offshore wind farms in the United Kingdom and is pushing ahead with the 230 MW Humber Gateway off the coast of Yorkshire. The east coast of England is not the United Kingdom's only suitable location for utility-scale projects. On the other side of Britain, German power company RWE's UK subsidiary, RWE Npower Renewables, aims to have its 160-turbine 576 MW Gwynt y Mor project off the coast of north Wales in full production by 2014.

Europe's Renewable Commitment

These large-scale wind farms are just a small part of the push for renewable energy sources around the world—particularly in Europe where most countries are well advanced in their commitment to get 20 percent of their power from a mix of wind, solar, tidal, hydro, geothermal, and biomass by 2020. Globally, renewable energy supplied an estimated 16 percent of final energy consumption in 2010 and almost 20 percent of the world's total electricity production, according to the 2011 global status report by the Renewable Energy Policy Network (REN21). It said renewable capacity now accounted for about a quarter of the world's total power-generating capacity.[2]

According to Steve Sawyer, secretary general of the Brussels-based Global Wind Energy Council (GWEC), wind power led the renewable electricity sector in 2010, with more new capacity installed that year than for any other technology, and with 450 GW of wind power likely to be available by 2015. For the first time, he said, more wind power was added in developing countries and emerging markets than in the industrialised world.[3] By that, essentially he means China, China, and China, with a long gap to India. GWEC figures show China added 16.5 GW in 2010 to take its cumulative wind capacity to 42.3 GW. The United States added 5.1 GW to move to a total of 40.2 GW, while India added 2.1 GW for a total of 13 GW. But that puts it still well behind the big European users, Germany with 27.2 GW of cumulative capacity and Spain with 20.7 GW. Companies such as Vestas of Denmark, Siemens of Germany, Gamesa of Spain, and German engineering tycoon Aloys Wobben's Enercon lead the way in Europe and in many other parts of the world, but they are being rapidly caught and passed by the Chinese makers who have burst on the scene in the past decade. Four of the world's top 10 wind turbine brands are now Chinese: Sinovel Wind, Xinjiang Goldwind Science & Technology, Dongfang Turbine, and Guodian

United Power Technology. The other two top-ten makers are GE Wind Energy of the United States and Indian billionaire Tulsi Tanti's Suzlon Energy (see Exhibit 8.1).

After a massive ramp-up of wind power capacity in China in 2009 and 2010, the Chinese government called for a breather in 2011, dropping subsidies and putting pressure on the entire supply chain to move a little slower. That prompted Sinovel founder Han Junliang and early investor Wei Wenyuan—who both became paper billionaires after Sinovel's initial share offer in January 2011—to look abroad for opportunities. An early example was Sinovel's deal in April 2011 with Greece's largest power producer, Public Power Corp SA, to work together on wind farms and other projects in the Greek renewables market.

While the Chinese companies have made rapid strides in the past decade, Tulsi Tanti has led the Indian charge with Suzlon Energy since 1995, with more than 10,500 wind turbines and 15 GW of installed capacity in 25 countries. In 2006, Suzlon bought Belgian gearbox maker Hansen Transmissions for $565 million (a stake since sold down to 25 percent), and in 2007 outbid French nuclear power company Areva for control of German turbine maker REpower. These acquisitions and the 2008–2009 global financial crisis strained Suzlon's finances, but recent big turbine orders make the future look more promising. A new range of 2 MW turbines released in 2011 aims to hit the sweet spot for low-wind sites around the world. Tanti acknowledges that some of the best wind technology comes out of Europe, but for him the wind power epicenter is clearly in the east, where costs are lower and markets are bigger. Research and development activity for all the top makers is following production to China and India.

1. Vestas Wind Systems, Denmark	6. Gamesa Technology Corp., Spain
2. Sinovel Wind Co., China	7. Dongfang Turbine Co., China
3. GE Wind Energy, United States	8. Suzlon Energy, India
4. Xinjiang Goldwind Science & Technology Co., China	9. Siemens Wind Power, Germany
5. Enercon, Germany	10. Guodian United Power Technology, China

Exhibit 8.1   Top 10 global wind power companies
Source: MAKE Consulting, March 2011

Wind power works as a business, says Tanti, because it is good for people and good for the environment—there are no greenhouse gas emissions, no fuel, no mining, no costs other than maintenance over a turbine's 20-year life. Plus a good wind site can be reused by repowering with a more efficient turbine down the track. As for carbon emissions created during construction of a wind turbine generator, the Global Wind Energy Council says these are offset within the first year of operation. Wind power costs have fallen sharply in the past three years as turbine hubs and blades become bigger and more efficient, and large-scale wind farms of 500 MW size become practicable. Even so, critics of wind power cite its cost, fluctuating availability, and the lack of grid connection infrastructure. Other issues include bird deaths, landscape pollution, and health concerns for people living close to wind farms.

Although onshore wind farms have been around for years, it is the offshore farms that are gaining favour in Europe, North America, and Asia. There is less of the "not-in-my-backyard" opposition. They are usually far enough away to be less visually polluting, and there are no land lease issues or pesky neighbours complaining of headaches. But offshore fields are hideously expensive, and have many more construction issues. These include footings to construct, substations, and power links to the land-based grid. Cost overruns are common—cabling problems at the UK's Greater Gabbard project cost the contractor Fluor a fortune. Floating wind turbines, which don't require footings, offer a chance to keep costs down by onshore assembly. The first example, a 2 MW unit built in Portugal, was towed to a site in the Atlantic Ocean in late 2011 for testing. Scale is important, but it comes at a hefty cost—South Korea's ambitious plan to create what would be the world's biggest wind farm off its southwest coast by 2019 comes with an equally ambitious price tag of $9 billion for 2.5 GW of capacity, in a project led by Korea Electric Power Corp.

Facing the Intermittency Factor

The most forthright skeptics of renewable energy dismiss its progress and prospects with just two words: baseload power. Only nuclear, oil, coal, or gas-fired power plants, they say, can deliver the continuous, reliable power that industrial and residential consumers demand, day-in and day-out. In their view, *intermittency*, the variability factor of windless days and clouded skies, means that wind and solar power can never be genuine replacement sources. But according to Dr. Klaus Rave, president of the Global Wind Energy Council, that is old-style thinking. "The baseload power era is over," he says, noting that in Europe a lot of baseload power capacity stands idle for part of the day. "The modern grid is part baseload, part medium load, and part low load. It is about smoothing the push of supply, so that eventually we get to the era of the virtual power station." But he acknowledges that the electricity distribution grid is not yet up to speed. "A smart grid is the key to the energy market," he says.[4]

GWEC Secretary General Steve Sawyer concurs, while pointing out that Spain is now 60 percent renewable and Denmark is close to 100 percent. "Connectivity and the smart grid is always the key. It is not so much about baseload as supply-demand management."[5] As well, the goal of cost parity—where generating power from renewable sources costs the same as fossil fuels such as coal and gas—is getting closer in Europe. By 2014 to 2015, there is likely to be parity in much of northern Europe.

The situation is far different in China, where its more efficient supercritical coal-fired power plants will stay well ahead of the cost curve for decades to come. Even so, many of the fastest-moving practitioners of green energy technologies in the 2010s are in China, where the government until recently has encouraged the sector with easy approvals and finance. Along with the promoters of Sinovel, Goldwind, Dongfang, and Guodian United Power in the wind sector, some of the key Chinese identities in solar have made massive paper fortunes on the strength of stock market listings at home and abroad. They include Suntech Power founder Dr. Shi Zhengrong, known as the Sun King; young business luminary Peng Xiaofeng of LDK Solar; Wu Jianlong of Zhejiang Sunflower; Zhu Gongshan of GCL Poly Energy; Jin Baofang of JA Solar; Gao Jifan, founder of early industry PV leader Trina Solar; Miao Liansheng of Yingli Green Energy; Lu Tingxiu, chairman of China Sunergy; Li Xianshou of solar wafer maker ReneSola; and Wang Chuanfu and Lu Xiangyang, co-founders of battery and electric car maker BYD Co. Since 2008, Warren Buffett's MidAmerican Energy has held a 10 percent stake in BYD, which was set up by Wang and Lu in 1995. They both hold stakes in BYD that put them in the paper billionaire class.

Like the wind sector, solar power—both thermal and PV—faces a shakeout in the years ahead as consolidation follows the first rush of enthusiasts and fortune-seekers. Globally, some of the big oil companies such as Exxon, Shell, Chevron, and BP have been major players in the solar industry since the 1980s. BP, for example, has a joint venture with India's Tata Group that has made Tata-BP the largest solar panel maker there. India plans to add 20 GW of solar power to its grid by 2020. In mid-2011, French oil major Total paid $1.3 billion for a majority stake in leading U.S. solar panel maker SunPower—a deal that marked another step in the sector's progression in that it matched a global industrial player with a solar technology leader. SunPower CEO Tom Werner offered the bullish view that the alliance would "change the way the world is powered" (see Exhibit 8.2).[6]

In Japan, Masayoshi Son, the one-time Internet investment pioneer turned telecom corporate stalwart, is directing his own multi-billion dollar fortune to the pursuit of solar power. Son, whose company SoftBank is the No. 3 mobile phone operator behind NTT DoCoMo and KDDI Corp., has set up the Japan Renewable Energy Foundation to work on his proposed renewable energy project encompassing at least ten solar plants, each of 20 MW.

Reflecting the rapid changes in the industry through 2011, two more Chinese module producers, JinkoSolar and LDK Solar, had replaced REC and SolarWorld in the top 10 list released by PVinsights for the third quarter of the year in December 2011.

---

1. Suntech, China
2. First Solar, United States
3. Sharp, Japan
4. Yingli Green Energy, China
5. Trina Solar, China
6. Canadian Solar, Canada
7. Hanwha Solarone, China*
8. SunPower, United States**
9. Renewable Energy Corp. (REC), Norway
10. SolarWorld, Germany

Exhibit 8.2   Top 10 solar module producers (by MW shipped in 2010)

*Joint venture between Hanwha of South Korea and Solarfun Power of China.

**In 2011, French oil major Total agreed to buy 60 percent of SunPower for about US$1.3 billion.

Source: PVinsights, May 2011

The building blocks of photovoltaic (PV) solar panels are solar cells, either made from a thin slice of semiconductor material known as a wafer, or created using a thin-film technology that uses material such as cadmium telluride, amorphous silicon, or copper indium gallium selenide. Thin-film technology has a cost advantage over silicon wafers but is not yet as efficient. Some solar panel companies make their own wafers, but most rely on specialist solar wafer producers. The top three wafer makers are the Chinese companies GCL Poly Energy, LDK Solar, and ReneSola, followed by REC of Norway, SolarWorld of Germany, another Chinese maker Comtec, ahead of two Taiwanese companies: Green Energy Technology and Sino American Silicon. The lone U.S. entrant in the top ten is Missouri-based MEMC—a 50-year veteran of the semiconductor wafer industry—followed by South Korean maker Nexolon.[7]

Big Geographic Variations

In Europe, about half of all renewable energy comes from hydro, about a quarter is wind and solar, geothermal, wave, and biomass make up the rest. There are big variations, depending on geography. Norway—where hydro accounts for 98 percent of power—and other parts of Scandinavia are well on their way to an almost complete reliance on renewables-based energy. Austria could be 70 percent renewable by 2020 because of its abundant hydropower, and a similar case applies in Switzerland, where hydropower's share stands at 59 percent. Justin Wilkes, policy director for the European Wind Energy Association, believes the aspirational target of 100 percent renewable energy set for 2050 in Europe is a real possibility if the grid is upgraded and interconnected, distribution is smoothed, and regulators get together on pricing. He sees an energy environment where 50 percent will be wind power and 50 percent will be other renewables—for example, hydropower in the Nordic countries and Austria, maybe biomass in eastern Europe, solar power in Germany, Spain, and southern Europe, and a preference for offshore wind in the United Kingdom, Denmark, and Spain. Wilkes said, "We need grid-friendly renewable energy sources. Flexibility is the key to success—flexible generation and storage, and demand-side management."[8]

Hydropower is by far the most widely used of the renewable energy sources, despite its often-heavy initial costs in dam construction, community dislocation, and environmental impact. It is the only form of renewable energy able to compete on price with fossil fuels. Once built, a hydro dam is likely to have a long working life and has no ongoing fuel costs. In some cases it will serve multiple roles, including flood mitigation, irrigation, aquaculture, and recreation/ water sports. In terms of electricity generation, hydropower globally accounted for 86.5 percent of all renewable sources in 2007, according to the EIA's International Energy Outlook, and by 2035 will still have a 68 percent share despite big advances by wind, solar, geothermal, and biomass.[9]

Hydropower's Role

According to the REN 21 Global Status Report for 2011, China was the top hydropower producer in 2010 with about 200 GW of installed capacity, ahead of Canada (90 GW), the United States (80 GW), and Brazil (70 GW). If China is to achieve its 2020 target of 15 percent primary energy consumption from renewables (up from 8.3 percent in 2010), hydropower will have to play a major role, with a nominated target of 400 GW of capacity by then. Already China is home to the world's biggest hydroelectric project, the 20.3 GW Three Gorges Dam on the Yangzi River, which required the relocation of 1.25 million people. The dam's operator, the China Three Gorges Corporation, plans to spend as much as $60 billion over the next few years building several large dams upstream on the Jishan River, including the Xiluodu project (12.6 GW, due in 2013) and the Xiangjiaba project (6.4 GW, also due in 2013).

The only other countries with similar mega projects planned or under construction are Brazil with its environmentally contentious 11.2 GW Belo Monte Dam on the Xingu River, and India's 11 GW Upper Siang project, which has been plagued by delays and concerns over its sensitive location on the Siang River in Arunachal Pradesh, close to the Chinese border. Venezuela operates one massive hydropower project, the 10.2 GW Guri Dam on the Caroni River, which provides more than 70 percent of the country's electricity. Some of the biggest hydropower plants are in North America, including the Grand Coulee Dam built on the Columbia River in Washington state in the 1930 to 1940s.

The largest hydro plant in Russia, the 6.4 GW Sayano-Shushenskaya Dam operated by RusHydro, suffered a catastrophic turbine failure in August 2009 that flooded the main turbine hall and engine room, leaving 75 workers dead. A four-year repair program began in 2010. Russia is home to two other large hydropower facilities: Rusal's 6 GW Krasnoyarsk Dam (which powers Rusal's associated aluminum plant) on the Yenisey River in Siberia, and the 4.5 GW Bratsk Dam on the Angara River near Irkutsk, Siberia. As with Krasnoyarsk, most of Bratsk's output goes to an associated aluminum plant. The Russian government is also looking at projects in the Russian Far East, which might have export potential to Japan and South Korea. Elsewhere, large parts of Central Africa, South America, and Southeast Asia are considered to have good hydropower potential. New Zealand also uses hydropower extensively (see Exhibit 8.3).

It is not just in hydropower where China reigns. In virtually every category of renewable energy except geothermal, China has either the greatest installed capacity or is likely to be near the top within a decade. In 2010, out of $211 billion invested globally in renewable energy, China accounted for $50 billion, followed by Germany with $41 billion, the United States $30 billion, India $14 billion, and Brazil $7 billion. These top five accounted for two-thirds of all renewables investment. China has made it clear there is more spending to come. In his March 2011 report setting out the main objectives for China's twelfth five-year plan covering 2011–2015, Premier Wen Jiabao said one goal was to "comprehensively build our capacity for sustainable development." Wen said the share of nonfossil fuels in China's primary energy consumption should reach 11.4 percent; energy consumption and CO_2 emissions

1.	Three Gorges Dam, China 20.3 GW, expanding to 22.5 GW	6.	Sayano–Shushenskaya Dam, Russia, 6.4 GW (under repair)
2.	Itaipu Dam, Brazil 14 GW	7.	Krasnoyarsk Dam, Russia 6 GW
3.	Guri Dam, Venezuela 10.2 GW	8.	Robert-Bourassa Dam, Canada 5.6 GW
4.	Tucurui Dam, Brazil 8.4 GW	9.	Churchill Falls Dam, Canada 5.4 GW
5.	Grand Coulee Dam, United States 7.0 GW	10.	Longtan Dam, China 2 GW, expanding to 6 GW

Exhibit 8.3   World's largest hydropower plants

Source: Company reports, UN World Water Development Report

per unit of GDP should be reduced by 16 percent and 17 percent, respectively; and the release of major pollutants should be reduced by 8 to 10 percent. As well, "We will substantially improve water conservation facilities; make progress in better controlling important tributaries of large rivers as well as lakes and small and medium-sized rivers; and significantly improve agricultural irrigation, the efficiency of water resources use and resistance to flooding."[10]

China's energy plans are not only breathtaking, but potentially game changing in terms of prices. According to a Brookings Institution briefing delivered by Trevor Houser, a partner at the Rhodium Group, China would have to generate between 320 and 480 GW of non–fossil fuel energy over the next decade to meet its 15 percent renewable target. That would equate to between a third and a half of all new global non–fossil energy capacity. Houser said he would be surprised if China could reach the upper end of these figures, but he noted that "even if they get halfway there, this will transform, fundamentally, the global market for clean energy technology . . . It will change the relative economics of low-carbon technology versus high carbon technology, and not just in China."[11]

Interest in Biofuel

Aside from power-generating renewables, there is massive interest in biofuel for transportation, particularly in Brazil and the United States, the two biggest producers of ethanol. Brazil has a thriving sugarcane-based ethanol industry to fuel its automobiles, with at least 12 global makers—VW, Ford, GM, Toyota, Honda, Mitsubishi, Nissan, Renault, Peugeot, Citroen, Fiat, and Kia—offering flex-fuel models for the Brazilian market that are capable of running on any blend of gasoline and ethanol. In the United States, pioneering automaker Henry Ford was an early advocate of biofuel, with some of his Model T Fords capable of running on ethanol as well as petrol or kerosene. Under U.S. energy security legislation, by 2022 at least 36 billion gallons (136 billion litres) of fuel used in the United States must come from renewable sources. Although the United States produces more ethanol than Brazil, it mainly uses corn as its feedstock rather than sugarcane. As more people question whether producing biofuel from the cornfields of Iowa and Nebraska is the best use of fertile croplands, some companies are starting to look beyond traditional feedstocks. One such alternative involves cellulosic ethanol technology. There have been some expensive setbacks in this field (ventures such as E3 Biofuels and Range Fuels), but in July 2011, the U.S. Department of Energy announced its Project Liberty, which is designed to help ethanol plants make the switch from corn to other feedstocks such as crop residues, native grasses, and woody materials. There are numerous other sources for cellulosic ethanol, including human waste. For example, Israel-based Applied Clean Tech recycles sludge from sewage treatment plants into pellets it calls Recyllose, which can be used as an ethanol feedstock. Massachusetts-based biofuel developer Qteros has a partnership with India's Praj Industries to develop what it hopes will be "multiple feedstocks by late 2012."[12] Other U.S. companies such as Amyris, Codexis, and Gevo also are exploring commercialization opportunities, but cost remains an issue when biofuels are measured against other energy sources and technologies. In a mid-2011 report on biofuels, the International Energy Agency said that with Brazil and the United States at the forefront, by 2016 ethanol and biodiesel should displace 5.3 percent and 1.5 percent, respectively, of total global gasoline and gas-oil demand. But the IEA noted that its research also suggested it might be 2030 before advanced biofuels achieve "widespread cost competitiveness with hydrocarbon-derived fuels."[13]

Notes

1. Khalid Al-Falih, speech on Saudi Aramco's Accelerated Transformation Program, Mellon Auditorium, Washington DC, (19 May 2011), www .saudiaramco.com/en/home/news/speeches/unlocking-human-potential-saudi-aramcos-accelerated-transformati.html#news%257C %252Fen%252Fhome%252Fnews%252Fspeeches%252Funlocking-human-potential-saudi-aramcos-accelerated-transformati.baseajax .html
2. Renewable Energy Policy Network, Global Status Report 2011, Paris, (12 July 2011). www.ren21.net/REN21Activities/Publications/Global StatusReport/GSR2011/tabid/56142/Default.aspx.
3. Steve Sawyer, secretary general, Global Wind Energy Council, press conference, Wind Power India conference, Chennai, 7 April 2011.
4. Klaus Rave, chairman, Global Wind Energy Council, press conference, Wind Power India conference, Chennai, 7 April 2011.
5. Sawyer, press conference.

6. SunPower media release, "Total and SunPower Partner to Create a New Global Leader in the Solar Industry," Paris and San Jose, California, (15 June 2011), http://us.sunpowercorp.com/about/newsroom/press-releases/?relID=41809.

7. "List of Top 10 Wafer Makers—Growing Bigger," *Green World Investor* (March 2011), www.greenworldinvestor.com/2011/03/01/list-of-worlds-top-solar-wafer-companies-growing-bigger/.

8. Interview with Justin Wilkes, policy director for the European Wind Energy Association, Chennai, India, 8 April 2011.

9. U.S. Energy Information Administration, "International Energy Outlook" (19 September 2011), www.eia.gov/forecasts/ieo/index.cfm.

10. Premier Wen Jiabao, Report on China's 12th Five-Year Plan 2011–15, Beijing, 14 March 2011. http://en.ndrc.gov.cn/hot/t20060529_71334.htm.

11. Trevor Houser, Rhodium Group, "Low-Carbon Chinese Development? Making Sense of Current Policy and Market Trends," presentation to Brookings Institution, Washington, DC, (31 May 2011), www.brookings.edu/~/media/Files/events/2011/0531_china_carbon/20110531_china_carbon_houser.pdf.

12. Media release, "Praj Industries and Qteros Announce Broad Strategic Partnership," Pune, India, (5 January 2011), www.qteros.com/news-events/news-detail.cfm?id=29.

13. International Energy Agency, "Technology Roadmap: Biofuels for Transport," Paris (20 April 2011), www.iea.org/papers/2011/biofuels_roadmap.pdf.

CHAPTER 9

Coppery Red, the Colour
of Earth's True Love

Over the next 30 years it is projected that the world will consume as much copper as it has over the last 10,000 years.
    —Rio Tinto chief executive Tom Albanese,
    14 April 2011 (Address to Rio Tinto annual
    general meeting in London)

The large-scale intrusion of the financial sector, with the apparent support of most large producers, creating a structure that makes the copper market seem tight and thus able to push prices continuously higher, is destroying the very foundations of the industry.
    —Veteran copper analyst Simon Hunt,
    "The likely pattern for copper prices in 2011
    and beyond," 7 January 2011, on www.mineweb.com

Every iPhone, iPod, Xbox, laptop, TV set, microwave oven, and other electronic device that fires the imagination and captures the wallets of buyers around the world contains copper (along with other metals such as silver and rare earths). Every new car contains at least 20 kg of copper—and much more in the case of electric/ hybrid cars. Every new construction site, apartment building or individual house uses copper, as does every ship, every aircraft, every piece of electrical equipment, every engineering project, every industrial enterprise. And the renewable energy sector, with its wind turbines, generators, fuel cells, and solar panels, is a major consumer. Global demand is growing at better than 10 percent a year. In 2010, the world consumed 19.4 million tonnes of refined copper, worth almost $150 billion at an average price for the year of just over $7,500 a tonne. By the end of 2011, copper was around $7,800, with a price above $8,000 forecast for 2012. Morgan Stanley estimated the refined copper supply shortfall in 2012 would be 300,000 tonnes.

The centre of demand has shifted inexorably to Asia. Back in 1990, when copper traded at $2,400 a tonne, North America, Europe, and Japan between them consumed 68 percent of the world's copper. China's share was just 5 percent, even though it had about 20 percent of the world's population. By 2010, the pendulum had swung sharply: Japan's share was now just 5 percent, North America and Europe were 27 percent combined and China was by far the single bigger user, with a 37 percent share. Its building and automotive industries, its appetite for consumer electronics, its massive investment in renewable energy and transport infrastructure— every high-speed train in China uses up to four tonnes of copper—and its huge industrialisation and urbanisation push means that its position as the world's bigger copper user will continue for years to come. And behind it, India, too, is starting to consume the red metal at a gathering pace as more of its 1.2 billion people reach income levels that support smartphones, motor vehicles, modern housing, and the copper-intensive comforts of twenty-first-century life.

Not surprisingly, the world's two biggest copper smelters—each of 900,000 tonnes capacity—are in China and India: Jiangxi Copper Corp.'s Guixi smelter, and the Aditya Birla Group's Hindalco operation at Dahej in Gujarat. Nobody else comes close in scale; the biggest smelters in Germany, Japan, Russia, and Chile are all in the 450,000-tonne range. Similarly, the three biggest copper refineries are in China and India—the 900,000-tonne Guixi refinery operated by Jiangxi Copper; Yunnan Copper's 500,000-tonne plant, and Hindalco's 500,000-tonne Dahej complex. China and India have their own copper mines, but they lack the super-sized copper resources that abound in the Andes Mountains in South America, which means they must import raw copper concentrates and also be on the lookout for opportunities to exploit new resources in emerging supply zones such as Africa. Already, Zambia and the Democratic Republic of Congo—the two fastest-growing copper supply sources in the world—are the focus of Chinese mining investments. Invariably, the Chinese companies making these moves are large, state-owned entities with government backing. Their competitors are global mining names such as Rio Tinto, Xstrata, Glencore, Freeport McMoRan, Anglo American, Vale and Vedanta, plus a host of junior miners who have had the exploratory gumption or the political connections to (maybe) strike it rich. Some of this is murky territory indeed; deals are done and undone as administrations change, mining leases are torn up, new partners are invited in, and a "free carry"—where one party (usually a state-backed agency) gets free equity—is the order of the day.

Despite the recent focus on Africa, the world's richest copper deposits are in Chile, which accounts for about a third of global production and where mines such as Chuquicamata and El Teniente—both held by Chile's state-owned Codelco since the 1971 nationalization of the copper industry—have been among the top producers for more than 50 years. Codelco is the world's biggest producer, with output in 2010 of 1.7 million tonnes of refined copper; it also holds about 20 percent of the world's reserves of copper. Peru is home to such big mines as Cerro Verde, Antamina, and the forthcoming Conga. Indonesia, China, the United States, Australia, Russia, Zambia, and the Democratic Republic of Congo are all significant producers, while expectations are growing that Mongolia and Kazakhstan also will become big suppliers in future. Although there are plenty of deposits around the world with tremendous potential, two names resonate with the magic ring of "100-year mines"—Escondida in Chile and Olympic Dam in Australia. Both are operated by BHP Billiton (though Rio Tinto has a 30 percent stake in Escondida) and both came into the BHP fold through acquisitions in which copper was not the main attraction (see Exhibit 9.1).

In the early 1980s, Jack Welch, then head of the U.S. conglomerate General Electric, decided he no longer wanted to be in commodities. He set about divesting GE's commodity assets, which included selling its coal mining arm Utah International for A\$2.4 billion in 1984 to an Australian company then called BHP, which was primarily a steel maker and coal miner (after a 2001 merger, the company became BHP Billiton). The deal's value was mainly in some coal mines in New Mexico and the Australian state of Queensland, but it also included iron ore deposits in Western Australia and a new copper resource called Escondida in Chile that Utah and its

1. Chile 5966	**6.** Australia 922
2. Peru 1375	**7.** Zambia 865
3. China 1313	**8.** Russia 775
4. United States 1223	**9.** Canada 575
5. Indonesia 962	**10.** Poland 469

Top 10 account for 14.445 million tonnes, or 81.5 percent of world total production of 17.717 million tonnes. Total world resources of copper are estimated to be around 2.3 billion tons. Future high-growth zones are Kazakhstan, DR Congo, and Mongolia.

Exhibit 9.1   Top 10 copper producing countries (2010, thousand tonnes of copper concentrates and SX-EW*)

*SX (solvent extraction) and EW (electro winning) process, which is used in about 18 percent of copper output.

Source: International Copper Study Group

partner Getty Minerals had found in 1981. The deposit had its share of logistical challenges, 160 km (100 miles) from the nearest port and perched at an altitude of more than 3,000 metres (10,000 feet) in the Atacama Desert in northern Chile. It would take until 1991 before the first copper came out of Escondida, but today it is the world's biggest copper mine, the source of 786,000 tonnes of copper concentrate in 2010, and on track for a $540 million expansion to 2.2 million tonnes a year by 2013.

Olympic Dam a Bargain Buy

BHP Billiton's other "100-year" mine is its copper-gold-uranium deposit at Olympic Dam in the desert country of South Australia, picked up in 2005 as part of its $9.2 billion takeover of Australian mining company WMC. BHP's former chief financial officer, Alex Vanselow, would later characterise the Olympic Dam asset as like "finding a Rembrandt" in a flea market. Certainly, BHP got a bargain—Olympic Dam is rated the world's fourth-largest copper deposit, the fifth-largest gold deposit, and the biggest uranium deposit, equal to a third of the world's known uranium resources. It will take $30 billion and more than a decade to expand Olympic Dam from the existing underground operation to a full open cut, with a four-to-sixfold increase in capacity. BHP expects the quantity of ore recovered to grow from 12 million tonnes a year to 72 million tonnes, while copper concentrate will rise from 600,000 tonnes to 2.4 million tonnes. Refined copper—including overseas production—will rise from 235,000 tonnes to 750,000 tonnes, worth $7.5 billion at current prices. It is a similar story with silver and gold—2.9 million ounces of silver bullion, up from 800,000 ounces now, and 800,000 ounces of gold, up from 100,000 ounces. Uranium oxide will grow from 4,500 tonnes a year to 19,000 tonnes. To get some idea of the scale of the Olympic Dam project, it will take about five years of mining just to remove the 350-metre thick layer of overburden and expose the upper surface of the ore body. During this time, more than 400 million tonnes of rock a year will be moved from the open pit to a storage site that eventually will be 150 metres high and cover about 6,700 hectares. By the time the expanded mine has been going for 40 years, the open pit will be 1 km deep, 4 km long and 3.5 km wide—bigger even than Rio Tinto's Bingham Canyon copper mine in Utah, which can be seen from space.

Copper hasn't always been an easy ride for the Australian miner; its opponents hooted derisively when BHP bought a Tucson, Arizona-based company called Magma Copper for $2.6 billion at the beginning of 1996. Less than six months later, the company and the rest of the industry endured "Red Tuesday," when the price of copper crashed more than 40 percent to just $0.80 a pound after a Japanese copper futures trader, Yasuo Hamanaka of Sumitomo Corporation, was found to have been rigging the market. Another source of trouble was BHP's majority ownership of the big Ok Tedi copper mine in Papua New Guinea, built in an area subject to massive rainfall and erosion. A partial collapse of a tailings dam and pollution caused by the mine's operators discharging tailings into the Ok Tedi and Fly River system led to a class action suit over environmental damage. BHP settled out of court for $400 million in 1996, quit the mine in 2002, and put its stake into a trust-style holding company, PNG Sustainable Development Program Ltd. (PSDP), set up to fund future development projects in Papua New Guinea. Ok Tedi continues producing copper, but is likely to close in 2013. The PNG government holds 30 percent and Canadian miner Inmet holds the remaining 18 percent.

It will be at least 2018 before Olympic Dam's open pit begins production, so for now, Escondida is the copper jewel in BHP's metals crown. The company has a 57.5 percent stake in the mine and is the operator. Rival miner Rio Tinto (which BHP tried unsuccessfully to take over in 2008) holds 30 percent, and a Japanese consortium led by Mitsubishi Corp. holds the remaining 12.5 percent. BHP's expects to complete an expansion of Escondida by the middle of 2012 that will give it another 1.5 million tonnes of copper concentrate a year. In July 2011, it announced that after a four-year $381 million exploration program, it was able to increase the ore resource surrounding the Escondida mining complex by 129 percent to 19.5 billion tonnes. That amount of ore potentially could yield more than 100 million tonnes of copper worth about $1 trillion.[1]

Along with Codelco and BHP Billiton, the other big copper miners and investors include Rio Tinto (which owns Kennecott in the United States, a stake in the Grasberg mine in Indonesia, the mothballed Panguna mine on PNG's restive Bougainville island, and a Mongolia resource); Anglo American (with 44 percent of the Collahuasi mine in Chile and 75.5 percent of the expanded Los Bronces resource, also in Chile); Xstrata (which has 44 percent of Collahuasi, plus projects in Peru); Freeport-McMoRan in Peru, DR Congo, Indonesia and the United States; the Russia-focused Norilsk Nickel; the Luksic family's Antofagasta Minerals in Chile with four mines—Los Pelambres, Esperanza, El Tesoro, and Michilla—that produced more than 520,000 tonnes in 2010; Nippon Mining and the Japanese trading houses Mitsubishi, Sumitomo, and Mitsui (see Exhibit 9.2). As global demand for copper increases, UK-registered miner Kazakhmys (currently mining 300,000 tonnes a year), Swiss-based commodities trader Glencore (which owns the Katanga and Mutanda projects in DR Congo and Mopani in Zambia), and the Canadian miner First Quantum (which has copper mines in Zambia, Mauritania, and Peru) all have the potential to be significant suppliers.

Mongolia's Oyu Tolgoi Promise

There is another 100-year mine possibility outside of Chile and Australia, though its developer, Rio Tinto CEO Tom Albanese,

1. Codelco	6. Xstrata
2. BHP Billiton	7. Glencore
3. Rio Tinto	8. Antofagasta
4. Freeport McMoRan	9. Norilsk Nickel
5. Anglo American	10. Nippon Mining

Exhibit 9.2   Top 10 copper mining companies

Source: Company reports

is conservative enough simply to call Mongolia's Oyu Tolgoi resource "one of the most promising copper-gold deposits in the world."[2] Rio Tinto's effective stake in the $6 billion project is through its 51 percent holding in Ivanhoe Mines, which in turn holds 66 percent of Oyu Tolgoi. The Mongolian government holds the remaining 34 percent. Under an agreement with Ivanhoe's CEO Robert Friedland, Rio Tinto is the project developer and operator, with first ore production expected to be in 2013. Chinese smelters are expected to buy some of Oyu Tolgoi's output of concentrates; the mine's location about 80 km north of the Chinese border makes it a natural supply fit, though Mongolia has excluded Chinese investment in the project itself. Albanese is a great believer in copper's future. At Rio Tinto's AGM in London in April 2011, he said the continued demand for copper would be driven by "global electrification and growth in China and India, along with a greater focus on renewable sources of energy."[3] Plus, there's the little matter of the 2012 Olympic Games in London. Rio Tinto's Bingham Canyon mine in Utah and the Oyu Tolgoi mine in Mongolia will provide the metal to produce the 4,700 gold, silver, and bronze medals for the Olympics and the associated Paralympic Games.

The world's major importers of copper ore, concentrates, and refined copper are China, Japan, India, South Korea, and Germany. The United States, which is the world's second-largest consumer, is able to source about 60 to 65 percent of its own requirements from domestic copper mines, mainly in Arizona, Utah, New Mexico, Montana, and Nevada. Its single biggest mine is Freeport McMoRan's Morenci operation in Arizona, which produces about 390,000 tonnes of copper cathode a year. Along with Freeport McMoRan, the major copper miners in the United States are Rio Tinto's Kennecott Utah Copper, Grupo Mexico's Asarco, The Washington Companies' Montana Resources, Canadian mid-tier miner Quadra FNX Mining, and BHP Billiton's BHP Copper.

On a per capita basis, the world consumes about 2.7 kg of refined copper per person, with much higher figures in North America, Europe, Japan, South Korea, and Taiwan. In the big emerging markets, India is not yet a major user, with per capita consumption of only 0.4 kg a year, compared to 3 kg in China. This reflects the different level of industrialisation; agriculture remains a significant part of India's economy, whereas China has a very heavy industrial and manufacturing base. So while copper demand in India is forecast to grow strongly, it will not be at the same pace as China. Demand drivers will be housing and construction, copper-intensive electrical products, motor vehicles—by 2015 Indian car production is likely to reach 5 million units a year, plus 20 million motorcycles and scooters—and consumer goods.

India's Big Three Producers

India's three big names in copper are Hindalco, Sterlite, and Hindustan Copper. Hindalco Industries, part of the diversified Aditya Birla Group run by billionaire Kumar M. Birla, is India's major private enterprise integrated copper producer, sourcing copper from mines it owns in Australia, and then smelting, refining, and further processing it at its Dahej complex. While Hindalco's main business is aluminium (it bought the U.S. aluminium producer Novelis in 2007 for $6.2 billion), Birla says he is also on the lookout for more world-class copper assets in his quest for group turnover of $65 billion by 2015. He identifies Brazil and Africa as "interesting" for mining and other resource ventures.[4]

Sterlite Industries, the Indian flagship of tycoon Anil Agarwal's London-based metals group Vedanta Resources, operates a 400,000-tonne smelter at Tuticorin in the south of India and two copper rod plants in western India. It also owns Australia's oldest working mine, the Mt. Lyell copper mine in Tasmania, which it bought in 1999. Mt. Lyell provides about 7 percent of Sterlite's copper concentrate needs. Vedanta Resources, which produces mainly aluminium, zinc, lead, iron ore, and copper, operates four copper mines in the African state of Zambia: one at Konkola, two at Nchanga, and one at Nampundwe, plus a tailings leach plant at Nchanga and a smelter at Nkana. Vedanta's copper cathode production was 507,000 tonnes in 2010. It is spending about $1 billion to expand the Konkola resource through its "Deep Mine Project," which is scheduled for completion during 2012. But outside of India and Africa, Sterlite and Vedanta have some legal fence-mending to do. In October 2008, with copper prices plunging amid the onset of the global financial crisis, Sterlite pulled out of a $2.6 billion deal to buy U.S. copper miner Asarco, which had filed for bankruptcy. Asarco's parent, the Mexican miner Grupo Mexico, eventually retained Asarco in a $2.5 billion scheme. Asarco has since filed suit against Sterlite for damages.

India's biggest domestic copper producer is state-owned Hindustan Copper, which mines about 3.7 million tonnes of ore (32,000 tonnes of concentrate) a year from sites in Madhya Pradesh, Rajasthan, and Jharkhand. An expansion plan aims to lift output to 12 million tonnes by 2016–2017, but the company's applications for new mining leases within India have yet to move forward. Hindustan Copper also has looked at buying mines in Naimibia, in Chile, and in Afghanistan. India overall lacks good-quality copper reserves—unlike China, it is not in the top-20 copper producing countries—and must import the bulk of its needs. But with India's power, tele-communications, automotive, and rail transport sectors all geared for large-scale investment over the next decade, Hindustan Copper believes there is a "huge opportunity" in greenfield copper explora-tion and development.

China's Production Shortfall

China produced about 1.16 million tonnes of copper concentrate in 2010. But that is far from enough to meet its smelting and refin-ing needs, so it imported 6.47 million tonnes of concentrate and another 4.36 million tonnes of copper scrap. These imports enabled China to produce 4.57 million tonnes of refined copper. Even so, this was not enough to meet domestic apparent consumption of 7.47 million tonnes. As a result, China imported just over 2.9 million tonnes of refined copper in 2010.

There are half a dozen major state-owned Chinese producers, led by Jiangxi Copper Corp., which in 2010 mined 172,000 tonnes of copper concentrate from its six mines. In 2010 it lifted the out-put of its main Dexing copper mine in Jiangxi province to 130,000 tonnes, and also upgraded its Yongping and Chengmenshan mines to take its total combined production capacity above 200,000 tonnes. Its Guixi smelter and refinery complex is the largest in the world, with production in 2010 of 900,000 tonnes of copper cathode and 450,000 tonnes of copper products. Jiangxi Copper is also one of the largest rare metal producers in China.

Chairman Li Yihuang told the group's annual meeting in April 2011 the goal for the year was to mine 200,000 tonnes of copper concentrate and produce 940,000 tonnes of copper cathode and 489,000 tonnes of copper products such as rods and wires. Other targets were 25 tonnes of gold and 510 tonnes of silver, worth about $2 billion at prevailing market prices.

Jiangxi Copper has two overseas projects—a copper mine in northern Peru and its Aynak copper mine venture in Afghanistan. In both cases, it has partnered with China Minmetals Corporation, the country's largest international metals and mining group. Separately, Minmetals has a joint venture with Chile's state-owned Codelco to develop copper resources there.

The country's No. 2 copper producer is Tongling Non-Ferrous Metals Group, with 852,000 tonnes of copper cathode in 2010. Tongling teamed up with China Railway Construction Corp. to buy the Corriente copper project in Ecuador for about $680 million in 2010. Another large Chinese producer is Jinchuan Group Ltd., which primarily focuses on nickel but also produces about 125,000 tonnes of copper domestically. Jinchuan Group signed a memorandum of understanding with London-listed Kazakhmys in 2010 to buy a 49 percent stake in the large Aktogay copper project in Kazakhstan, but this deal was subsumed a year later by Kazakhmys agreeing to borrow $1.5 billion from China Development Bank to fund the Aktogay development. Jinchuan has stakes in three offshore nickel projects in Australia, Canada, and Zambia, and in late 2011 made a $1.36 billion bid for copper and cobalt miner Metorex, which has mines in Zambia and the Democratic Republic of Congo. Brazil's Vale was also interested in Metorex but withdrew after Jinchuan's bid. Yunnan Copper is another Chinese domestic producer, based in Kunming in Yunnan province. China's state-owned aluminium giant Chinalco paid about $1 billion to buy a 49 percent stake in Yunnan Copper in 2007 and later increased this to 58 percent. Yunnan Copper controls Australian-listed Chinalco Yunnan Copper resources, which has projects in Australia, Chile, and Laos. Separately, Chinalco has won approval for its Minera Chinalco venture in Peru, where it plans to spend $2 billion developing the Toromocho resource from 2013. State-owned China Non-Ferrous Metals Mining Corp. (CNMC) runs the largest copper mine in northeast China, the Fushun Hongtoushan mine, in Liaoning province. Daye Non-ferrous Metals Co., based in Hubei province, produces about 100,000 tonnes of copper cathode and 150,000 tonnes of copper cathode a year.

China's total copper smelting capacity is 3.47 million tonnes, while refining capacity is 5.88 million tonnes. But it has no single world-class deposit at home on the scale or quality of the Escondida, Chuquicamata, or Collahuasi mines in Chile, or Grasberg mine in

Indonesia. The annual output at the Dexing mine, for example, is only one-tenth that of Escondida. In a bid to offset that, Chinese companies have looked for opportunities in South America (Jiangxi Copper and Chinalco in Peru) and in Africa, particularly copper-rich Zambia and DR Congo. China Non-Ferrous Metals acquired Chambishi Copper Mines in Zambia in 1998, and expanded the site significantly in 2007 with the opening of the $100 million Chambishi West ore body project. A further $250 million expansion is underway that will double output to 300,000 tonnes of copper concentrate by the end of 2012. Chambishi also has a 150,000-tonne a year smelter.

But not all Chinese bidders are successful. Hong Kong-listed Minmetals Resources dropped its $6.3 billion bid for copper miner Equinox Minerals in April 2011 after Toronto-based Barrick Gold, the world's largest gold producer, trumped it with an offer of $7.5 billion. The win gave Barrick control of the Lumwana mine in Zambia—one of the richest in Africa, with annual output of 145,000 tonnes of concentrate—and a large copper deposit at Jabal Sayid in Saudi Arabia. Minmetals, which is part of state-owned China Minmetals Group, said it would be "value destructive" to try to compete with Barrick.[5]

Whatever Barrick is able to achieve with the Lumwana mine, it is clear that Zambia—the world's bigger copper producer in the 1970s, before the oil shock, a copper price slump, and massive debt ravaged its economy—is back on a growth trajectory and is what Barrick calls a "mining friendly jurisdiction." By 2015, the country's copper output could more than double from about 680,000 tonnes in 2010 to 1.44 million tonnes by 2015, according to the London-based metals consultancy Brook Hunt. Copper projects in the pipeline include Vale's Konkola North joint venture with African Rainbow Minerals, Vedanta's Konkola Copper expansion project, Glencore's Mopani investment, and First Quantum's Trident and Kansanshi mines.

"Deal of the Century"

Minmetals's failure to win Equinox means that the most significant Chinese investment in the African copper sector is by China Railway Engineering Corp. and SinoHydro in the Democratic Republic of Congo. There, they struck the controversial "deal of the century" in 2007 with the DR Congo state-owned mining entity Gecamines. The two Chinese companies and Gecamines set up the Sicomines joint venture, under which China would invest $6 billion (reduced from an original $9 billion after International Monetary Fund pressure) in a "minerals for infrastructure" plan; the Chinese side would fund and build roads, railways, hospitals, schools, and universities, in return for 68 percent of the copper and cobalt Sicomines would extract from five rich deposits in the "copper belt" in Katanga province. The first ore is likely to be mined in 2014. Back in 2008, the Swiss bank Credit Suisse noted in an outlook that while copper production could be delayed because of poor infrastructure, it believed the Katanga region alone "could host an industry of 1.5 million tonnes of copper by 2021." The latest projections are that DR Congo overall could produce as much as 1.9 million tonnes of copper concentrate by 2015, up from 300,000 tonnes in 2009. In May 2011 the DR Congo began a $600 million project to rebuild 700 km of rail track in Kasai and Katanga provinces. The five-year project is part-funded by the World Bank, with $200 million to come from the government's China infrastructure deal. One of the tracks to be restored would link Katanga to the Atlantic coast port of Lobito in Angola via the Benguela line, much of which was rendered unusable during the conflict in Angola over the past 30 years. As part of its aid to Angola, China began rebuilding the Benguela line in 2006.

One of the largest corporate investments in DR Congo's copper sector is by Freeport McMoRan Copper & Gold and its partner Lundin Mining, which jointly spent $2 billion to develop the Tenke Fungurume project 180 km northwest of Lumumbashi in Katanga. The first copper cathode was produced in March 2009, and Freeport expects annual output over the mine's 40-year life to average about 115,000 tonnes of copper cathode and about 8,200 tonnes of cobalt (DR Congo has about a third of the world's cobalt, which is used in batteries, alloys, pigments, and medical technology). Freeport now trucks most of its output to Durban, South Africa, 3,500 km away, but a switch to Africa's east–west rail link—once it becomes available—would shorten that considerably. Tenke, potentially one of the world's biggest copper and cobalt mines with ore reserves of 137 million tonnes, is held 56 percent by Freeport, 24 percent by Toronto-based Lundin Mining, and 20 percent by Gecamines[6] (see Exhibit 9.3).

1. Escondida, Chile	**6.** Oyu Tolgoi, Kazakhstan
2. Olympic Dam, Australia	**7.** Las Bambas, Peru
3. Grasberg, Indonesia	**8.** Lumwana, Zambia
4. Tenke Fungurume, DR Congo	**9.** Conga, Peru
5. Los Bronces, Chile	**10.** Katanga, DR Congo

Exhibit 9.3   Ten mines of the future
Source: Industry, company reports

Global commodities trader Glencore has a long-standing interest in DR Congo's copper resources. It has two key assets there—a 40 percent interest in Mutanda Mining, a rich new project that could be producing 110,000 tonnes of refined copper and 23,000 tonnes of cobalt in 2012, and a 74.75 percent interest in Toronto-listed Katanga Mining, which runs Kamoto Copper and DRC Copper & Cobalt, which between them produce 130,000 tonnes of copper and 8,000 tonnes of cobalt, with expansion capacity to 310,000 tonnes of copper and 30,000 tonnes of cobalt by 2015. In neighbouring Zambia, Glencore plans to spend $500 million on expanding its 73 percent-owned Mopani copper and cobalt mine, an integrated operation producing 250,000 tonnes of copper metal. Glencore's ambitions in copper extend far beyond Africa, with other copper assets in Kazakhstan, the Philippines, Australia, and Argentina. But in December 2011, it dropped plans to buy a 70 percent stake in the Mina Justa copper project, 400 km southeast of Lima in Peru, from Hong Kong-listed CST Mining Group (formerly China Sci-Tech Holdings).

Glencore has a 34 percent stake in Xstrata,* which in mid-2011 said it would spend about $5.7 billion on its Antapaccay and Las Bambas mines in Peru over the next few years to lift its output of copper concentrate by 2014 to world-leading levels. Xstrata might also invest up to $6 billion in Argentina, where its proposed Agua Rica and El Pachon projects have the potential to add another 600,000 tonnes of copper concentrate a year by 2016. But Argentina rates poorly on the International Finance Corporation/World Bank's ease of doing business index, ranking 115th out of 183 nations. That compares to a ranking of 36 for Peru, 39 for Colombia, and 43 for Chile. A weak financial and regulatory system and a perception of

---

*Glencore and Xstrata plan to merge in the third quarter of 2012.

corruption weigh on Argentina's business reputation. For example, it ranked 168th in the subcategory of "dealing with construction permits." Still, overall it ranks ahead of India at 134 and the copper-rich Democratic Republic of Congo at 175. Zambia, the other big African investment destination for copper miners, ranks 76th. China itself was 79th.[7] Xstrata is working on another large, long-term copper play in a difficult environment—the 450,000-tonne a year Tampakan project in the southern Philippines, where environmental groups and the communist-led guerillas of the New People's Army oppose it.

Alternatives to Copper

Amidst all the hype of billion-dollar expansion projects in Africa, South America, Australia, and Mongolia, is there any likelihood of a collapse in copper demand and, consequently, prices? Virtually every outlook—except that of veteran copper analyst and China expert Simon Hunt (see below)—is bullish based on continued Chinese and Indian demand, with supply shortages expected in 2012. But there is the real prospect of alternatives to copper emerging to fill the gap. Some manufacturers are looking to design copper out of their products, because of supply and price concerns. According to the U.S. Geological Service, there are various substitutes for the red metal. Aluminium could replace it, for example, in power cables, electrical equipment, car and truck radiators, and in cooling and refrigeration tubes. Titanium and steel are alternatives in heat exchangers, while optical fiber already has replaced copper in some telecommunications uses. Plastics are a substitute for copper in water pipes and some plumbing fixtures. Another issue for big miners is that copper ore grades and production levels are both declining. London-based research company CRU estimates that grades worldwide have fallen from 0.9 percent Cu (copper) in 2002 to 0.76 percent Cu in 2009.

Simon Hunt, who co-founded metals consultancy Brook Hunt in 1975 and left in 2005 to set up Simon Hunt Strategic Services, has long believed that China has massive amounts of copper stockpiled in warehouses as a financial investment rather than for industrial consumption, and that when the time is right (or wrong, depending on your point of view), this material will flood back into circulation. At the start of 2011 he wrote: "A return to global recession, deflation, and the destruction of large end uses of copper will see prices crashing to levels long since forgotten—to under $1,500 by 2016. It will be at that point that the real restructuring of the industry will take place."[8] Hunt argued that the future trend growth rates for world refined copper consumption would fall below 2 percent a year, with the implication that marginal producers would have to close down. "It is not a shortage of supply that will shape the future of copper but a shortage of required material for furnaces," he wrote. "Today's focus on short-term copper prices has sown the seeds for its own destruction. History does not always repeat itself but it frequently rhymes. As in the mid-1980s, material warehoused outside the reporting system will be thrown onto markets as investors/speculators will demand cash against their investments."[9]

Copper has known its share of upheaval since the great African wave of independence in the 1960s, the South American industry nationalizations of the 1970s, the price collapse of the 1980s, the Sumitomo trading scandal of the 1990s, and the great globalisation advances of the 2000s. As to whether the market will crash and burn in the 2010s, the industrialisation and urbanisation of China, India, Brazil, and other emerging economies such as Mexico, Turkey, Indonesia, and South Africa should be strong enough to keep demand high. More cars, more houses, more electricity generation, and more consumer electronics should all mean more copper. The swing toward renewable energy sources will also help; as the European Copper Institute notes, "When it comes to solar-heated water systems, copper's resistance, workability and conductivity remain unrivalled."[10] Even so, the big global miners are certain to face challenges from new suppliers and copper substitutes.

Notes

1. BHP Billiton annual exploration and development report, (20 July 2011), www.bhpbilliton.com/home/investors/reports/Documents/110720_BHP%20Billiton%20Exploration%20and%20Development%20Report%20for%20the%20Year%20Ended%2030%20June%202011.pdf.
2. Address to Rio Tinto annual general meeting London, (14 April 2011), www.riotinto.com/documents/Investors/Rio_Tinto_plc_AGM2011_Tom_Albanese.pdf.
3. Ibid.

4. Hindalco profile, "Capacity doubled at Birla Copper." www.hindalco .net/media/features/birla_copper.htm.

5. Media release, "Minmetals Resources Limited Withdraws Intention to Offer to Acquire Equinox Minerals Limited and Resumption of Trading" (26 April 2011), www.mmg.com/en/Investors-and-Media/ News.aspx?pn=11.

6. Freeport McMoRan, half-year results, (21 July 2011), www.fcx.com/ news/2011/072111.pdf.

7. International Finance Corporation/World Bank, "Doing Business Index" (June 2010), www.doingbusiness.org.

8. Simon Hunt, "The Likely Pattern for Copper Prices in 2011 and Beyond" (7 January 2011), www.mineweb.com.

9. Ibid.

10. European Copper Institute, "Renewable Energy," www.eurocopper .org/copper/copper-renewable-energy.html.

10

Finding Steel's Essential Ingredients

Simandou Blocks 1 and 2 and Zogota are one of the world's best undeveloped sources of high-grade iron ore with potential to support the development of a large-scale long-lived project.
—Brazilian miner Vale on its Simandou joint venture in Guinea ("Vale acquires Simandou iron ore assets," Rio de Janeiro, 30 April 2010)

When completed, Simandou will be the largest private integrated iron ore mine and infrastructure project ever developed in Africa. At capacity the project will produce 95 million tonnes of ore per year.
—Anglo-Australian miner Rio Tinto on its part of the Simandou prospects (Statement by Rio Tinto, 23 December 2010)

Israeli diamond trader and arts patron Beny Steinmetz sits comfortably on the Forbes billionaires list, with a net worth of around $6 billion. Steinmetz controls the Geneva-based BSG Group, one of the largest customers of the De Beers diamond marketing organization and an enterprise whose other arms have interests in mining, engineering, investment, and real estate. Steinmetz, who joined his father's diamond business in Tel Aviv in 1978, has shown himself to be a man with an uncanny knack for finding the right deal in such difficult business environments as the African states of Guinea,

Sierra Leone, and the Democratic Republic of Congo. He is the pivotal figure in what is the biggest iron ore experiment of the early twenty-first century—the development of the massive Simandou prospect in the mountainous southeastern hinterland of Guinea. His partner in one half of Simandou is Brazil's Vale—the world's biggest iron ore producer—which is keen to burnish its African mining credentials. Vale's competitor in the race to bring the first Simandou ore to market is one of the other gorillas of the global iron ore trade, Anglo-Australian miner Rio Tinto, which has Chinese state-owned metals giant Chinalco [Aluminium Corp of China] as its partner in Blocks 3 and 4, in the other half of the prospect that stretches over the 110 km-long [68-mile] Simandou mountain range. Before we get into the complexities of how Rio Tinto lost half—and almost lost all—of the Simandou mining concession it thought it held, and how Steinmetz fits into this puzzle, it's worth looking at some of the background to steel and the iron ore trade.

In the twentieth century, first the United States, then Japan, and later South Korea led the way in steel production. Now it is all China, with India waiting in the wings. In the first decade of the twenty-first century, the world produced more crude steel—11.5 billion tonnes—than it made in the first 70 years of the twentieth century. Of that 11.5 billion tonnes, China produced a third of it—3.8 billion tonnes—and its growth rate is accelerating to the point where in 2011 it is responsible for almost 45 percent of total world output. Nobody else comes close—China's output is almost six times that of Japan, the No. 2 producer, and almost eight times that of third-place United States, which dominated steel production for the first 60 years of last century. China's output is nine times greater than its other great Asian competitor for resources, fourth-placed India, and 10 times that of South Korea (see Exhibit 10.1).

Although India has no chance of catching up to China, it will likely become the world's second-largest producer within five years, with the country's steel ministry eyeing output of 145 million tonnes a year by 2016. But it will need a herculean effort to reach that ambitious target; global steelmakers such as POSCO and ArcelorMittal that are looking to build new plants in India have found it heavy going when they confront the country's many regulatory, environmental, and social challenges. Still, in an optimistic report on the global steel outlook in mid-2011, Ernst & Young offered the view that India's domestic steel demand would grow by 10 to 12 percent a year over the next two years. "As steelmakers invest in the latest

1. China 626.7 [573.6]	**7.** Germany 43.8 [32.7]
2. Japan 109.6 [87.5]	**8.** Ukraine 33.6 [29.9]
3. United States 80.5 [58.2]	**9.** Brazil 32.8 [26.5]
4. India 68.3 [63.5]	**10.** Turkey 29.0 [25.3]
5. Russia 66.9 [60.0]	World total 1413.5
6. South Korea 58.5 [48.6]	

Exhibit 10.1   Top 10 steel producing nations 2010 [million tonnes, 2009 figures in brackets]

Source: World Steel Association

generation of steel-making equipment, the profitability of Indian steel could possibly lead the world," it said.[1]

Meanwhile, in late 2011 China is making crude steel at a rate of about 700 million tonnes a year—and possibly more, because of underreporting. The raw materials required for this are staggering: An integrated steelmaking operation using basic oxygen furnaces would consume just under 1.2 billion tonnes of iron ore, 450 million tonnes of coking coal, 105 million tonnes of limestone, and 96 million tonnes of recycled steel to produce 700 million tonnes of crude steel, according to the Brussels-based World Steel Association. The other steelmaking route, via electric arc furnaces, has a different mix but a still-substantial appetite. These furnaces would need 735 million tonnes of recycled steel, about 45 million tonnes of coking coal, and 30 million tonnes of limestone.[2]

Most of the world's iron ore comes from Brazil, Australia, China, India, North America, and Russia, with Brazil and Australia dominating the export trade and China and India using their ore for their domestic steel industries. Until 2010, India was a major supplier to China, but has cut back sharply since then. Africa and Canada are potentially big new supply sources. In coking coal, China, India, the United States, Australia, and Indonesia are the top five producers. Australia again clearly leads the export trade, ahead of the United States, Canada, and Russia. Various African nations are viewed as emerging suppliers, along with Indonesia, Colombia, Mongolia, and Kazakhstan.

China Looking to Diversify

The China Iron and Steel Association (CISA) has long wanted to escape what it regards as the aggressive pricing of the big three iron ore suppliers, Vale of Brazil, and the two Anglo-Australian miners

Rio Tinto and BHP Billiton. Its goal is threefold—it wants to diversify supply sources to include second-tier countries such as Russia and Canada, it wants to back new mining ventures in emerging locations such as West Africa (which means occasionally partnering with Vale, Rio, or BHP), plus it wants to create home-grown iron ore champions who can compete globally. By the end of 2015, the association wants China to have two or three "super large" producers in the 200–300 million tonnes a year range and half a dozen other groups able to mine 30 million tonnes each. China may be the world's single biggest iron ore producer with 2010 output above 1 billion tonne, but the problem with CISA's scenario is that iron ore from Brazil and Australia has a purity (or iron content) that domestic producers cannot match. Where Vale, Rio, and BHP can supply millions of tonnes of ore with an iron content of around 62 percent or higher—meaning it can be fed directly into blast furnaces—Chinese ore averages only 25 percent, which means it has to be *beneficiated,* or upgraded, before it can be used. It is what mining analysts call the "ore of last resort"—low quality and high price, with proximity its only advantage. China has thousands of iron ore mines, but they are often inefficient and "captive" producers that supply the smaller provincial plants among the country's 700 steel mills. Still, the China Metallurgical Mines Association hopes that more than 20 large new mines in the 5- to 10-million tonne a year range will come on stream by 2015, enabling domestic output to reach 1.5 billion tonnes and supplying 40 percent of China's iron ore needs.[3]

> The demand for base metals, essentially iron ore, tends to stabilize at the per capita income level of $15,000 per year, which in China could happen in the year 2020.
> —*Dr Mauricio Cardenas, head of the Latin America initiative at the Brookings Institution, in "Is China the New North" discussion on trade between Latin America and China, 17 August 2011*

No single producer dominates China's iron ore mining scene. The three biggest producers are AnBen Group, with 2010 output of 45 million tonnes, Shougang Beijing Group with 26.5 million tonnes and Wuhan Iron & Steel Group with 19 million tonnes. AnBen, formed in 2005 through the merger of Anshan Iron & Steel and Benxi Iron & Steel, holds about a quarter of China's known iron ore reserves, including the large Nanfen mine. Its goal is to lift output to 68 million tonnes by 2015 and 92 million tonnes by 2020. AnBen aims to have a role in developing China's single largest iron ore deposit, at Dataigou near the steel city of Benxi in Liaoning province. Work on the 3 billion-tonne resource began in 2009 through a joint venture led by Shenzhen-based Glory Harvest Group, founded by construction and property entrepreneur Li Weibo.

China's "Big Five" Steel Producers

On the steel production front, China's "big five" are all state-owned entities that have been brought together by government direction, to lift the efficiency and scale of the domestic industry. The biggest is Hebei Iron & Steel (Hegang) with 2010 steel output of 53 million tonnes, followed by Baoshan Iron & Steel (Baosteel), Wuhan Iron & Steel (Wugang), Shandong Iron & Steel Group (SISG), and Anshan Iron & Steel (Ansteel). Each of them has sought resource security through ventures in Australia, Africa, and South America covering both iron ore and coking coal.

Hebei Iron & Steel, for example, in early 2011 agreed to buy iron ore supplies from the 223 million-tonne Cerro Negro Norte project in Chile being developed by Compañía Minera del Pacífico (CMP). CMP is a subsidiary of the Chilean iron and steel producer CAP S.A.

Second-ranked Baosteel, with annual output of 26.5 million tonnes, has always bought from the big three iron ore suppliers, but by 2007 it had found a potential fourth supplier. It came in the shape of Australian mining maverick Andrew "Twiggy" Forrest, who created Fortescue Metals Group (FMG), specifically as a "new force" that would challenge the iron ore majors. Forrest had the ore in the rich Pilbara region of Western Australia, and by sheer persistence, skilful lobbying and the implicit financial credibility that came with big potential customers such as Baosteel, was able to secure and build the rail and port links he needed to bring his Cloud Break and Christmas Creek mines onstream. In 2010, Baosteel signed a 10-year agreement under which FMG would supply it with 20 million tonnes a year of its high quality ore. The first shipment of 170,000 tonnes left Western Australia's Port Hedland in May 2011. From the outset, Forrest had tried hard to secure Baosteel as an equity investor, but when that failed he looked elsewhere. In 2009, he struck a deal for a smaller Chinese steelmaker, Hunan Valin Iron & Steel, to take a 17.4 percent stake in the project for $1.2 billion. United States fund Leucadia National and Russian steelmaker Magnitogorsk also were early investors in FMG, with 10 percent and just over 5 percent, respectively.

Another Baosteel linkage is the $6 billion Aquila Resources West Pilbara iron ore project, a 50–50 joint venture between Aquila and U.S. private group American Metals & Coal International (AMCI). In 2009, Baosteel paid about $265 million for a 15 percent stake in Aquila, which also has coking-coal projects in Queensland and an iron ore project in South Africa.

Third-ranked Wuhan Iron & Steel is one of four Chinese steelmakers in the Wheelarra joint venture with BHP Billiton to develop the Jimblebar mine, a high-grade iron ore resource in the Pilbara region that will supply 12 million tonnes a year for 25 years from 2014. Wuhan's Chinese co-venturers are Tangshan Iron & Steel, Maanshan Iron & Steel, and Jiangsu Shagang. Wuhan also is seeking to expand its Canada ties, linking up with Century Iron Ore to explore in Quebec, and working with Adriana Resources to develop another Quebec project at Lac Otelnuk. Wuhan already sources ore from "captive" projects in Canada and Brazil, involving Consolidated Thompson Iron Ore Mines and Eike Batista's EBX Group-controlled MMX. Wuhan has a 16 percent stake in MMX, which Batista set up in 2005 to mine iron ore at Corumba in Mato Grosso do Sul state near the border with Bolivia and Paraguay, and at Serra Azul in Minas Gerais state in the southeast of Brazil.

Shandong Iron & Steel is investing $1.5 billion for a 25 percent stake in UK-listed African Mineral's massive Tonkolili iron ore project and related infrastructure in Sierra Leone. It will take between 2 million and 10 million tonnes of ore a year from the project as it is ramped up from 2012 onwards. SISG joins another Chinese investor in this project, China Railway Materials Commercial Corp., which in 2010 agreed to work with African Minerals to develop Tonkolili, and invested $247 million for a 12.5 percent stake.

Ansteel has a long-term contract with mid-tier Australian miner Gindalbie Metals covering their $2.5 billion Karara joint venture in the Mid-West iron ore region of Western Australia. Beginning in late 2012, Ansteel will take ore worth up to $65 billion from Karara over the life of the mine.

China's largest private-sector steel company, Jiangsu Shagang Group, is about the same size as Ansteel, with output of about 26 million tonnes of steel a year. Its chairman and 30 percent shareholder is billionaire Shen Wenrong, an engineer, economist, "national model worker" and representative of the Chinese Communist Party Congress who set up the company in Jiangsu province in 1975. To help secure future resources, in 2009 Shagang bought a 45 percent stake in Grange Resources, an Australian miner whose Southdown project in Western Australia aims to produce 6.6 million tonnes a year of magnetite concentrate from 2013. There are numerous other iron ore projects in Australia with a Chinese connection, including the Sino Iron Project at Cape Preston, run by Citic Pacific Mining; Sinosteel Midwest Corporation's Koolanooka export mine; and China Metallurgical Group's Cape Lambert project near Karratha.

Forty years ago, there were no Chinese names to be seen in a list of the world's biggest steel producers. In 1972, Nippon Steel led the way with 33 million tonnes, while South Korea's Pohang Iron & Steel Co. (POSCO) was in its first year of production and would not make the top 10 for another decade. Instead, the other nine places were filled by two U.S. makers (U.S. Steel and Bethlehem), British Steel, Japanese makers Nippon Kokan, Kawasaki and Sumitomo, and European makers Thyssen, Estel, Arbed Group, and Finsider. Hindustan Steel, the forerunner of Steel Authority of India, ranked twenty-fourth and China nowhere. Even 20 years ago, the world's leading steel producer was still Nippon Steel with 25.4 million tonnes, ahead of POSCO with 20 million tonnes. Producers from France, Britain, the United States, Russia, Japan (three groups), and Germany rounded out the top 10. No producer from China or India made it—the closest was Steel Authority of India, placed twelfth with 1992 production of 9.9 million tonnes (mt). China's first entrant was Anshan, sixteenth with 8.4 mt, followed by Shanghai Baoshan 23rd with 6.5 mt, and Shougang 25th with 5.7 mt.

In 2011–2012, while Lakshmi Mittal's Luxembourg-based Arcelor-Mittal is a clear No. 1, it is followed by three Chinese makers (Hebei, Baosteel, Wuhan), ahead of POSCO, Nippon Steel, JFE, two more Chinese producers in Shandong and Shagang, and the lone Indian representative, Tata Steel (see Exhibit 10.2).

All of these companies buy iron ore from Australia—in fact the Japanese trading houses and the steel mills they represented were

1. ArcelorMittal 98.2 [77.5]	**6.** Nippon Steel 35.0 [26.5]*
2. Hebei Iron & Steel 53.0 [40.3]	**7.** JFE 31.1 [25.8]
3. Baosteel 37.0 [31.3]	**8.** Shandong Iron & Steel 23.2 [26.4]
4. Wuhan Iron & Steel 36.5 [30.3]	**9.** Jiangsu Shagang 23.2 [26.4]
5. POSCO 35.4 [31.1]	**10.** Tata Steel 23.2 [22.0]

Exhibit 10.2   Top 10 steel producers in 2010 [million tonnes, 2009 figures in brackets]

*Nippon Steel and Sumitomo Metal have agreed to a merger by late 2012, which would result in a higher ranking for the joint entity.

Source: World Steel Association, companies

the first big overseas investors in the iron ore trade in the 1960s. Mitsui, Nippon Steel, and Sumitomo Metal were all part of the 1965 joint venture that began the Robe River project in the Pilbara region of Western Australia. It would take another 20-plus years for the first Chinese investment in the Pilbara, when China Metallurgical Import and Export Corp. (the forerunner of state-owned mining company Sinosteel) in 1987 took 40 percent of a joint venture with Rio Tinto covering its Channar mine. About 97 percent of Australia's ore comes from the Pilbara, which is home to as much as 27 billion tonnes of EDR (economic demonstrated resources) iron ore. Along with the Carajas region of Brazil, it is regarded as one of the richest fields in the world. BHP Billiton and Rio Tinto both plan massive expansions of their Pilbara mining operations, with BHP aiming to lift output to 220 million tonnes a year and Rio aiming for 333 million tonnes by 2015. FMG's goal is 155 million tonnes. Those three expansions, along with Gina Rinehart's Hancock Prospecting (which has POSCO as an investor in its Roy Hill iron ore project) and a raft of smaller projects, will dramatically increase the Pilbara's depletion rate, which, according to the Australian Bureau of Agricultural & Resource Economics, was running at about 320 million tonnes a year in 2010. By 2020, mining in the Pilbara could reach 1 billion tonne a year, meaning that without further resource discoveries, the ore could be gone within 30 years.

African Projects on the Move

That is why the separate Vale and Rio Tinto investments covering the Simandou blocks in Guinea, along with other iron ore ventures in Africa and Canada, are so important. New projects such as ArcelorMittal's Yekepa mines in Liberia and its Baffinland resource in Canada, BHP Billiton's concession on the Guinea-Liberia border, the stake held by Indian miner Sesa Goa (part of the Vedanta Resources group) in the controversial Western Cluster in Liberia, African Minerals' Tonkolili site in Sierra Leone, Sundance Resources' Mbalam development in Cameroon and Congo, and Cape Lambert's Marampa in Sierra Leone will give Chinese buyers an alternative to the Pilbara and Brazil.

Of all the many African projects, none is so rich in potential (and intrigue) as the Simandou blocks, where at least 2.4 billion tonnes of high-grade iron ore lie beneath the Simandou mountain range. The main actors include the world's two top iron ore producers in Vale and Rio Tinto, the listed Chinese metals group Chalco (Aluminium Corp. of China) and its parent company Chinalco (which happens to be the single largest shareholder in Rio Tinto), a trio of Guinean presidents past and present, a U.S.-trained investment banker turned mining minister, and the billionaire Israeli diamond dealer, Beny Steinmetz. A bit player is the International Finance Corporation, the project-financing arm of the World Bank, which has a 5 percent stake in Rio Tinto's Simandou joint venture. Adding to the general air of derring-do, *The Times* of London reported in 2011 that U.S. diplomatic cables obtained by Wikileaks apparently show a rival of Rio Tinto paid a $7 million bribe to officials in Guinea to sideline the company's front-runner position. Guinea, which declared its independence from France in 1958, clearly is no place for the faint-hearted in business, despite its wealth of mineral resources such as bauxite and iron ore. Drugs, violence, and military strongmen have tainted its investment milieu for years and kept most of its people poor. Transparency International ranks Guinea 164th out of 178 nations in its corruption perceptions index while the UN Human Development Index scores it at 156 out of 169 countries surveyed.

According to Rio Tinto, the company made its first reconnaissance of the Simandou area in 1996 at the invitation of Guinea's then mining minister. Rio subsequently applied for exploration licences covering the Simandou range, and these were granted in 1997. A mining convention for Simandou was drawn up in 2002 and signed into law by Guinea's then president, military strongman Lansana Conte, in February 2003. In March 2006, Rio's local subsidiary, Simfer SA, was granted the mining concession stipulated in the convention. The plan was for Rio to develop the mine—which faced substantial logistical and engineering challenges—at its own cost, with the government having an option to buy a 20 percent stake.

But 2006 was also the year things started to go awry for Rio. Beny Steinmetz's BSG Group was already on the ground in Guinea, having signed a memorandum of understanding with the government in February covering iron ore and bauxite exploration programs. Essentially, the government in Conakry was hedging its bets, concerned that there might be little to show in the way of tangible mining development after almost a decade of Rio's involvement. There was talk of "use it or lose it" and of the requirement for Rio to hand back half of its concession area after 10 years. Meanwhile Steinmetz's mining arm BSG Resources was drilling in various places, leading to its discovery in early 2008 of what would become known as the Zogota iron ore deposit in Simandou South.

In June 2008, Rio Tinto said it had received a letter from Conte's office querying the validity of the decree issuing Rio Tinto's Simandou mining concession, but not the validity of the legally approved convention under which the concession was held. "Rio Tinto is confident that its Convention and Concession are in all respects in conformity with Guinean laws in their current form," it said in a statement.[4] The company said it was talking to government representatives to resolve "what it considers to be issues based on the misinterpretation of the Simandou Mining Convention."

But Simandou was a battle Rio was destined to lose. Conte died in office in December 2008, which led to an immediate military coup. The new military junta headed by Captain Moussa Dadis Camara was not inclined to give Rio more time. In the first half of 2009, the government in Conakry told Rio it needed to hand back 50 percent of the concession—specifically, Blocks 1 and 2. Guinea's mining minister Mahmoud Thiam said these blocks would be awarded to BSG Resources. Rio initially left its drilling equipment on site while it protested the move, maintaining that it still held a "valid legal claim to the northern concession" and that it needed all of Simandou to make the development viable. But when it was clear it had few friends in the Dadis Camara administration, Rio buckled. In July that year it said it would comply with Thiam's directive and remove its drilling rig. Thiam, an investment banker who served as mining minister from January 2009 to January 2011, noted that Rio's half was still a world-class asset. After the brutal crushing of an opposition rally in Conakry in September 2009, Dadis Camara was shot and wounded by one of his aides in December that year, and subsequently left the country for medical treatment. An interim government led by vice president Sekouba Konate took over to manage the transition to a civilian administration, and elections were held in November 2010, which saw Alpha Conde emerge as president.

Two Deals Change the Picture

In the meantime, two significant deals were done: in April 2010 Vale bought into Steinmetz's Guinea operation, agreeing to pay $500 million immediately and another $2 billion later, for a 51 percent stake in BSG Resources (Guinea); and in August 2010, Rio Tinto signed an agreement with Chinalco's listed subsidiary Chalco to set up a joint venture to develop and operate what was left of the Simandou project. Chalco would pay $1.35 billion over two or three years to get into the game.

Vale said its joint venture with BSG Resources (BSGR) would develop the Zogota (Simandou South) deposit, and would do a feasibility study on Simandou Blocks 1 and 2. The aim was to start at 10 million tonnes a year before reaching 50 million tonnes, with the potential to reach 75 to 90 million tonnes eventually. As part of the deal, the Vale-BSGR venture would rebuild the trans-Guinea railway from Conakry to Kankan for passenger use, and would have the exclusive right to export iron ore through Liberia (a much shorter route to the coast than through Guinea).

For its part of Simandou, Blocks 3 and 4, Rio said mining was expected to start within five years. A 650 km (400 mile) trans-Guinean industrial railroad would be built to transport up to 95 million tonnes a year of high-grade sinter fines to a new deepwater port to be built near Conakry. Rio made the most of the situation, declaring that "when the mine goes into full production, Simandou will be the largest integrated iron ore mine and infrastructure project ever developed in Africa."

It sounded positive, but it would be another eight months before Rio could reach a deal with the government that would allow the project to proceed. In April 2011, with President Alpha Conde at the helm in Conakry, Rio announced that to resolve what it called "all outstanding issues" and to finalise the new investment terms, its subsidiary Simfer SA would pay $700 million to the Guinea government in return for presidential decrees granting the mining concession over Simandou Blocks 3 and 4 and approving the Chalco-Rio joint venture. The first iron ore would be shipped by mid-2015, with "every effort" being made to reach that milestone earlier. Rio Tinto Iron Ore chief executive Sam Walsh hailed the agreement as giving Rio "the certainty we need to allow us to invest and move forward quickly." Rio, which has already spent $1.5 billion on Simandou, estimates another $10 billion will have to be spent to bring the mine and associated infrastructure on stream.[5]

Along with the $700 million up front, Guinea gets another sweetener—a free 15 percent stake in the project and the right to buy another 20 percent stake in three tranches over the next 20 years. The new rail line and four-berth wharf will be built and funded by the JV partners, with ownership reverting to the government in 25 to 30 years time. Chalco will acquire a 47 percent interest in the Simandou JV by providing $1.35 billion on an "earn-in basis" to fund development work over two or three years. Once that is done, the effective interests of Rio Tinto and Chalco in Simfer will be 50.35 percent and 44.65 percent, respectively. The remaining 5.0 percent will be held by the World Bank's project finance arm, the International Finance Corporation.

Is everybody a winner here? Guinea gets two large-scale mining operations run by the world's two biggest iron ore companies, new rail and port infrastructure, a $700 million immediate payday plus the taxes and royalties that will be payable later in the life of the projects, and a free 15 percent stake in Rio's joint venture. Vale gets its first investment in West Africa's iron ore province, one that it says will have low capital expenditure, low operating costs, and a high-quality product. It gives it more diversification away from its home base of Brazil, even though deposits such as its mighty Carajas mines in Para state have many more years to run. Chalco gets the African toehold it dearly wants, Rio gets some certainty for its truncated Simandou blocks, and Beny Steinmetz gets a healthy payment from Vale. But in February 2012, the Simandou saga took another twist, with Guinea's mines minister saying a commission might review BSG Resources' mining licence.

ArcelorMittal's Liberia and Canada projects

Liberia is the other West African state to catch the interest of global miners—specifically BHP Billiton, Vedanta Resources and steel-making giant ArcelorMittal, which also happens to be the world's fourth-ranked iron ore producer. ArcelorMittal has been working away quietly for five years at its $2 billion Yekepa greenfield site in northern Liberia, with the first ore shipped from Buchanan port in late 2011. Yekepa, which lies close to the border with Guinea, initially will provide 4 million tonnes a year of direct ore exports, with a likely second phase lifting that to 15 million tonnes a year by 2015. ArcelorMittal also has high hopes for its Mary River deposit on Canada's largest island, Baffin Island, where projected output could be 18 to 20 million tonnes a year from 2015 to 2016. The $4 billion Baffinland project, located about 1,000 km northwest of the Nunavut territory capital of Iqaluit, still needs to pass environmental hurdles and to secure an agreement with the region's indigenous Inuit people. About 11,000 people live on the island, which at more than 500,000 sq km, is the fifth largest in the world. Bringing the project on stream is a physical and logistical challenge of immense proportions. Much of the island lies above the Arctic Circle, and even at Iqaluit in the south, winter temperatures can drop below −30°C. During the winter months, Mary River is in complete darkness. A rail line of about 140 km has to be built from the mine site to a port, where ore will be loaded onto icebreaker-style bulk carriers and shipped through the Arctic waters to customers in Europe. Using the ice-reinforced carriers extends the shipping season to eight or nine months. As an interim measure, ArcelorMittal is looking at a plan that would allow it to truck about 2.5 million tonnes a year from the mine until the rail and port links are established, with a decision on the project's final configuration due in 2012. With high risk may come high rewards. Peter Kukielski, ArcelorMittal's head of mining, says the quality of the Baffinland iron ore is so good it could be the richest asset in the company's portfolio.[6] An iron content of 66 to 67 percent means it rates as direct shipping ore that needs no processing.

Indian Consumption Rising

India is the world's fourth largest iron ore producer, with output of about 213 million tonnes in 2011, and enough reserves (25 billion tonnes) to meet the needs of its domestic steel industry and to export up to 100 million tonnes a year to overseas buyers, mainly in China. But with domestic consumption rising, India's largest iron ore exporter, Sesa Goa, is looking for offshore supplies. It has invested in the Western Cluster project in Liberia, joining Israeli businessman

Jacob Engel and his Tel Aviv-based EngelInvest Group. In August 2011, Sesa Goa, which is a unit of Anil Agarwal's London-based metals group Vedanta Resources, said it would pay $90 million for a 51 percent stake in Western Cluster, a project that has the key attributes for export success: an ore base of up to 1 billion tonnes, reasonable grades (37 to 68 percent iron) and proximity to a port. It is expected that most of the ore will go to China.

India's largest iron ore producer is government-owned National Mineral Development Corporation (NMDC), which produces about 30 million tonnes a year of ore, or about 15 percent of total output, and has a resource base of 800 million tonnes. It too is on the overseas acquisition trail, though results have been mixed. It lost a chance to buy a half-share in Siberia-focused miner Kolmar Coal in mid-2011, with Russian billionaire Mikhail Prokhorov's Onexim Group opting to sell the stake instead to the privately held energy and commodities trader Gunvor Holdings, which has extensive Russian connections. Nor has NMDC seen much progress on its joint venture with ArcelorMittal to develop the Faleme iron ore mines in Senegal, Africa. But it has better prospects with its half-share in Legacy Iron Ore in Australia and a potential partnership in Mozambique. NMDC is also part of a consortium with three other state-owned entities, Steel Authority of India Ltd. (SAIL), Coal India Ltd. and Rashtriya Ispat Nigam Ltd. (RINL), in International Coal Ventures, which is looking to buy overseas coal assets.

SAIL is India's biggest steel producer, with 2011 output of about 16 million tonnes. That puts it well clear of private enterprise steelmakers JSW Steel (11 mt), Essar Steel (10 mt), and Tata Steel (6.8 mt), though Tata has much higher global output (28 mt) through its ownership of the former Corus Steel in Europe, NatSteel in Singapore, and Millennium Steel in Thailand. Tata Steel group, which has turnover of about $23 billion, is one of the world's top 10 steelmakers and is expanding capacity to 10 million tonnes a year at its original Jamshedpur plant and building a 6 million tonne greenfield site at Kalinganagar in Odisha (formerly Orissa) state.

> The company has always given great importance to its control of the iron ore and coal which it consumes. It continues to actively explore opportunities for growth in India and other parts of Asia.
> —*Tata Steel chairman Ratan Tata (Tata Steel 2010 Annual Report chairman's statement, 31 May 2011)*

According to Ratan Tata, the group's priorities include development of the Benga coal resource in Mozambique, its DSO (direct shipping ore) project in Canada and the Sedibeng iron ore mine in South Africa. Tata Steel also has offtake rights for the Carborough Downs coking-coal venture in Australia. Tata Steel made a handy profit on part of its Mozambique activities, when it sold its 26.2 percent stake in the Australia-listed Riversdale Mining to Rio Tinto for about $1.1 billion in mid-2011—or about twice what it had paid four years earlier.

Essar Steel, run by the Mumbai-based brothers Shashi and Ravi Ruia, also has ambitious expansion plans that will take domestic capacity to 14 million tonnes by 2012. It already owns the 4 million tonne former Algoma Steel business in Canada, and a smaller facility in Indonesia. In August 2011 it agreed to pay $750 million for a 60 percent stake in state-owned Zimbabwe Iron & Steel Co., which has been renamed NewZim Steel. That deal, to rehabilitate Zimbabwe's aging steel plant, also gave it 80 percent of the mining venture NewZim Minerals, which opens up the prospect of access to the estimated 45 billion tonnes of iron ore reserves held by NewZim Minerals' predecessor, Buchwa Iron Mining Co. (BIMCO). Essar saw off another Indian rival in Jindal Steel, along with ArcelorMittal and the Chinese-backed miner Sino Zimbabwe. Essar says it might export surplus iron ore, and if so, the logical shipment point would be through Mozambique.

Essar's Zimbabwe venture potentially brings it closer to the big league of iron ore producers. Although the three giants of Vale, Rio Tinto, and BHP Billiton are streets ahead of everyone else with combined capacity of 900 million tonnes, the next level down is led by Fortescue Metals with 55 million tonnes a year, China's AnBen on 45 million tonnes, and Anglo American with 41 million tonnes. Anglo American says its Kolomela project in South Africa and its Minas-Rio project in Brazil will add to that figure substantially in years to come. CEO Cynthia Carroll says Minas-Rio, which is on track to ship 26.5 million tonnes a year from late 2013, may have expansion potential of 80 to 90 million tonnes a year.[7] Two Russian metal groups, Evraz (controlled by Alexander Abramov and Alexander Frolov) and Alisher Usmanov's Metalloinvest, are also significant producers. Evraz uses its ore in its own steel mills, while Metalloinvest makes steel but also exports iron ore to customers such as Baosteel in China.

Supply Shortage Looms

Iron ore analyst Ronnie Cecil of Wood Mackenzie says that even with 240 to 250 new iron ore projects in the pipeline at mid-2011, a supply deficit until 2015 is inevitable. "China is at the heart of the supply deficit and price hikes until then. Over the next five years, global blast furnace production will rise by about 300 million tonnes—around the same amount of iron ore needed to build 5,000 Empire State buildings. China alone will account for 60 percent of this total, and therefore is critical to the evolution of the iron ore market."[8] Fortescue Metals Group chief executive Nev Power is even more bullish, expecting China's iron ore imports to reach 1 billion tonnes by 2015.

The other key requirement for the world's steel mills is metallurgical (coking) coal. Although China and India are the two biggest producers, they are not self-sufficient and imported 48 million tonnes and 30 million tonnes of coking coal respectively in 2010. India in particular suffers from a scarcity of domestic good-quality coking coal. Both countries are looking to diversify their supply sources away from the dominant exporter Australia, which shipped 155 million tonnes in 2010. Canada, Russia, and the United States are also major exporters. New players, some with Chinese and Indian backing, are emerging in Africa (Mozambique, Madagascar), Asia (Mongolia, Kazakhstan), and South America (Colombia). Globally, there is high demand for PCI (pulverized coal injection) coal, which can be fed directly into blast furnaces and reduces coking-coal usage by 25 to 30 percent. The largest seaborne supplier of what is known as low volatile PCI is Australian miner Macarthur Coal, now owned by Peabody Energy after it bought out other shareholders ArcelorMittal, POSCO of South Korea, and China's CITIC. Macarthur, which supplies steel mills in Europe, Asia, and Brazil, is just one of several miners operating in the rich Queensland coal basins of Bowen, Surat, and Galilee that have attracted the attention of resource-hungry suitors. China's Yanzhou Coal, for example, bought Felix Resources in 2009 to gain access to its PCI coal deposits. Japan's Nippon Steel, Mitsubishi, and Mitsui groups are allied with BHP Billiton and Anglo American, while Rio Tinto, Vale, and Xstrata are all present, along with independent miners such as Gina Rinehart's Hancock Coal and New Hope.

A similar story prevails in Mozambique's Tete province, which has been called "the next Bowen Basin." Vale shipped the first coking coal from its Moatize mine to the port of Beira in August 2011, and hopes to lift Moatize's production eventually to 11 million tonnes a year. Rio Tinto, which bought Riversdale Mining in mid-2011, aims to bring its Benga project into production in 2012. India's Jindal Steel and Coal India both have coal mining concessions in the same area. If all goes well with Tete's infrastructure, quality, and security— and, of course, global economic conditions—Mozambique could be the world's No. 2 source of seaborne coking coal by 2025. The other big contributor to the coking-coal trade could be Mongolia's massive Tavan Tolgoi block, which trucked its first coal south to the Aluminium Corp. of China in August 2011. With a possible 7.5 billion tonnes of high-quality coking coal under the vast South Gobi Desert, Tavan Tolgoi is a potential economic game-changer for Mongolia— if the government gets the development structure right. United States, Russian, Chinese, Japanese, and South Korean companies are all angling to develop Tavan Tolgoi's western arm. But its prospects, too, are dependent on better infrastructure and good political relations with neighbouring Russia and China.

Notes

1. "Global Steel: 2010 Trends, 2011 Outlook," Ernst & Young, 5 May 2011.
2. Fact Sheet, "Raw Materials," World Steel Association, www.worldsteel .org, May 2011.
3. China Mining Association, www.chinamining.com.cn.
4. Statement, "Simandou position," Rio Tinto, 11 June 2008.
5. Statement, "Rio Tinto and Government of Guinea sign new agreement for Simandou iron ore project," Rio Tinto 22 April 2011.
6. Interview with Peter Kukielski, ArcelorMittal, London 13 May 2011.
7. Media release, "AngloAmerican announces 45 percent increase in half year core operating profit to $5.9 billion," 29 July 2011.
8. Media release, "Wood Mackenzie Says That Iron Ore Suppliers Will Not be Able to Meet Market Demand Until at Least 2015," Sydney/ Edinburgh/Houston, 20 July 2011.

11

CHAPTER

U.S. Energy

Hail to the Shale

The resources of America and its future will be immense only to wise and virtuous men.

—Nineteenth-century American essayist
Ralph Waldo Emerson, *The Complete Works, Volume VIII, Letters and Social Aims,* "Resources" essay, 1876

As the second decade of the twenty-first century unfolds, it is clear the United States will have to cede some of its Asia-Pacific regional influence to China and learn to live in a world where there are two superpowers. But its technology, innovation, capital markets, capacity to evolve, and overall confidence will ensure it remains the "go-to" country when there's an energy, food, or water problem. Its formidable resources, and those of neighbouring Canada, keep it well and truly at the top of the economic big league, even with the recent advances of China, India, Russia, or Brazil. It is the world leader in natural gas production, it has the biggest reserves of recoverable coal, it is the third-largest crude oil producer behind Russia and Saudi Arabia, it has significant new petroleum prospects in the Gulf of Mexico and Alaska, it is the leading producer of nuclear electricity, and it has supply capacities in copper, other metals, food, and bioenergy that are either at or near the top of the tree. And in the evolving field of unconventional oil and gas, its vast shale reserves and gas-to-liquids conversion abilities have a "game-changer" whiff about them. At the same time, the U.S. government is pumping billions of dollars into alternative energy forms such as wind, solar, and wave power. Renewables are well and truly part of America's future energy mix, but for the next decade at least, the main U.S. energy story will be the shift from coal to natural gas. And that is where China comes in.

In 2005, state-owned China National Offshore Oil Corporation (CNOOC) sought to buy the U.S. oil company Unocal for $18.5 billion. It was supposed to be an investment masterstroke, doubling CNOOC's oil and gas output and giving it access to new technology. Instead, it proved a bitter and humiliating experience for the Chinese company, which was forced to drop out in the face of trenchant opposition from some U.S. lawmakers who raised national security objections. CNOOC's withdrawal in August 2005 opened the way for U.S.-based Chevron to snap up Unocal and its string of oil and gas assets in the Gulf of Mexico and Southeast Asia. CNOOC denounced Congressional opposition to its bid as "regrettable and unjustified."[1] But the California Republican who led the anti-CNOOC push, House Resources Committee Chairman Richard Pombo, was having none of it, issuing this statement: "I believe in a competitive, free market, global economy. CNOOC's communist government ownership and promise of virtually interest-free loans are not consistent with these principles. As such, CNOOC's withdrawal from this bidding process is good news for the free market, the American consumer and U.S. national security."[2] Potshots had been exchanged the previous month between the Chinese foreign ministry and another Republican, Richard D'Amato, chairman of the U.S.-China Economic and Security Review Commission. Beijing's statement on 4 July 2005 ran as follows:

> We demand that the U.S. Congress correct its mistaken ways of politicizing economic and trade issues and stop interfering in the normal commercial exchanges between enterprises of the two countries. CNOOC's bid to take over the U.S. Unocal company is a normal commercial activity between enterprises and should not fall victim to political interference.

A "demand" by the Chinese government was always going to evoke a sharp response. Appearing before the U.S. House of Representatives Committee on Armed Services on July 13, D'Amato said, "This proposed transaction gives every appearance of being an effort by the Chinese government to take over a private American oil company. This is true despite the rhetoric of the Chinese Foreign Ministry."[3] It was not the best of times for U.S.-China business relations.

Five years down the track, the business environment for CNOOC in the United States would prove much friendlier, with the company able to strike two landmark deals with shale gas industry standard-bearer, Oklahoma-based Chesapeake Energy. In November 2010, CNOOC bought a one-third interest in Chesapeake's leasehold acreage for the Eagle Ford shale project in South Texas for $1.1 billion, plus a commitment to fund another $1.1 billion's worth of drilling costs up to the end of 2012. The Eagle Ford project could produce up to 500,000 barrels a day of oil equivalent. CNOOC came back for more a few months later, agreeing to pay $570 million in March 2011 for a one-third interest in Chesapeake's leasehold acreage in the Denver-Julesburg (DJ) and Powder River Basins in northeast Colorado and southeast Wyoming, in what is known as the Niobrara shale formation. CNOOC also agreed to fund drilling and completion costs up to $697 million, which Chesapeake expected to occur by the end of 2014. The deals give CNOOC both a toehold in the United States and access to the complex technology of hydraulic fracturing and horizontal drilling that is the hallmark of U.S. shale gas and oil extraction.

Swing to Unconventional Resources

CNOOC's partner Chesapeake Energy is at the forefront of what is potentially the biggest trend in the U.S. energy market—the swing to unconventional resources such as shale gas and oil, and the associated higher-margin gas-to-liquids conversion technology. Chesapeake's co-founder and executive chairman, Aubrey McClendon, is the industry's most tireless promoter, pointing out that thanks to shale gas, the United States passed Russia in 2009 as the world's largest natural gas producer. He portrays the emergence of shale gas as an energy revolution so enormous that U.S. industry enjoys the lowest natural gas costs in the world. McClendon also tackles head-on the objections by environmental groups and some affected landowners that the hydraulic fracturing—or *fracking*—technique used to extract gas from shale deposits buried deep below the ground in a string of American states is bad for people's health and contaminates water supplies. In a speech in Philadelphia in September 2011, McClendon said that pulling the plug on natural gas because of antifracking protests would have a very bad economic effect. "The reality is that wind and solar can never be more than about 15 percent of our power requirements. So, 70 percent of American homes on natural gas heat—cold. And the 35 percent of American homes and businesses and factories that use electricity from natural gas—dark. All those crops that require natural gas based fertiliser—not grown. What a great vision of the future! We're cold, it's dark and we're hungry. I have no interest in turning the clock back to the Dark Ages as our opponents do."[4]

His opponents maintain that the consequences of pumping a high-pressure mix of water, sand, and chemicals into porous shale rock formations to release the hydrocarbons need more scrutiny. One of the most high-profile antifracking campaigners is Josh Fox, whose 2010 documentary *Gasland* outlined the apprehension many American communities living above gas deposits felt about the practice. "It is truly unfortunate that the gas-drilling industry continues to deny what is so obvious to Americans living in gaslands across the nation instead of taking responsibility for the damage they are causing," Fox wrote after the release of *Gasland* prompted a storm of counter-argument from the industry.[5] Fox also wrote that *Gasland* never contested that the target layers of fracking were far below underground drinking water sources. "We don't know why fracking chemicals and fugitive natural gas are getting into water supplies, we just know that they are," he said.[6] This is a global debate with some way to run yet, particularly as environmentally conscious Europe is thought to have huge shale gas potential—as much as 17.7 trillion cubic metres (624 trillion cubic feet). U.S. companies ExxonMobil and ConocoPhillips are among those drilling for gas in Germany and Poland. But in France, Parliament banned fracking outright in mid-2011 and the practice was put on hold in the United Kingdom after a couple of mild earthquakes. Some parts of Germany also have a moratorium on it. Outside of North America, Europe, Russia, and the Middle East, areas thought to have substantial shale resources include much of South America, South Africa, Algeria, Libya, China, India, Pakistan, Turkey, and Australia.

Back in the United States, where the U.S. Energy Information Administration estimates the technically recoverable shale gas resource is 24.4 trillion cubic metres (862 trillion cubic feet), McClendon says Chesapeake has the best assets in the business, pointing to its leading positions in most of the top U.S. unconventional liquids-rich fields such as the Anadarko Basin, Utica shale, and Niobrara shale, plus an array of natural gas shale fields. He professes to be not too concerned about the low price of gas in the United States, saying his priority for the future is liquids, and that gas prices will rise in the second half of the 2010s anyway as demand from industry, power generation, and the transport sector picks up. Thermal coal in particular is expected to cede ground to gas.

International Interest in Shale

CNOOC, which also has a stake in the Canadian oil sands industry, is not the only Chinese oil company enthused by American shale assets. In January 2012, China Petroleum and Chemical Corporation (Sinopec) agreed to pay $2.5 billion, including $1.6 billion in drilling costs, to take a 33 percent stake in four shale fields and one limestone field being developed by Devon Energy in Ohio and Michigan. France-based Total and Norway's Statoil have struck joint ventures with Chesapeake Energy, as has U.S. domestic player Plains Exploration & Production. BP bought two lots of gas assets from Chesapeake in 2008 for about $3.5 billion. But Chesapeake's biggest deal came early in 2011, when it agreed to sell the remainder of its Fayetteville, Arkansas, shale gas assets to Anglo-Australian energy giant BHP Billiton for $4.75 billion. The deal included 487,000 net acres of leasehold, production of about 11.75 million cubic metres (415 million cubic feet) of natural gas equivalent per day, and 680 km (420 miles) of pipeline. A few months later, BHP Billiton added to its U.S. investments when it agreed to pay just over $12 billion in July 2011 for PetroHawk Energy, in what would be its biggest acquisition since the 2001 merger between BHP and Billiton. PetroHawk has extensive shale gas and oil in Texas and Louisiana, and relatively low operating costs. BHP Billiton plans to spend about $80 billion over the next 10 years developing its U.S. shale gas and oil assets, in the process lifting its daily output from 500,000 barrels of oil equivalent to more than 1.5 million barrels by 2020.

Companies such as Chesapeake and PetroHawk may be the trendsetters in shale gas, but the biggest U.S. oil and gas plays still rest with the industry heavyweights. For example, ExxonMobil picked up a swag of unconventional oil and gas resources when it bought Houston-based XTO Energy in 2009 for about $41 billion, including $10 billion of debt. Buying XTO—at the time, the largest natural gas producer in the United States—was Exxon's biggest acquisition of the decade. Exxon now has stakes in all the major shale gas plays, including Barnett and Eagle Ford in Texas, Haynesville in Louisiana, Fayetteville in Arkansas, Bakken in North Dakota, and the Marcellus field, which runs beneath parts of Pennsylvania, New York, and West Virginia. Marcellus, where Exxon holds 700,000 acres, may well be the second largest gas field in the world after Qatar's North Field. By 2020 Exxon expects its output from unconventional sources such as shale and tight gas to reach 1 million barrels a day of oil equivalent. According to XTO Energy president Jack Williams, "The benefits of shale gas development have only begun to be realized," with enough natural gas in the United States to meet more than 100 years of current demand.[7]

Another of the global oil giants, Royal Dutch Shell, agreed in May 2010 to pay $4.7 billion for a private Pennsylvania company, East Resources, to gain access to acreage in the Marcellus and Eagle Ford fields. Shell plans to build a cracker plant to process ethane from Marcellus natural gas in the Appalachian region. Japan's Mitsui & Co. is another entrant, agreeing to pay $1.4 billion in 2010 for a one-third stake in Houston-based Anadarko Petroleum's assets in the Marcellus field. Indian entrepreneur Mukesh Ambani, who controls Mumbai-based energy and petrochemicals giant Reliance Industries, also sees a bright future for North American shale ventures. In April 2010 he paid $1.7 billion to enter a joint venture with Pittsburgh-based Atlas Energy covering its part of the Marcellus shale field, and two months later bought a 45 percent stake in Pioneer Natural Resources' acreage in the Eagle Ford shale field for about $1.3 billion. Indian state-run gas utility GAIL followed in Ambani's footsteps a year later, agreeing to pay about $300 million in September 2011 for a 20 percent stake in the Eagle Ford acreage held by Houston-based Carrizo Oil & Gas. GAIL chairman B. C. Tripathi said the deal marked a "major step" by the company to establish a presence in North America and to give it experience in shale gas projects ahead of possible Indian developments.

Malaysia's state-owned oil company Petronas and South Korean utility Korea Gas have bought into Canadian gas fields, but not all recent Asian forays into North America have gone to plan. PetroChina pulled out of a $5 billion-plus deal to buy a half share of Canadian natural gas company Encana's Cutbank Ridge shale gas assets in June 2011 after the two sides could not agree on a final price. It would have been PetroChina's first shale gas reserves in North America, following its $1.9 billion purchase of oil sands assets in Canada's Alberta province in 2010. PetroChina subsequently bought a 20 percent stake in Shell's Groundbirch shale assets in Canada in early 2012. Back home in China, its parent company, China National Petroleum Corp. (CNPC), has brought in Chevron and Royal Dutch Shell as partners to help it explore and assess some of China's own extensive shale gas deposits. Shell is not the only example of China's push to promote innovative gas projects. General Electric has tied up with a group of venture capital funds that include Citic Capital Partners to hunt for natural gas, shale gas, biogas, and coal-bed methane gas opportunities in China. Natural gas accounts for about 4 percent of China's total energy output in 2011, a share expected to double by 2015 (see Exhibit 11.1).

In its September 2011 International Energy Outlook covering the period out to 2035, the U.S. Energy Information Administration said it expected that sustained high oil prices would make unconventional resources—including oil sands, extra-heavy oil, biofuels, coal-to-liquids, gas-to-liquids, and shale oil—economically competitive, allowing them to grow by 4.6 percent a year out to 2035 in its base reference case. World production of unconventional liquid fuels would rise from 3.9 million barrels a day in 2008 to 13.1 million barrels a day in 2035, accounting for 12 percent of total world liquids supply. It said the largest components of this increase would be made up of Canadian oil sands, U.S. and Brazilian biofuels, and Venezuelan extra-heavy oil. World gas consumption would

1. Russia 46,000	4. Turkmenistan 8,340
2. Iran 33,000	5. Saudi Arabia 8,016
3. Qatar 25,201	6. United States 7,075

Exhibit 11.1   Proven natural gas reserves by country (billion cubic metres)
Source: OPEC Annual Statistical Bulletin, August 2011

rise 52 percent from 3.1 trillion cubic metres (111 trillion cubic feet) in 2008 to 4.8 trillion cubic metres (169 trillion cubic feet) in 2035. The EIA's outlook says the relatively low carbon intensity of gas compared with oil and coal "makes it an attractive option for nations interested in reducing greenhouse gas emissions in the power section." Within gas consumption, supplies of unconventional gas—tight gas, shale gas, and coal-bed methane—are expected to rise substantially, especially in the United States, Canada, and China. In its reference case, the EIA outlook expects shale gas will account for 47 percent of U.S. natural gas production in 2035, reaching 560 billion cubic metres (19.8 trillion cubic feet) when tight gas and coal-bed methane are included. The role of unconventional gas is even more important in Canada and China, where their share of total domestic gas production is 50 and 72 percent respectively by 2035, it says.[8] There is also a possibility the United States will become an exporter of LNG over the next decade, if liquefaction projects such as the one proposed for 2015–2016 by Cheniere Energy for its Sabine Pass terminal in Louisiana come on stream in time.

Pipeline Projects in the Mix

The North American low-cost shale gas revolution has already caused one alternative gas pipeline project to pull the plug; after three years of work and $165 million in development costs, partners BP and ConocoPhillips in May 2011 abandoned their Denali project—a plan to build a $35 billion gas pipeline to the main U.S. market from Alaska, where plentiful North Slope gas is lying untapped for want of an economically feasible delivery mode. The third big Alaska gas producer, ExxonMobil, has aligned itself with TransCanada Corp. in a similar plan known as the Alaska Pipeline Project that remains alive for now. Since 2009, Exxon and TransCanada have been working to win approvals and customers, but like the Denali project they face a U.S. market flooded with much cheaper and closer gas suppliers. If the $40 billion project gets the go-ahead, construction will start in mid-2015, with the first gas to flow from Alaska in 2020–2021.

Part of the problem for the Alaska gas suppliers is that according to the American Petroleum Institute, there could be much more oil and natural gas in the United States than previously thought. It points to the Bakken shale formation in North Dakota and

Montana (which also extends north into Canada's Saskatchewan and Manitoba provinces) as one example, where the U.S. Geological Survey (USGS) said in 2008 as much as 4 billion barrels of recoverable oil may exist there. That figure was 25 times greater than the original estimate back in 1995, but is still well below more recent estimates. The formation may contain 160 billion barrels or more, but recovery rates with existing technology—the solid oil shale must be mined and heated—have kept estimates of the field's maximum recoverable potential to 24 billion barrels. That still rates it as one of the world's largest discoveries, with oil being produced from the Bakken field at a rate of more than 450,000 barrels a day in 2011. Because natural gas prices are so low in the United States, much of the gas associated with the Bakken oil play so far has been flared off, but that is expected to change as infrastructure to better capture the gas is built up. Rising oil prices began to make Bakken look economically feasible in the mid-2000s, and its ramp-up since 2006 has been so rapid that producers have struggled to ship the oil to refineries efficiently, in some cases using rail until enough pipeline capacity comes onstream.

One pipeline project in the wings is that of Canadian operator Enbridge, which aims to add 145,000 barrels a day of Bakken crude capacity to its network by 2013. TransCanada's Keystone XL pipeline between Alberta and U.S. Gulf refineries would also pick up Bakken oil if it goes ahead. Also betting big on shale's potential is U.S. pipeline giant Kinder Morgan, which struck a deal in October 2011 to buy rival El Paso Corp. for $38 billion (including debt), creating an entity with a network of more than 100,000 km of natural gas pipelines. Kinder Morgan chairman Richard Kinder said if America was serious about cutting carbon emissions and reducing its dependence on foreign oil, "natural gas is absolutely the best readily available option."[9]

Reserves of U.S. conventional oil elsewhere also are being upgraded. Advances in seismic technology and deepwater drilling techniques have lifted estimates for the U.S. share of Gulf of Mexico offshore fields to 45 billion barrels. Likewise, in Alaska, the giant North Slope field at Prudhoe Bay (discovered in 1967) had produced more than 16 billion barrels by mid-2011, and while production has declined, it is still reckoned to have 10 billion barrels left, with some estimates putting its reserves at 40 billion barrels. BP and other operators are using new technology to reach previously untouched oil in the North Slope fields, where more than 1,000 active wells exist. At its peak in 1988, the 1285-kmTrans Alaska Pipeline from Prudhoe Bay in the north to the port of Valdez in the south carried 2.2 million barrels of crude a day. The daily flow now hovers around 570,000 barrels, and as it steadily drops closer to its minimum flow rate of 200,000 barrels a day, the pipeline owners—BP, ExxonMobil, ConocoPhillips, Chevron, and Koch Industries—are worried that the cooler, more sluggish oil will enable wax to build up, ice crystals to form inside, and metal corrosion to set in. Oil once flowed from Prudhoe Bay to Valdez in four days; the same journey in 2011 takes 14 days. That slow flow means the pipeline needs more maintenance, raising the per-barrel transport cost.

But if the North Slope is declining, the waters off Alaska still hold immense promise and could extend the working life of the pipeline, with the U.S. government estimating Alaska's offshore reserves at 27 billion barrels of oil and 3.73 trillion cubic metres (132 trillion cubic feet) of natural gas. Much of this is in the Chukchi Sea, an area off Alaska's northwest coast that is the same size as the Gulf of Mexico and which environmentalists fear could be ruined by oil spills if drilling is allowed to go ahead. The U.S. government raised $2.6 billion (including $2.1 billion from Royal Dutch Shell) from the sale of Alaskan oil leases in 2008, but exploration in the Chukchi Sea was put on hold after a U.S. court ordered more environmental work there. Shell holds permits to drill six wells in the Chukchi Sea and another four in the adjacent Beaufort Sea, where it hopes to begin drilling in mid-2012. If Shell is successful and can bring oil ashore and into a proposed connection to the Trans Alaska pipeline by 2020, then the area's economy will enjoy a significant boost. ConocoPhillips and Norway's Statoil also aspire to drill in the Chukchi Sea, though in Statoil's case it will be 2014 at the earliest. Overshadowing all Alaskan development is the memory of the 1989 *Exxon Valdez* tanker oil spill in Prince William Sound, which had devastating consequences for birds and marine life.

Gulf of Mexico Prospects

The Arctic is a relatively long-term play. There are more immediate prospects in the Gulf of Mexico, despite BP's disastrous Macondo well blowout in April 2010 that set off an explosion on the Deepwater Horizon drilling rig. The rig sank in 1,525 m (5,000 ft) of water, causing massive oil pollution and taking the lives of 11 workers on the platform and injuring 17 others. The Macondo spill brought U.S. deepwater exploration in the Gulf to a six-month halt, and it would take until the second half of 2011 before BHP Billiton brought online the first deepwater well there since the disaster. But the potential of the Gulf of Mexico is just too vast to deny or delay—particularly when big new fields such as Chevron's Jack/St. Malo and Moccasin prospects, BP's Mad Dog extension, Shell's Great White field and the associated Perdido ultradeepwater development, and ExxonMobil's Keathley Canyon finds are adding to the resource tally. According to the U.S. EIA, offshore oil production in the Gulf accounts for 29 percent of total U.S. crude oil production, while about 12 percent of total U.S. gas production comes from offshore Gulf platforms. Over 40 percent of total U.S. petroleum refining capacity and 30 percent of natural gas processing capacity is on the Gulf coast. But this can be a hazardous environment; apart from dangers such as the Deepwater Horizon explosion, which caused 11 deaths and environmental havoc, there is the seasonal threat of hurricanes, which can mean shutting down and evacuating rigs. In 2005, the super-storm Hurricane Katrina became America's costliest natural disaster, devastating the city of New Orleans, causing more than 1,800 deaths, running up a damages bill of $80 billion and putting much of the Gulf's oil facilities out of action for months. Thirty rigs were damaged or destroyed, and nine refineries were shut down.

The new rigs that operate in the Gulf must be engineered to contend with wind speeds of 300 km/h and wave heights of 30 m or more. An example is Shell's 55,000-tonne $3 billion Perdido spar, a floating production facility that is moored in water 2,450 m (8,000 ft) deep about 320 km (200 miles) off the coast of Texas and began producing in March 2010. Perdido—Spanish for "lost"—is the world's deepest offshore drilling and production unit, able to produce 100,000 barrels of oil equivalent a day drawn from three fields within a 50 km radius. The 150 workers on the platform do 12-hour shifts for 14 days straight, before spending 14 days off. Two large helicopters can evacuate the workforce if a hurricane threatens. About 80 percent of Perdido's production is to come from the Great White field, with the remainder from the Silvertip and Tobago fields. Not far from Great White in the area known as Lower Tertiary is BP's Tiber field, which it discovered in 2009 after drilling to a total depth of 10,685 m (35,055 ft)—one of the deepest wells on record. BP, the single largest producer in the Gulf with about 400,000 barrels a day of oil equivalent, aims to lift output to as much as 650,000 barrels by 2025 as Tiber and another massive field, Kaskida, come on stream, and existing fields such as Mad Dog and Atlantis are extended. Tiber holds about 3 billion barrels of oil, of which about 450 million barrels are economically recoverable.

For more than 60 years, oil companies in the United States and Mexico have been exploiting Gulf of Mexico resources, growing its capacity to a point where it now supplies about a third of the world's needs. U.S. production from the Gulf reached just over 1.5 million barrels a day in 2003 but by 2008 had declined to just 1.15 million barrels before new fields such as Thunder Horse, Great White, and Jack reversed the trend. At the end of 2011, for example, BP was producing from 20 fields and had 11 projects underway in the Gulf. Chevron aims to have a startup for the $7.5 billion first stage of its Jack and St. Malo fields in 2014, with a production capacity of 170,000 barrels of oil and 1.2 million cubic metres of natural gas a day. Along with BP and Chevron, other majors such as Exxon, Shell, ConocoPhillips, and partners Anadarko, Petrobras, Statoil, and BHP Billiton have scores of wells in production or being brought on stream.

The Cuba–China Connection

In recent years, Cuba has entered the Gulf picture, along with a potential China connection. A U.S. Geological Survey in 2004 suggested that there could be as much as 4.6 billion barrels of oil and 277 billion cubic metres (9.8 trillion cubic feet) of gas off Cuba's northwest coast in the deep waters of what is known as the North Cuba Basin. Because U.S. oil companies are unable to operate in these waters, any proposal for Chinese involvement in Cuba's oil industry provokes an intense political reaction in America, as evidenced by a flurry of inaccurate (or premature) reports between 2005 and 2010 that Cuba and China had reached a deal for China to drill for offshore oil, potentially within 100 km (60 miles) of the Florida coast. That might yet eventuate: in mid-2011, Chinese Vice President Xi Jinping and China National Petroleum Corp. president Jiang Jiemin visited Havana, where Jiang signed an expanded energy cooperation agreement with Cubapetroleo (Cupet) chief executive Raul Perez. Under the agreement, CNPC will use its technology and engineering prowess to help boost Cuba's crude oil production, and will also help Cupet in "exploring and developing new onshore and offshore oil blocks in Cuba."[10]

The CNPC agreement may include helping to expand a Cuban refinery jointly owned by Cupet and Venezuela's state-owned PDVSA. Cuba produces about 80,000 barrels of oil a day, or about half its needs, and imports the remainder from Venezuela. Another Chinese state-owned entity, Sinopec, signed an agreement in 2005 with Cupet covering onshore resources only. Canadian company Sherritt International has had oil and gas operations in Cuba since 1992, and it is that country's largest independent energy producer. Brazil's Petrobras has drilled in Cuban waters, as has the Spanish oil company Repsol-YPF, in which Mexico's Pemex holds a strategic stake of almost 10 percent. Repsol has chartered a Chinese-built submersible rig to further explore Cuban waters in 2012. State-owned oil companies Gazprom of Russia and Petronas of Malaysia struck a deal with Cupet in mid-2011 to drill in four offshore blocks. Gazprom Neft Chairman Alexander Dyukov said at the time that by 2020 the company wanted 10 percent of its production to come from overseas projects, and the Cuba partnership would help expand its deepwater expertise. India's ONGC of India also plans to drill in Cuban waters.

U.S. politicians have always been nervous about overseas investors who might somehow impinge on U.S. energy, minerals, transport, or food security. In the 1980s and 1990s, there were various bouts of trade friction with Japan, particularly as the strong yen encouraged Japanese automakers, real estate investors, and technology companies to set up plants or buy trophy buildings in the United States. In 2006, U.S. legislators intervened after the United Arab Emirates-owned company DP (Dubai Ports) World took over UK-based P&O Shipping, which would have given it control of several large U.S. ports. DP World ended up reselling the U.S. assets in response to the political pressure. In the case of Chinese direct investment, U.S. suspicion manifested itself in the outcry against CNOOC's proposed purchase of Unocal in 2005 and later in several failed deals requiring approval by the Committee on Foreign Investment in the United States (CFIUS). For example, the committee indicated national security concerns over a 2009 proposal by Northwest Nonferrous International Investment to buy gold miner Firstgold Corp. and a 2010 bid by Tangshan Caofedian Investment for solar PV technology company Encore.

Opening the U.S. Investment Door

In May 2011, the Asia Society released a major report on Chinese investment in the United States, "An American Open Door?" In it, the authors, Daniel Rosen and Thilo Hanemann, wrote that if China followed the pattern of other emerging nations, more than $1 trillion in direct Chinese investment would flow worldwide by 2020, and a significant part of that would go to advanced markets such as the United States. They noted that China's direct investment in the United States had reached a takeoff point and was starting to boom. "But at the same time, it has stoked worries about what it will mean to have China as the owner next door rather than just a distant contract manufacturer," they said.[11]

China already holds almost $1.2 trillion in U.S. Treasuries, another $450 billion in U.S. government agency debt, and portfolio equity investment in U.S. companies of about $80 billion, as opposed to direct investment, which usually means an investment of 10 percent or more. The U.S. Bureau of Economic Analysis found that in 2009 the world's total direct investment in the United States was $2.3 trillion, of which China's share was a miniscule $2.3 billion, or 0.1 percent, compared to Japan's 11.7 percent. Australia, Singapore, and Korea are all bigger direct investors in the United States than China. Japan and the rest of Asia Pacific account for only 16 percent of foreign direct investment (FDI), with the bulk coming from Europe at 63 percent, Canada with just under 11 percent, and Latin America at 6.7 percent. Although these figures don't account for third-country conduits used by some Chinese investors, they do show the very low starting point for Chinese FDI. In the Asia Society report, Rosen and Hanemann identified 230 Chinese investments in the United States between 2003 and 2010 worth about $11.7 billion, split between 109 greenfield projects and 121 acquisitions. They included such big-ticket investments as Tianjin Pipe's 2009 decision to spend $1 billion to build a greenfield steel pipe plant in Corpus Christi, Texas, and the purchase of a 15 percent stake in Virginia power utility AES by sovereign wealth fund China Investment Corporation for $1.58 billion in 2010. Since then, CNOOC has agreed to spend $3.5 billion on U.S. shale assets and Sinopec has signed up for a $2.5 billion investment.

Among the world's other big emerging energy players, Brazil's Petrobras has made a number of U.S. investments, including a Texas refinery and stakes in several oil fields in the Gulf of Mexico. India has Reliance Industries, GAIL, and ONGC in the U.S. picture, while Russian independent producer LUKOIL said in March 2011 it was keen to find an opening in U.S. shale fields. The U.S. energy-trading arm of Russia's state-owned Gazprom signed its first long-term natural gas supply contract in Missouri in October 2011.

Notes

1. Statement by Chinese Foreign Ministry, 4 July 2005.
2. Statement by Richard Pombo, chairman, House Resources Committee, 2 August 2005.
3. Statement by Richard D'Amato, chairman, U.S.-China Economic and Security Review Commission, before the House Committee on Armed Services, 13 July 2005.
4. Aubrey McClendon, CEO, Chesapeake Energy Corporation, speech to Marcellus Shale Insights Conference, Philadelphia, 7 September 2011.
5. Josh Fox, "Affirming Gasland," July 2010, http://1trickpony.cachefly.net/gas/pdf/Affirming_Gasland_Sept_2010.pdf, retrieved 3 October 2011.
6. Ibid.
7. Jack Williams, speech to the SPE Unconventional Gas Conference, "Shale Gas: The Keys to Unlocking Its Full Potential," Houston, Texas, 14 June 2011.
8. U.S. Energy Information Administration, "International Energy Outlook 2011," 19 September 2011, Highlights, page 2. http://www.eia.gov/forecasts/ieo/index.cfm.
9. Kinder Morgan press release, "Kinder Morgan to purchase El Paso for approximately $38 billion," 16 October 2011.
10. CNPC press release, "CNPC and Cupet sign expanded oil cooperative framework agreement," 8 June 2011.
11. Rosen, Daniel H. & Hanemann, Thilo, "An American Open Door? Maximising the Benefits of Chinese Direct Investment," Asia Society and Woodrow Wilson Centre for Scholars, May 2011.

CHAPTER 12

Japan after the Deluge

When one looks at GDP growth to working age population (defined as population aged 20–60), one gets a surprising result: Japan has actually done better than the U.S. or most European countries over the last decade.
—Daniel Gros, director of the Centre for European
Policy Studies, January 6, 2011

Japan may be softly receding into nonimportance in the eyes of the more strident backers of Chinese or Indian twenty-first-century economic supremacy, but its global influence remains significant. Although the Japanese consumer juggernaut that bedazzled the world in the 1980s and 1990s has lost some of its allure and spending power, the ideas and trends that roll out of Japan in fields such as energy innovation, science and technology, medicine, industrial design, manufacturing prowess, communications, culture, finance, and retailing can still set the global benchmark. And because Japan has never had much in the way of conventional low-cost energy resources, it is a market of substance for energy and metals suppliers around the globe. That alone ensures that wherever its demographic future may take it, Japan still carries enough geopolitical weight to upset archrival China.

In the second half of 2011, Japan released a military report that infuriated China. In its annual White Paper, Japan's Ministry of

Defense called China "overbearing" in the way it dealt with conflicts in disputed waters such as the East and South China Seas, saying it was making the neighbours anxious about the future direction of China's rapid military buildup. For good measure, Japan said it was concerned about the real size of China's defense budget and its overall assertiveness. China, it said, should be aware of its responsibility as a major power and abide by international rules.[1]

As expected, the Chinese response was swift and tart. China's economic development had brought important opportunities to countries around the world, including Japan, Foreign Ministry spokesman Ma Zhaoxu responded on August 3. "The development of China has not and will never pose a threat to any country," Ma thundered, before adding the obligatory reference to Japan's invasion of China and brutal treatment of its citizens in the lead-up to World War II. "We hope Japan can regard history as a mirror, earnestly reflect on its own defense policy and do more to deepen mutual trust with neighbouring countries and maintain regional peace and stability, not the contrary."[2]

Along with Japan's treatment of China in the first half of the twentieth century, the biggest impediment to a smoother relationship is territorial friction in the East China Sea, where there is an overlap of about 40,000 sq km in the exclusive economic zones claimed by China and Japan. Aside from fishing resources, there is a potential energy resource dispute covering the Chunxiao gas field (known as the Shirakaba field by Japan), which lies within Chinese territory and is being developed by the state-owned oil companies CNOOC and Sinopec. The first gas flowed from Chunxiao in 2006. Japan acknowledges that the Chinese drills are operating in Chinese waters, but says they might tap into a gas field that extends into the disputed territory, in which case Japan might have a claim on some of the gas.

China has dismissed the Japanese position, in much the same way as it refuses to acknowledge various territorial claims further south in the oil-rich South China Sea by Vietnam, Malaysia, the Philippines, Brunei, and Taiwan. These waters, it constantly reminds its neighbours, always have been and always will be Chinese. A recent study prepared for the U.S. Army by the RAND Corporation on possible regional conflicts involving China found that "an ongoing territorial dispute over the Senkaku/Diaoyu islands and overlapping claims to exclusive economic zones in the East China Sea are persistent irritants to the (China-Japan) relationship. Conflict could arise from an at-sea incident in the East China Sea, or from the escalation of a war of words amplified by some sort of maritime encounter."[3] Just such an incident happened in September 2010, when Japanese authorities arrested the captain of a Chinese fishing trawler after his vessel rammed a Japanese coastguard ship near the Senkaku/Diaoyu islands. The resultant uproar in China ended only when Japan agreed to release the trawler skipper.

This sort of sparring between the world's No. 2 and No. 3 economies has been going on for decades, but Foreign Ministry spokesman Ma's point about the importance of China's growth to the Japanese economy is well made. China is Japan's No. 1 trade partner for goods and services, with the two-way trade relationship in 2011 worth about $320 billion. That makes it one of the biggest bilateral trade flows in the world, exceeded only by China's trade with the United States and the European Union, and America's trade with Canada, Mexico, and the European Union. China is also a key destination for Japanese investments. Japanese companies have set up more than 43,000 projects in China over the past three decades, with much of this investment in finished products such as electronics, other consumer goods, and motor vehicles that are destined for global markets (see Exhibit 12.1).

The political and economic weight of China, Japan, and their cultural cousin South Korea grew substantially in the postwar era, creating what the Australian academic Ross Garnaut called the "Northeast Asian Ascendancy" in his 1989 report of that name. Defining Northeast Asia for the purposes of his study as Japan, South Korea, China, Taiwan, and Hong Kong, Garnaut wrote, "Never before in human history have economies grown as fast for so long

1. United States-EU $868 billion	5. United States-Mexico $429 billion
2. United States-Canada $589 billion	6. China-Japan $320 billion
3. European Union-China $565 billion	7. European Union-Japan $190 billion
4. United States-China $481 billion	8. United States-Japan $181 billion

Exhibit 12.1   The world's biggest trade flows in goods and services (for 2010 calendar year)

Source: EU, United States, China, Japan governments

as in Northeast Asia over the past four decades. As a result, there has been an historic shift in the centre of gravity of economic production and power towards Northeast Asia."[4]

Garnaut, whose later output would include editing *China: The Next 20 Years of Reform and Development* with Jane Solley and Ligang Song in 2010, was not alone among economic commentators in noting the rise of the Northeast Asia economies, but he was among the first to look forward and map out specific strategies that would allow the region's trading partners to make the most of the opportunities emerging from this massive growth spurt.

Garnaut noted that Northeast Asia's economic output had more than doubled each decade in the periods of sustained rapid growth in the five economies. While Japan was at the peak of its financial power and could expand more rapidly than other advanced industrial countries through the 1990s if "structural changes allow increasingly scarce labor and skills to be channeled to the most productive industries,"[5] he sounded a warning note on China: "It is not yet clear whether China is set firmly on sustained growth in the Northeast Asian pattern, or whether shifts in the political order will cause the uneven experience of the first three decades of the People's Republic to recur."[6]

Political Shifts in North Asia

Shifts in the political order were fresh in Garnaut's mind when he completed his report in October 1989. It was a few months after the June political crackdown in China, when tanks and troops of the People's Liberation Army fired on prodemocracy demonstrators in Beijing, and two months before Japan's Nikkei 225 share index reached its record closing high of 39,915 points on December 29 that year. Japan entered 1990 with an exultancy that knew no bounds. The Tokyo stock market already had a greater market capitalization than New York, and there was a brief moment when Japan looked as if it might become the richest country in the world. But within a year, the Nikkei had almost halved to be below 21,000 points, and within three years it was below 16,000 as Japan's asset bubble burst and the country sank into what some economists—perhaps erroneously—would come to call its "lost decade." Big-city real estate prices collapsed, some Japanese consumers grew more cautious (but not all—the over-55 retirees known as "silvers" started to spread their wings), domestic manufacturers moved more plants abroad, and a series of corporate crises linked to bureaucratic cronyism sapped business confidence. Policy failures abounded and Japan's political leadership appeared incapable of meeting the challenge. Overseas investors turned their sights on more lucrative opportunities, particularly as China opened up. With demography against it and catastrophes such as the 1995 Kobe earthquake exacerbating the pressures on its financial system, Japan struggled to regain momentum.

There was a spurt inspired by the information and communications revolution of the late 1990s and early 2000s that lifted GDP growth to 3 percent in 2004, but it was not enough to inspire the market. The Nikkei reached its nadir in March 2009, falling below 7200 as the economy struggled along in the low single-digits, sometimes dropping into negative territory as the turbulence of the late 2000s swept through.

Even in this difficult environment, Japan remained the world's second-largest economy until 2010; its domestic demand, its science and technology, its proven manufacturing expertise—including its ability to establish world-class plants offshore—its trading networks and its intellectual and financial capital ensured its continued importance in global business circles. Meanwhile, China's paramount leader Deng Xiaoping (who died in 1997) had reinvigorated the reform process at the beginning of the 1990s, and his new team led by President Jiang Zemin, joined later by Premier Zhu Rongji, was presiding over a long period of 8 percent or better growth that catapulted China's economy into the major league. The special economic zones that began in the early 1980s with the sleepy fishing village of Shenzhen, just across from Hong Kong on the Chinese mainland, were beginning to deliver on their trade and investment potential. In 2000, the city of Shenzhen—by then its population swollen past 10 million people—marked Deng's role as a "great planner and contributor" to its development, unveiling a 6 m bronze statue in Lianhua (Lotus) Mountain park that shows Deng in a purposeful pose. Today, Shenzhen's economic zone has expanded to take in the container port of Yantian and it forms part of the powerful Pearl River Delta region with Guangzhou and Hong Kong.

China's gross domestic product overtook that of Japan midway through 2010 for it to become the world's No. 2 economy, though per capita income, even on the basis of purchasing power parity, is only about one-fifth of Japan's. According to the International

Monetary Fund, U.S. nominal gross domestic product in 2010 was $14.5 trillion, compared with $5.88 trillion for China and $5.46 trillion for Japan. Brazil and India ranked seventh and ninth, with GDP of $2.1 trillion and $1.6 trillion, respectively. Japan will continue to be an economy of immense size over the next four decades, even as its population declines. According to the global bank HSBC in its 2011 forecast of *The World in 2050,*[7] Japan's population will fall to just 102 million people, compared to 1.61 billion for India, 1.42 billion for China, 404 million for the United States, and 219 million for Brazil. Japan's economy will still rank fourth in size behind China, the United States, and India, with a GDP of $6.43 trillion in constant 2000 U.S. dollars. HSBC's estimate for China's GDP is $24.6 trillion, followed by the United States on $22.3 trillion and India on $8.16 trillion. Brazil will rank seventh, behind Germany and the United Kingdom, on $2.96 trillion. Goldman Sachs sees a somewhat different outcome for 2050, with Brazil, Mexico, and Russia ranking fourth, fifth, and sixth behind China, the United States, and India, and Japan consigned to eighth spot behind Indonesia.[8]

Player of Consequence

Japan's demand for energy, minerals, and food ensures it remains a player of consequence in the scramble for resources. It is the world's No. 3 net oil importer after China and the United States, buying about 8.5 percent of the global trade in crude oil and more than 30 percent of traded LNG. About 45 percent of its total energy needs come from crude oil imports, sourced mainly from Saudi Arabia, the United Arab Emirates, Qatar, Kuwait, and Iran. Japan is the world's biggest coal importer. In iron ore, coking coal, and steaming coal, its web of investments, financing muscle, long-term trading relationships, and information networks in minerals and energy are so strong that Japan cannot be overlooked when a new project seeks backers or customers. It is one of the world's biggest food markets, particularly for seafood, meat, grains, soybeans, and vegetable oil sourced mainly from the United States, China, Southeast Asia, and Australia. And while the world knows Japanese consumer brands such as Toyota, Sony, Canon, Honda, Shiseido, and Nintendo, it is these less familiar names that are at the forefront of the global resources battle:

- JX Holdings (created from the merger of Nippon Oil and Nippon Mining in 2010)

- State-owned Japan Oil, Gas and Metals National Corp. (JOGMEC), which took over the sourcing functions of Japan National Oil Corp. and the Metal Mining Agency of Japan in 2004
- Inpex Corp., in which the Japanese government holds a 19 percent stake
- Japan Petroleum Exploration Co. (Japex), in which the Japanese government owns 34 percent
- Private players Cosmo Oil and Idemitsu Kosan
- The big trading companies Mitsubishi Corp., Mitsui & Co., ITOCHU Corp., Marubeni Corp., Sumitomo Corp., and Sojitz Corp.

They invest in, produce, and supply oil, gas, coal, metals, and a vast array of other commodities from sources around the world to a range of Japanese and third-party customers, including the country's main steel makers Nippon Steel (which aims to merge with Sumitomo Metal Industries by late 2012), JFE Holdings and Kobe Steel, and the main power utilities Tokyo Electric Power Co., Kansai Electric Power Co. in Osaka, Chubu Electric Power Co. in Nagoya, Tohoku Electric Power Co. in Sendai, and Kyushu Electric Power Co. in Fukuoka. Sometimes the trading companies work together: In the 1980s, Mitsubishi Corp. and Mitsui & Co. joined forces to take a one-sixth share in one of Australia's biggest resources developments, the North West Shelf Venture. And sometimes, they bring in their Japanese customers as co-investors: Mitsubishi Corp. formed a 50–50 joint venture with Canadian oil and gas explorer Penn West Exploration in 2010 to exploit the Cordova shale gas project in British Columbia, and then brought in JOGMEC, Chubu Electric, and Japan's two biggest natural gas distributors, Tokyo Gas and Osaka Gas, to hold a total 30 percent stake. The Japanese gas companies are also investors in LNG projects around the world, in Qatar, Malaysia, Brunei, Australia, and Canada.

The trading companies take a very wide-ranging approach to energy commodities. ITOCHU, for example, is the world's second-largest nuclear fuel trader, behind Germany's NUKEM, but is also a key investor with agrifood giant Bunge in the Brazilian bioethanol venture Pedro Afonso, in Colombian steaming coal, and in U.S. solar thermal power projects. Sojitz trades and invests in everything from woodchips in Africa and stock feed in Vietnam to helping build a 5.5 million tonne hotstrip steel mill in India for the Indian steel giant Tata.

Equity Partners around the Globe

Typical of the resources approach taken by Japanese industrial companies is that of Nippon Steel, which sources its steel-making ingredients mainly from iron ore suppliers in Australia and Brazil, and coking- (metallurgical) coal suppliers in Australia, the United States, Canada, and China. To ensure the security of those supplies, Nippon Steel usually takes an equity stake in new mine ventures, partnering with global miners such as Rio Tinto, Vale, Xstrata, and Anglo American. Sometimes its equity partners include Korean steel rival POSCO. Other times it forms a consortium with other Japanese steel makers. Some of these relationships go back for decades; for example, Nippon Steel was a key investor in Robe River Iron Associates (along with Mitsui and Sumitomo Metal Industries), the venture that helped start the buildup of the massive Pilbara iron ore export operation in Western Australia in the late 1960s. And sometimes its suppliers are the Japanese trading companies themselves, which have formed their own joint ventures with miners; the BHP Billiton Mitsubishi Alliance (BMA) based on the Queensland coalfields in Australia is the world's biggest coking-coal exporter and a major supplier to Nippon Steel. BHP also has an alliance with Mitsui covering Queensland coking coal. Similarly, Mitsubishi is a shareholder in Rio Tinto's Iron Ore Co. of Canada. Another of the trading companies, Sojitz, is a partner with Nippon Steel, Sumitomo Metal, JFE Steel, Kobe Steel, and Nisshin Steel in Nibrasco, the Brazilian iron ore pellet company in which Vale holds 51 percent.

Japan's leading oil and gas explorer is Inpex Corp., which completed a takeover of smaller rival Teikoku Oil in 2008. Inpex, which began life in 1966 as North Sumatra Offshore Petroleum, has stakes in 70 projects around the world, including the following developments:

- Tangguh LNG project (with Mitsubishi) and South Natuna block in Indonesia
- Kitan and Bayu-Undan oil and gas fields in the Timor Sea
- Oil fields known as the ADMA block off Abu Dhabi in the United Arab Emirates

- West Bakr block in Egypt (in which Mitsui also has a stake)
- Off the coast of the Democratic Republic of Congo

Inpex is a partner with Total and Occidental in the Joslyn oil sands upstream project in Alberta, Canada, and with trading house Sojitz in a Brazilian offshore block known as Frade, where Chevron and Petrobras are major shareholders. Inpex has stakes in several Gulf of Mexico fields covering the United States and Mexican sectors, is also involved in Venezuela with PDVSA, and has small stakes in several Caspian Sea ventures.

But it also knows when to beat a strategic retreat. In October 2010, Inpex relinquished its interest in Iran's massive Azadegan oil field in the face of U.S. sanctions that would have hindered its ability to raise funds from U.S. banks. Inpex at one stage held 75 percent of the Azadegan field—one of the world's largest, with reserves estimated at 26 billion barrels—but cut that to 10 percent in 2006. It returned the final 10 percent to the state-run National Iranian Oil Co. for free, after spending about $150 million on development. While the write-off was costly, there looked to be little upside for Inpex in the politically charged environment of Iran, and it decided it could better spend its funds on projects such as the $30 billion Ichthys LNG development in northern Australia. Inpex, which holds 76 percent of Ichthys, expects its first gas supplies to go to its customers in Japan and Taiwan in 2016.

JX Holdings Builds Energy, Metals Business

JX Holdings is Japan's largest integrated energy and resources company, with turnover of about $115 billion in the year to March 2011 from its petroleum exploration, refining, and marketing operations and its metals business built around copper and electronic materials. It has overseas oil and gas interests in Vietnam, Malaysia, Myanmar, Indonesia, Papua New Guinea, Australia, the North Sea, Gulf of Mexico, Abu Dhabi, and Qatar. JX is a relatively new creation, formed through the merger of Nippon Oil and Nippon Mining into the operating unit Nippon Oil & Energy in 2010. The company is held 42 percent by Japanese financial institutions, while overseas investors, including the government of Singapore, hold 31 percent.

Nippon Oil began life in 1888. It merged with Mitsubishi Oil in 1999. It went through a series of consolidations with various refining, petrochemicals and gas producing companies during the 2000s, before merging with Nippon Mining. It has by far the greatest number of gasoline retail outlets in Japan, with market share of about 34 percent. On the metals side, Nippon Mining is one of the world's largest copper smelters and has interests in the Escondida, Collahuasi, and Los Pelambres copper mines in Chile. It also has a joint venture, Pan Pacific Copper (PPC) with Mitsui Mining, covering development of the rich Caserones copper and molybdenum deposit in northern Chile. It is a major player in the world's electronic materials business that includes copper foil for printed circuit boards, thin film materials such as indium for flat panel displays, and precision-fabricated products such as gold plating.

Japex, now held 34 percent by the Japanese government, was set up by the state in 1955 and part-privatized in 1970 before listing in 2003. It is considerably smaller than Inpex and is one of 16 energy companies in which the Japanese government retains an interest. The company's focus is on domestic gas sales and offshore operations in Canada, Indonesia, Iraq, and Russia. Japex president Osamu Watanabe said in early 2011 that he was confident the group's proven reserves of 254 million barrels of oil equivalent at March 2010 could be lifted to 350 million barrels by the target of March 31, 2013, given "steady progress" in its ventures. That includes an expansion project in Canada's Athabasca oil sands region, where Japex expects to boost production from its Hangingstone block. In southern Iraq, Japex and its partner, Malaysia's Petronas, expect their Garraf field to be producing 230,000 barrels a day by 2017. On the Russia Far East island of Sakhalin, Japex is a shareholder (along with the Japanese government and trading houses ITOCHU and Marubeni) in Sakhalin Oil & Gas, which owns 30 percent of the Sakhalin 1 project. This project produces 250,000 barrels a day for export, plus gas that is sold into the Russian domestic market. Likewise, Mitsui and Mitsubishi have a 22.5 percent combined stake in the Sakhalin 2 project, which went online in 2009.

Other Japanese energy players include Idemitsu Kosan, which holds stakes in several UK and Norwegian fields in the North Sea, and is an investor there with Osaka Gas. It is also exploring west of the Shetland Islands, where it made oil and gas discoveries from 2009 onward. In non-oil energy business, Idemitsu mines about 10 million tonnes of coal a year through its Australian subsidiaries, and also has a stake in the Cigar Lake uranium venture in Canada's Saskatchewan province. Oil importer, refiner and retailer Cosmo

Oil had sales of about $32 billion in 2011, with oil and gas exploration interests in Abu Dhabi, Qatar, and Australia, and agreements with suppliers in Saudi Arabia, Kuwait, and Iran. Like Idemitsu (which has wind power, geothermal, biofuel, and fuel cell projects), Cosmo is looking at renewable energy for the future. It has a concentrated solar power generation venture with the Abu Dhabi government, a photovoltaic cell project, a biomass to liquid process, and a wind power business in Japan.

SoftBank's "New Energy" Vision

One company that does not yet figure in a list of Japan's biggest energy producers is Internet and mobile phone conglomerate SoftBank, the group created by the billionaire maverick entrepreneur Masayoshi Son. But if Son gets his way, that may change. He wants Japan to shift 60 percent of its electricity requirements to renewable energy sources over the next 20 years, cut down on nuclear power, and build a Japan "super-grid" that would move power around the country, with an expansion eventually to the Asian mainland. That potentially would put Japan on a pan-Asia power grid linking up with China, Russia, and perhaps even India. As a starting point, Son launched the Japan Renewable Energy Foundation in Tokyo in September 2011, and said he and SoftBank would invest in new energy ventures.

After the March 2011 earthquake and tsunami that precipitated the Fukushima nuclear power plant disaster, Son involved himself in the extensive energy debate that followed in Japan. He said that three beliefs about Japan's nuclear power—that it was stable, safe, and reasonably priced—had collapsed. His analysis was on target: the Fukushima disaster caused massive damage to Japanese agriculture, fishing, and tourism, aside from its public health costs and the financial burden that plant operator Tokyo Electric Power Co. (Tepco) would have to bear for years to come in cleaning up the mess. But finding a cost-effective solution is another matter. In the short-term, Tepco and other power utilities scrambled to source LNG as a quick fix for their fuel needs, creating a bonanza for suppliers in the Middle East, Europe, and Australia but putting stress on processing and port-handling facilities.

Meanwhile, Yoshihiko Noda, who took over from Naoto Kan as Japanese prime minister in September 2011, pledged to get some of the country's nuclear power stations running again while the politicians and the bureaucrats worked on a long-term recovery plan. Noda reaffirmed that no new nuclear power stations would be built, and existing plants would be decommissioned at the end of their useful life.[9] Kan had set the wheels in motion soon after Fukushima, declaring that Japan's previous goal of 50 percent nuclear power by 2030 was out the window and the country would need to start from scratch on a new energy plan.

Son, like other observers, noted that while nuclear power was supposed to supply 30 percent of Japan's energy needs, by midyear the country was making do with only 16 of its reactors operating (a figure that would fall even lower to five in January 2012, with capacity of just over 5 GW, compared with 54 commercial reactors generating 49 GW before the earthquake). The other plants were offline for regular maintenance or undergoing stress tests in the wake of Fukushima. With power demand in Japan falling as people became more energy conscious, Son posed the question: Was nuclear power truly necessary? He suggested a nuclear "minimalist" approach: Do an audit to determine how much nonnuclear energy could be generated in Japan, match it to a demand already trimmed back through extensive use of energy-saving devices, and then make up any shortfall from nuclear power until new energy could be found to replace it. Son concedes that the cost of renewable energy is high, but argues than in 10, 20, or 30 years' time, technology will have reduced that cost substantially.

> The extensive debate about energy that emerged in the aftermath of the disaster has made me keenly aware of something that is obvious, but easily taken for granted: that telecommunications, and the information revolution itself, depend by their very nature upon the availability of energy. . . in pursuit of our vision we have therefore started a new initiative to examine the possibilities of developing a business around power generation from renewable energy sources.
> —*Masayoshi Son, Internet entrepreneur and SoftBank founder, August 2011*

Indicative of Son's approach is his suggestion that farmland contaminated by seawater from the tsunami be revitalized not for agriculture but as an "East Japan Solar Belt" that would create jobs and exploit Japan's capability in solar technology. He argues that the government should take the lead in creating a recovery project built on producing new energy, in which "ports of the past could gain new life as ports of solar and wind energy."[10]

After the Fukushima disaster, Japan's nuclear power plant usage plummeted. It hit a record low of 10.3 percent in January 2012, down from 67 percent a year earlier. There was other damage too, to the country's energy infrastructure from the earthquake and tsunami: refineries and gas and oil-fired power plants and the electricity grid itself were all affected. For Son and others such as SunEdison, which has a five-year $4.6 billion plan to build solar power plants in Japan, the clear answer was alternative energy—primarily solar and wind. But fossil fuel dominates the electricity mix in Japan, and weaning producers and consumers away is likely to be a slow process. Even hydropower plays a relatively small role in Japan, despite a water-rich, mountainous environment that is ideal for this form of power. Hydro accounts for about 3 percent of Japan's energy needs, though the installed capacity is closer to 8 percent. A number of large hydro projects are in the wings, including Tepco's 2,820 MW Kannagawa twin-dam pumped-storage plant on the Minamiaiki River between Nagano and Gumma prefectures in central Japan. Tepco put the plant's first 470 MW unit into production in December 2005 and aims to have all six units operating by 2020. It is the world's largest pure pumped-storage plant, with water pumped from the lower dam to the higher one during off-peak hours and then released later to meet peak power demand.

Renewable Potential

With about 4 GW of installed capacity, solar, wind, and geothermal provide less than 1 percent of Japan's energy, but may offer the most potential. The Japanese government's targets are 28 GW of solar power by 2020, increasing to 53 GW by 2030, and 10 percent of domestic primary energy demand to be met by solar by 2050. Japan already has a strong solar PV industry, ranked third in the world behind Germany and Spain in installed capacity. Solar panel producers Kyocera, Sharp, Mitsubishi Electric, and Sanyo are among the top global makers. But in installed wind power capacity—an area dominated by the United States, China, India, and Europe—Japan ranks only thirteenth, and apart from Mitsubishi Heavy Industries it has no maker on a scale to rank with global turbine producers

Vestas, GE, Sinovel, Goldwind, Gamesa, Suzlon, and Siemens. The Japan Wind Energy Association has set its own targets of 11 GW by 2020 (up from 2.3 GW in 2011), rising to 50 GW by 2050, or about the same scale as solar power.

Son's entrepreneurial spirit is a powerful change agent in Japan, but whichever directions the country's energy supply needs take over the next 30 years, almost certainly its biggest trading houses and corporations will have a role in the sourcing, finance, technology, and distribution of energy. An example is the backing given by oil company Inpex and Mitsubishi Chemical to the energy and environment-focused Kaiteki Institute and its work on a hydrogen generation process led by Professor Kazunari Domen of Tokyo University's School of Engineering. The process, where a photocatalyst is driven by sunlight to split water into hydrogen and oxygen, is viewed as a promising medium to long-range renewable energy alternative.[11]

Notes

1. Japanese Ministry of Defense, 2011 White Paper, Tokyo, 2 August 2011.
2. Chinese Foreign Ministry spokesperson Ma Zhaoxu, Beijing, 3 August 2011, reacting to Japan's Defense White Paper.
3. James Dobbins, David Gompert, David Shlapak, Andrew Scobell, Occasional Paper, *Conflict with China: Prospects, Consequences, and Strategies for Deterrence*, (Santa Monica: RAND Corporation), October 2011.
4. Ross Garnaut, *Australia and the Northeast Asian Ascendancy* (Canberra: Australian Government Publishing Service, 1989), p. 36.
5. Ibid., p. 13.
6. Ibid., p. 36.
7. HSBC, "The World in 2050," Hong Kong, January 2011.
8. Goldman Sachs, "BRICs and Beyond," 23 November 2007.
9. Remarks at Prime Minister Yoshihiko Noda's press conference, 2 September 2011.
10. Son, Masayoshi, "Tsunami Clears Way for Solar-Powered Japan," *Asia Times*, 23 September 2011.
11. Prof. Kazunari Domen, "Development of Photocatalysts for Energy Conversion," www.domen.t.u-tokyo.ac.jp/english/index_framepage_E .html.

CHAPTER 13

BRACQK (Brazil, Russia, Australia, Canada, Qatar, Kazakhstan) Is the New BRIC

Russia cannot be great and will not remain a great power if we do not develop the Far East region.
—former Russian Prime Minister Yevgeny Primakov, November 1998 (ITAR-TASS report)

Brazil, Russia, Australia, Canada, Qatar, and Kazakhstan (the BRACQKs) have one thing in common: an abundance of energy resources, including oil and gas, that make them attractive investment targets for big energy consumers such as China and India. While Saudi Arabia, Kuwait, Iraq, Iran, and Venezuela continue to be the main short-term oil plays, every oil and gas major is keen to have a piece of the long-term BRACQK action. In some cases, the operating challenges they face are enormous—Brazilian pre-salt oil, Russian Arctic gas, Australian LNG (liquefied natural gas) from the cyclone-prone North West Shelf, or Canadian oil sands all have technological and environmental difficulties. Qatar's bountiful North Dome gas field looks a walk in the park by comparison, while Kazakhstan's Caspian Sea reserves suffer from a combination of logistical, financial, and political pressures in a geographic setting that is unusually harsh.

We start with Russia, because that is perhaps where the greatest challenges and rewards lie, particularly in the area above the Arctic

203

Circle. In 2008, the U.S. Geological Survey completed its resource appraisal for the entire circum-Arctic region, which it said covered more than 21 million sq km (8.2 million sq miles), or 6 percent, of the Earth's surface, including almost 8 million sq km (3.1 million sq miles) of onshore land and more than 7 million sq km (2.7 million sq miles) on continental shelves under less than 500 m of water. "The extensive Arctic continental shelves may constitute the geographically largest unexplored prospective area for petroleum remaining on Earth," it said.[1]

To fully appreciate the significance of the Arctic, we need to step back a century. In October 1904, Russian Tsar Nicholas II ordered his Baltic fleet to leave its northern European base and make its way to the Far East, where a land war with Japan over economic and strategic interests in Manchuria and Korea was going badly. Eight months earlier, the Russian Pacific squadron based in Port Arthur (modern-day Dalian in China) had been hard-hit by a surprise Japanese torpedo-boat attack. Now, after a couple of disastrous forays that caused further losses, the Russian ships were reluctant or unable to run the Japanese blockade. Port Arthur was under siege from Japanese land-based gunners and would fall by January 1905. With the Suez Canal unavailable to the Russian warships because of British opposition, the 45 vessels in the Russian Baltic fleet were forced to sail down the coast of Africa, around the Cape of Good Hope, stopover in Madagascar for provisions, then head east across the Indian Ocean to French Indo-China, before turning north for the run to Vladivostok. After an arduous eight-month voyage of 18,000 nautical miles (33,000 km), the fleet's commander, Admiral Zinovy Rozhestvensky, was out of luck and out of time. His crews were fatigued and unhappy and his ships were slow. The Japanese fleet commanded by Admiral Heihachiro Togo intercepted the Russians in the Straits of Tsushima (between Korea and Japan) on May 27, 1905, and virtually wiped out its opponents in a battle that brought the Russo-Japanese war to an end. All of Rozhestvensky's eight battleships were lost, and only three Russian ships out of 38 involved in the battle made it to Vladivostok. It would be another three decades before ships of the Baltic fleet were to be seen again in these waters.

Transporting hydrocarbons through the Northern Sea Route is expected to reduce the costs and delivery time for shipments from Russia's northern ports to consumers in the Asian-Pacific region.

—*Russian independent gas producer Novatek, 15 July 2011*

In the 2010s, Russian ships seeking to make fast time to the Far East have a choice of routes, and the speediest of them all is the NSR, or Northern Sea Route, that in the summer months allows an ice-ready bulk carrier to sail from Murmansk on the Kola Peninsula, along the Russian north coast through Arctic waters to the Bering Strait, into the Pacific Ocean and on to a Japanese, Korean, or Chinese port in just three weeks. The NSR, also known as the North East Passage, has been a dream of explorers and traders since the sixteenth century. For most of those adventurers, the icebound seas and harsh climate of Siberia proved impenetrable, but Danish navigator Vitus Bering and other seafarers in the seventeenth, eighteenth, and nineteenth centuries showed that in favorable conditions it could be done. By the early 1930s, Soviet expeditions had mapped out a course for commercial shipping, and in 1936, warships of the Baltic fleet for the first time sailed through the Bering Strait into the Pacific. The route was used both by the Germans and the Allies during World War II. In the postwar Soviet era, cargo ships helped by nuclear-powered icebreakers sometimes used the route, and in the 1960s it was touted as an alternative to the Suez that could save two weeks on a run between Hamburg and Yokohama. Because of the ice, the escort cost and the special ship requirements, the NSR has not been a popular choice, but the coming development of Russia's vast gas fields in the Yamal-Nenets region of northern Siberia has revived interest in its potential. Using the NSR, Murmansk to China's Ningbo port near Shanghai is just 7,000 nautical miles (13,000 km), compared with 12,000 miles (22,000 km) via the Mediterranean Sea, Suez Canal, Indian Ocean, and Straits of Malacca.

In the northern summer of 2011, Russian gas producer Novatek opened the NSR sailing season early, sending a 60,000-tonne cargo of gas condensate aboard the MV Perseverance from Murmansk on June 29, arriving at Ningbo three weeks later. It was the first of seven tankers it would send to Asia via the NSR in 2011, aided by icebreakers such as the nuclear-powered NS Yamal. The NSR has its limitations— a short sailing season, the cost of hiring icebreakers, and the hazards of extreme northern waters—but Novatek says the route is an integral part of the company's logistical strategy to develop prospective gas fields in the Yamal peninsula, an area that holds as much as 83 percent of Russia's gas reserves.[2]

Novatek, controlled by billionaire chief executive Leonid Mikhelson, took a major step forward for its $15 billion Yamal LNG development in early 2011 when it secured French oil major Total as its main international partner. Total took a 12 percent stake in the project for $4 billion, with a commitment to lift that to 20 percent within three years. Novatek's key shareholders with Mikhelson (27.2 percent) include state-owned gas major Gazprom (10 percent) and Volga Resources (23.5 percent), the Luxembourg investment vehicle of Gennady Timchenko, owner with Torbjörn Tornqvist of the oil trading firm Gunvor. The Yamal LNG project will develop Novatek's South Tambey field, which contains an estimated 1.25 trillion cubic metres (44 trillion cubic feet) of gas. First production is due in 2016, with output expected to reach 15 million tonnes of LNG a year by 2018. Mikhelson says Novatek will hold 51 percent of the Yamal project and that other overseas investors will be invited to join. Yamal is not Total's only Russian investment. It also has a 25 percent stake in Gazprom's huge Shtokman field, which is due to deliver its first LNG in 2017. As a deepwater field about 600 km north of the Kola Peninsula in the Barents Sea, Shtokman poses extreme engineering and environmental challenges, not least the risk of iceberg collisions. To overcome this, the developers plan to use floating removable platforms. Shtokman's reserves are estimated at 3.8 trillion cubic metres of gas and 37 million tonnes of gas condensate.

Yamal and Shtokman are just two of the many energy projects that could deliver substantial wealth to Russia and the overseas bidders it allows in. Russian Prime Minister Vladimir Putin approves all of the country's major energy deals and is destined to remain the country's pivotal political figure, if he resumes the presidency after the March 2012 presidential election. The best oil and gas prospects are to be found in five broad areas—the Arctic Shelf (Shtokman and the Kara Sea), the Yamal-Nenets autonomous region (South Tambey), the Krasnoyarsk region of Eastern Siberia (Rosneft's Vankor field), the Caspian Sea in the south, where LUKOIL—Russia's largest nonstate oil producer—has the Korchagin and Filanovsky projects, and the enormous Sakhalin 1–5 projects in the Russian Far East where Gazprom and Rosneft have a swag of partners who include ExxonMobil, Shell, India's ONGC, and Japanese trading companies Mitsui and Mitsubishi. In Nenets, state-owned Zarubezhneft and its partner PetroVietnam began producing in 2011.

As well, several existing Russian oil fields in the West Siberian basin are ranked among the biggest producers in the world, including the Samotlor field, owned by the Russia-UK joint venture TNK-BP, and the Priobskoye field run by Rosneft and GazpromNeft. Oil and gas exports account for almost half of Russia's budget revenues, and that share may rise as more of the mega-projects come on stream over the next decade.

Uncertainty for Foreign Investment

But uncertainty is likely to continue to plague the foreign investment scene, given that parts of the Russian oil and gas sector still do business in mysterious ways, and the oligarchs who bought the best energy assets for a song from the state in the 1990s have no intention of relinquishing their privileged positions. BP, for example, lost its $16 billion asset swap and chance to work with Rosneft in the Arctic's Kara Sea exploration because the AAR consortium that is BP's partner in TNK-BP thought it should control what BP does in Russia. Putin had backed the BP-Rosneft alliance, but when that deal fell through, he was happy to endorse ExxonMobil as Rosneft's new partner a few months later. Exxon agreed to invest $2.2 billion in Arctic exploration of the East Prinovozemelsky blocks and another $1 billion in the Black Sea. Rosneft gained a notable first for a Russian state-owned company: access to U.S. energy projects, including Texas "tight" oilfields and deepwater fields in the Gulf of Mexico.[3]

The biggest issue for investment in Russia remains official corruption and bureaucratic inertia, with "no pay, no play" even more endemic in Moscow and its far-flung administrations than in China or India. That is borne out by Transparency International's corruption perception rating for Russia of 154 out of 178 nations, compared to 78 for China and 87 for India. Putin and his protégé Dmitry Medvedev, who are due to swap roles as prime minister and president in the first half of 2012, have the task ahead of them if they are to stage successfully the October 2012 APEC summit in Vladivostok and the 2014 Winter Olympics at Sochi on the Black Sea, the two international events they envisage as a showcase of glorious modern Russia.

Brazil's Pre-Salt Independence

Glorious modernity is not a goal restricted to the Russians. When former Marxist guerilla Dilma Rousseff took over as Brazilian president on January 3, 2011, she named alleviating poverty as the focal point of her economic policy. It was a recognition that while Brazil may be on a fast track to international prestige with the World Cup in 2014 and the Olympic Games in 2016, many of Rousseff's 195 million fellow countrymen and women still don't have enough food to eat, nor decent housing, education, or affordable health services. What Brazil does have is a resources pool deep enough and rich enough to fund all this and more, if it is handled well. Those resources include iron ore, manganese, bauxite, other minerals, vast timber and agricultural estates, and on the energy front, hydropower and biofuels such as ethanol. But most of all, Brazil has oil—a fact that has attracted the attention of ExxonMobil, Shell, Chevron, Total, BP, BG, Spain's Repsol, China's Sinopec, India's ONGC, Norway's Statoil, and even the Russian consortium TNK-BP.

In 2006, then state-controlled oil company Petrobras and its partners BG Group of the UK and Portugal's Galp Energia discovered the Tupi pre-salt oil and gas field (so named because the oil lies below a salt layer) in the deepwater Santos basin, an area of the South Atlantic Ocean about 250 km (155 miles) south of Rio de Janeiro. It was a find destined to turn the oil world upside down, as further discoveries lifted the size of the possible resources in Santos and the neighbouring Campos and Espirito Santo basins to as much as 80 to 100 billion barrels of oil equivalent, rendering it the biggest new hydrocarbon field of the decade. Petrobras had already found oil in these waters as far back as 1985, starting with the Marlim fields in the Campos basin, but the depth of the pre-salt discoveries put it at the outer limits of the company's logistical and technical capacity. If Petrobras and its partners could master the technology and the economics of bringing up the high-quality, low-sulfur oil, held as much as 7 km below the sea surface and buried beneath rock and layers of salt, it would transform Brazil into one of the largest oil producers in the world. Rousseff's predecessor as president, Luiz Inacio Lula da Silva, called the Tupi field Brazil's "second independence."

By 2011, Petrobras—which raised $70 billion in a 2010 share offer that delivered 51 percent of the company to private investors—had renamed the Tupi field "Lula" (Portuguese for "squid" and the nickname of the country's recent president) and was preparing to spend $73 billion with its partners over the ensuing five years to develop the Santos basin pre-salt cluster. Petrobras was compelled to pick up another asset along the way; as part of the 2010 share sale, it was required to pay the Brazilian government $42.5 billion in Petrobras stock for a "transfer of rights" that gave it access to another 5 billion barrels of recoverable oil equivalent in adjoining pre-salt areas. The government also changed the investment dynamic, bringing in a new law for the pre-salt regions that specified Petrobras would have a 30 percent stake in all future consortia and would be the lead operator of all new projects. The industry grumbled, but Brazil's government was adamant that it would control the way the pre-salt riches were to be shared. On the technical front, Petrobras moved to expand its deepwater experience from the 1,000 m of the 1985–1987 Marlim fields to depths of 2,000 m and beyond. At the same time, it began work on the extra onshore logistics needed to handle the building of the deepwater production platforms it would position in the South Atlantic. It refreshed the helicopter fleets—mainly Sikorsky S76 and S92 crew-carriers that would be taking workers to the rigs on return trips of 600 km over water. All of these elements would become a regular part of pre-salt life.

By late 2010 Petrobras had its first floating production, storage, and offloading (FPSO) platform sitting in the Lula Pilot field, moored 300 km off the coast in water more than 2,000 m deep. Another seven FPSO platforms, each able to produce 150,000 barrels of oil and 6 million cubic meters of gas a day, are being built at the Rio Grande Shipyard Complex for Lula, with two more planned for the Lula Nordeste and Guará fields. Along with the FPSOs and multiple drilling rigs, there will be hundreds of kilometres of under-water gas pipelines to link the production units. By 2017, Petrobras expects to have 13 production platforms in the Santos basin pre-salt cluster, with production activity focused on Lula's 6.5 billion barrels of recoverable oil and gas, and Guará's 2 billion barrels. Another new field, Franco, may have 4.5 billion barrels. Waiting in the wings for the right development window in the Santos basin is the Libra field, potentially the biggest of them all with possible reserves of 15 billion barrels, according to Brazil's petroleum industry regulator ANP. If and when it is developed, Libra will be held 40 percent by Brazil's newly formed state oil company, Pre-Sal Petroleo, and 30 percent by Petrobras. All of this means that for the next decade at least, the epicentre of the world's deepwater oil activity will be Brazil.

The demand for what Petrobras terms critical resources, cover-ing drilling rigs, supply vessels, FPSO platforms and jackets is simply immense—more than 700 of these resources will be in operation by 2020. The pre-salt areas are taking 45 percent of Petrobras's total

$127.5 billion budget for exploration and production in 2011–2015, but the rewards are expected to soon become apparent.

Petrobras is learning how to keep costs down as it goes along. Eduardo Molinari, exploration and production strategy coordinator for Petrobras, told an oil conference in London in 2011 that back in 2006, it took 270 days to drill the first well in the pre-salt area. "We did have problems drilling through the salt. We have learned from that experience. It cost us $240 million for that first well. Now we can drill a well in 90 days at $1 million a day."[4] According to Molinari, the breakeven for pre-salt oil is $40 to $45 a barrel, including both capital and operating costs. Pre-salt's share of the company's domestic oil output will rise from 2 percent in 2011 to more than 40 percent by 2020, when Petrobras expects to be producing almost 5 million barrels a day of oil equivalent in Brazil, and another 1.5 million barrels from its fields outside Brazil—mainly Argentina, Bolivia, and Nigeria.

Although Petrobras is far and away the frontrunner in Brazil's oil and gas sector, there are several smaller local companies, including OGX Petroleo & Gas, owned by resources and infrastructure tycoon Eike Batista. Batista, a flamboyant billionaire industrialist, set up OGX in 2007 as part of his EBX industrial group. The company raised $4 billion in an initial public share offer in June 2008, and now holds licences for 29 offshore blocks in the Santos, Campos, Espirito Santo, Para-Maranhao, and Parnaiba basins. Successful finds in the Campos basin sent the company's market capitalization soaring above $40 billion, before it halved in late 2011. OGX positioned its first FPSO platform in the Campos basin in January 2012. Batista wants Petrobras and iron ore giant Vale to use the Acu port complex that his logistics arm LLX is building about 200 km east of Rio de Janeiro. In April 2011 OGX said potential resources for all of its fields in Brazil and Colombia totalled 10.8 billion barrels of oil equivalent. OGX says it expects its first natural gas to flow from its Parnaiba basin field in 2013, and hopes to produce its first oil outside Brazil from one of its Colombian wells in 2012. Another name in this sector is HRT Participacoes em Petroleo, a company set up by former Petrobras staff in 2004. It raised about $1.5 billion in a 2010 initial share offer to fund its exploration work in Brazil and Africa. It is drilling for oil on land in the Solimoes Basin of Amazonas state, in the northwest of Brazil, and off the coast of Namibia in southern Africa.

China, in the shape of Sinopec and CNPC, has come late in the rush to explore the oil and gas riches of South America. So far,

Brazil and Argentina are Sinopec's main investment destinations there, following two key purchases in 2010. In October of that year it agreed to buy 40 percent of Spanish oil major Repsol's Brazilian operations for $7.1 billion, and followed that two months later with a deal to buy U.S.-based Occidental's assets in Argentina for $2.45 billion. In mid-2011 Sinopec and its joint venture partner Repsol-YPF found high-quality crude at Gavea in the Campos basin, one of the six Brazilian blocks where Repsol Sinopec is the operator. Repsol called the find the "most significant" yet in the Campos pre-salt area. A few months later, Sinopec added another Brazilian asset: 30 percent of Portuguese energy company Galp Energia's assets there, which include offshore oil blocks. Sinopec is paying $5 billion for the stake. In contrast, CNPC (PetroChina) has had most of its success in Peru and Venezuela, where it has been the operator of several large fields such as Intercampo and Caricoles since the late 1990s. In Brazil, CNPC struck an agreement in 2005 with Petrobras to look for business opportunities together, but nothing much came of it until 2011, when CNPC's oil equipment unit Baoji Oilfield Machinery said it was setting up a joint venture with two Brazilian companies that are key suppliers to Petrobras.

Compared to China, India has a relatively small presence in Brazil. ONGC has invested about $400 million in Brazil and operates several oil fields in the Santos, Campos, and Espirito Santo basins with Petrobras that produce about 40,000 barrels a day.

Australia's Foot on the Gas

Good luck, good timing, good geography, good government, or good investors? Whatever the reason, Australia's reputation as a lucky country blessed with more natural resources than it knows what to do with is set to continue as the world enters what the International Energy Agency suggests is a "golden era" for gas. The sharp turn away from nuclear power after the Fukushima disaster in Japan simply accelerated what was a gathering trend toward gas as an apparently safer, cleaner energy source. Qatar is the world's LNG export powerhouse, but it may be joined at the top or even overtaken within the decade if a string of proposed Australian gas projects come to life. Where Brazil goes for marine life in naming its fields, the Australian ones run the gamut from the prosaic—Goodwyn, North Rankin—to the mythic: Perseus, Pluto, Gorgon, Xena. As many as 12 gas export terminals are planned around the Australian coastline, boosting supply capacity to somewhere between 60 and 100 million tonnes of gas a year by 2020.

That would give it the potential to become the world's largest LNG exporter, particularly if power utilities in China, Japan, and Korea keep the contracts rolling in. Asian buyers favour Australian LNG because it is cheaper to ship than gas from Qatar or other Middle East fields, and they can get project equity to further ensure the security of their supply. As well, the route from Australia to North Asia can avoid the Strait of Malacca, a chokepoint where oil tankers and bulk carriers can be vulnerable. But talk is cheap, and all the potential in the world comes to naught without finance and project execution skills. To bring all of these proposed terminals onstream would require thousands of skilled workers and massive technology and infrastructure upgrades within an investment cost of about $200 billion over the next decade. As much as $75 billion of that could come from projects on the books of Australia's Woodside Petroleum, operator for the past 25 years of the major North West Shelf (NWS) oil and gas fields.

As the name implies, the NWS fields sit on the continental shelf off the remote northwest coast of Australia, stretching for hundreds of kilometers across the Carnarvon Basin in the warm waters of the Indian Ocean. The depths here are nowhere like those of the Brazilian pre-salt fields; most of the platforms stand in water less than 200 m deep, though a few go up to about 1,000 m and the gas itself is up to 3,500 m below the seabed. What makes the North West Shelf a difficult working environment is that this area is part of Australia's *cyclone alley*. In the cyclone season that begins as early as November and can run as late as April–May, powerful tropical storms with winds up to 250 km/h can swirl in from the Indian Ocean, shutting down the platforms—some of which are 250 km or more offshore—and dumping vast amounts of rain onto the onshore communities that support the NWS oil and gas industry.

Woodside brought its first gas ashore in 1984, and shipped its first gas to Japan in 1989. Woodside has five equal partners—each with a 16.67 percent share—in what is known as the North West Shelf Venture: BHP Billiton, BP, Shell, Chevron, and Japan Australia LNG (MIMI). The last entity is a 50–50 joint venture between Mitsubishi Corp. and Mitsui & Co. Since 2006, China National Offshore Oil Corp. (CNOOC) has had an interest in the North West Shelf Venture's reserves, but not its infrastructure. CNOOC pioneered the Australia-China gas trade with a 25-year contract that sees LNG imported through a terminal in southern China operated by Guangdong Dapeng LNG. The main producing fields are Perseus, Goodwyn, North Rankin, Angel, and Cossack Pioneer, with a new project known as Pluto expected to start sending gas to Japanese customers in 2012. Pluto will start with a single LNG processing train of 4.3 million tonnes a year, but more trains are likely to be added. Further to the north in the Browse Basin, Woodside has three fields in planning, 400 km off the coast, with a proposed LNG onshore processing plant about 60 km north of the town of Broome. Its equity partners in Browse include BHP Billiton, BP, Chevron, and Shell. A Deutsche Bank report in August 2011 estimated that the two-stage Pluto project and the Browse project between them would cost $63 billion.

Japan's Inpex—which has the Japanese government as its biggest single shareholder—and its partner Total also have a $34 billion development in the Browse Basin named Ichthys (Greek for "fish"). The field contains an estimated 12.8 trillion cubic feet of gas and 527 million barrels of condensate. Inpex plans to pipe the gas to a new LNG processing facility in the north Australian city of Darwin. The city already has substantial gas infrastructure—since 2006, ConocoPhillips has run Australia's second operational LNG export terminal from Darwin, drawing gas through a 500-km subsea pipeline from its Bayu-Undan field in the Timor Sea and sending it to Japan. ConocoPhillips's customers (and equity holders in the project) are Tokyo Gas and Tokyo Electric Power Co. Italy's Eni, the Australian gas explorer and producer Santos and Inpex are also shareholders.

Australia's gas potential has drawn the attention of all the oil majors, with Chevron taking the lead in the single biggest new development, the $43 billion three-train Gorgon project that will likely draw its first gas in 2014 from the Greater Gorgon fields about 130 km off the coast of Western Australia. The project includes a 15 million tonne a year LNG plant on Barrow Island and a domestic gas plant to supply Western Australia. Chevron has 47 percent; its partners include Shell and ExxonMobil, each with a 25 percent stake, and three Japanese utilities. The customer base covers Japan, China, and India.

Shell is the lead operator of the $10 billion Prelude project, which will use the world's first floating LNG production facility, drawing gas from the Prelude and Concerto fields in the Browse Basin, about

475 km from Broome on the north coast of Western Australia. Shell says that the relatively small size of the gas fields (3 trillion cubic feet/85 billion cubic metres) and their remote location make them an "ideal candidate" for a floating LNG processing plant. The Prelude plant being built by Samsung Heavy Industries in South Korea will be the world's largest floating structure at 488 m long, 74 m wide, and 600,000 tonnes in weight when fully loaded. About 260,000 tonnes of that weight will be steel. The floating plant has been designed to handle a Category 5 tropical cyclone (wind speed above 250 km/h), and will be anchored by four sets of massive chains in water 250 m deep. This project, off the north coast of Western Australia, is expected to begin production in 2016 or 2017, with South Korean state-owned utility Korea Gas (KoGas) taking a 10 percent stake in Prelude and committing to buy 3.64 million tonnes a year for 20 years.

> The Prelude floating LNG plant is being called a "facility" rather than a "ship," though it can be moved to a new location if necessary. The largest ship ever built was the oil tanker Seawise Giant, which was 458 m long and weighed 657,000 tonnes when fully loaded. Built in Japan in 1979 for C.Y. Tung's Island Navigation Corp, the Seawise Giant went through four name changes and one sinking during the Iraq-Iran war before ending its life as a floating storage tanker in the Persian Gulf. The vessel was sent to India and scrapped in 2010.[5]

Chevron is the operator for another large LNG export project, known as Wheatstone, that it proposes to build near Onslow in Western Australia, with a first-phase capability of 8.9 million tonnes a year. Tokyo Electric Power Co. has agreed to buy 3.1 million tonnes a year for up to 20 years. Chevron plans to start the $30 billion two-train project in 2016 and make first gas deliveries in 2017 to Tokyo Electric Power and two other customers, Kyushu Electric Power and KoGas. Shell bought a 6.4 percent stake in the Wheatstone project in 2011 and will also take a stake in Chevron's Wheatstone and Iago fields that will supply gas to the export terminal. The other equity participants in Wheatstone are U.S.-based Apache Corp. (13 percent) and Kuwait Foreign Petroleum Exploration (Kufpec) with 7 percent, leaving Chevron with 73.6 percent.

Pluto, Gorgon, Prelude, and Wheatstone are all based on Australia's west coast, but there is also activity on the east coast, near the industrial city of Gladstone in Queensland, where at least four large LNG plants are proposed using coal-seam gas from the southern and central Queensland gas fields. Coal-seam gas (CSG), also known as coal-bed methane (CBM), is methane trapped underground, and is one of several sources of unconventional natural gas, along with shale gas and "tight" gas (usually found in sandstone reservoirs) that require hydraulic fracturing, or fracking (see Chapter 11 for a description of fracking). As in the United States, there is opposition in Australia to the fracking process. The technology for converting CSG to LNG for export is at an early stage, but the various groups planning to ship from Gladstone are pushing ahead with their plants. The two most advanced projects are known as Queensland Curtis (led by BG Group) and Gladstone LNG (led by Santos). Between them, they have a range of equity and supply deals with customers in China, Japan, South Korea, and Singapore. The $15 billion two-train project at Queensland Curtis will produce around 8.4 million tonnes a year from 2014, using CSG brought from the Surat basin by pipeline to Curtis Island at Gladstone for processing, while the $16 billion Gladstone LNG project will have two trains producing up to 7.8 million tonnes from 2015. Queensland Curtis has signed three 20-year supply agreements with China National Offshore Oil Corp. (CNOOC), Tokyo Gas and a group of customers in Singapore. It also has a 21-year supply deal with GNL Quintero in Chile, in which BG Group is a shareholder. The Gladstone LNG partners are Santos of Australia, Petronas of Malaysia, Total of France, and KoGas, which has agreed to take 3.5 million tonnes of gas a year. This project will bring CSG from southern Queensland gas fields. Separately, CNOOC has invested $50 million in junior explorer Exoma Energy, which holds petroleum exploration permits in Queensland's Galilee Basin and is looking for CSG and shale gas there.

A third project known as Australia Pacific LNG involves ConocoPhillips in a joint venture with Origin Energy. It envisages bringing CSG from the Surat and Bowen basins via a 450 km pipeline to Gladstone for processing into LNG, before shipment to Asia. Sinopec is the first customer, signing two 20-year agreements to buy up to 7.6 million tonnes a year from 2014–2015. Sinopec also has a 25 percent stake in the project, which could eventually grow to four trains with processing capacity of 16 million tonnes a year. At $35 billion, it is the largest gas project on the Australian east coast.

A fourth proposal, known as Shell Australia LNG, is a joint venture between Shell and PetroChina, the two companies that bought Australian midsize gas producer Arrow Energy in 2010 for $3.4 billion. Through their Arrow Energy joint venture, Shell and PetroChina paid $520 million in September 2011 for Australian coal-seam gas producer Bow Energy. The $10 billion Shell proposal is for two processing trains, each of 4 million tonnes a year capacity, to be built on Curtis Island.

While a flurry of oil and gas activity convulses the Australian east and west coasts, down in Bass Strait, a wild stretch of water that separates the Australian mainland from the southern island of Tasmania, ExxonMobil and partner BHP Billiton continue with their Gippsland Basin fields that pioneered the country's offshore industry in the late 1960s. These fields still produce substantial amounts of oil and gas more than 40 years after their discovery, and they account for 30 percent of Australia's total cumulative gas production and almost two-thirds of cumulative oil production. BHP, Santos, and Woodside have all made more recent discoveries in the Otway Basin to the west of Bass Strait.

Canada's Athabasca Challenge

> We were devastated by what we saw and smelled and experienced. The air is foul, the water is being drained and poisoned and giant tailing ponds line the Athabasca River.
> —Maude Barlow, Canadian environmentalist and senior advisor to the United Nations on water, after visiting the Alberta oil sands in October 2008 (Edmonton Sun, 2 November 2008)

Oil sands are deposits of bitumen (thick, heavy crude oil) mixed with sand, clay, and water. At various times considered too expensive, too hard to get at, and leaving too big a mark on the environment (an argument that is not likely to go away), the oil sands of Canada's Athabasca basin in Alberta province rank as the world's biggest deposit of its type. For 40 years, Athabasca has been the standard-bearer of the unconventional oil industry, and now looms as a resource coming into its own as the global oil price equation changes. According to the International Energy Agency, between now and 2035, unconventional oil will play an increasingly important role in world oil supply, "regardless of what governments do to curb demand."[6] The IEA expects unconventional output to rise from 2.3 million barrels a day in 2009 to 9.5 million in 2035, with Canadian oil sands and Venezuelan extra-heavy oil dominating the mix. Coal-to-liquids, gas-to-liquids, and oil shales also will make a contribution.

The world's unconventional oil resources are huge—in the case of Canada, 170 billion barrels of its estimated total oil reserves of 175 billion barrels are in oil sands, lying under about 140,000 sq km of land spread over three main deposits: Athabasca, Peace River, and Cold Lake.

Critics of oil sands say that their production process—either by in-situ drilling or by surface mining—uses large amounts of water, pollutes the ecosystem, and emits more greenhouse gases per barrel than conventional oil fields. But, the IEA says, on a "well-to-wheels" basis, carbon dioxide emissions from Canadian oil sands are only between 5 and 15 percent higher than for conventional crude oil.

The pioneer of the Athabasca oil sands is Canada's third-largest listed company, Suncor Energy, which began commercial develop-ment there in 1967 as Great Canadian Oil Sands (GCOS), part of the original Sun Oil. Other major companies operating in the oil sands include Canadian Natural Resources, Syncrude Canada (a syn-thetic oil joint venture between seven companies), Shell, ExxonMobil, Chevron, ConocoPhillips, Total, Statoil, Devon Canada, and Imperial Oil. Petro-Canada, formed in 1974 by the Canadian government, was active in the oil sands until its merger in 2009 with Suncor. Scores of smaller prospectors also are in the mix, along with some heavy-weight international investors. China's Sinopec has a 9 percent stake in Syncrude, bought from ConocoPhillips in 2010 for about $4.65 billion, and 50 percent of Total's as-yet undeveloped Northern Lights project. PetroChina is an investor in Athabasca Oil Sands Corp., which hopes to develop oil sands properties with potential output of 500,000 barrels a day. China Investment Corp. has a 45 percent stake in Penn West Energy Trust's Peace River projects, while CNOOC holds a 16.7 percent stake in MEG Energy's northern Alberta project. Thailand's PTT Exploration and Production agreed to pay almost $2.3 billion in 2010 for 40 percent of Statoil's Kai Kos Dehseh project. Japanese and South Korean energy and investment companies also have taken positions in various oil sands projects. Indian companies ONGC Videsh, GAIL, and Reliance Industries have looked at the oil sands, but there have been no commitments so far. The IEA, in its energy outlook to 2035, says that the rate at which the Canadian oil sands and other unconventional oil deposits are exploited will be determined by "economic and environmental considerations, including the costs of mitigating their environmental impact."[7] The cost may be high—oil extracted from the oil sands needs to be upgraded before it can be transported by pipeline or used in conventional refineries—but the resource base is enormous. One example is Canadian Natural Resources' Horizon Oil Sands operation north of Fort McMurray in the Athabasca basin, where the company produced its first synthetic crude oil (SCO) in 2009. Canadian Natural says its Horizon mine and plant facilities are expected to produce for decades to come without the production declines normally associated with crude oil fields. "At full production, we target the operating cost for the life of the mine to be between $25 and $35 per barrel of SCO," it said in 2011.[8] Rival Syncrude Canada runs the world's largest oil sands facility and has been producing since 1978 at its Mildred Lake plant, where the raw oil is upgraded into sweet light crude and sent by pipeline to refineries in the Edmonton area, or further afield. At peak pipeline rates, it takes three days for oil to travel the 450 km from Fort McMurray to Edmonton.

The Canadian Association of Petroleum Producers (CAPP) maintains that mining could affect only 3 percent of the oil sands land in Alberta because the rest is recoverable by in-situ drilling. Drilling uses about half a barrel of fresh water for every barrel of oil produced, while mining requires two to four barrels of water, according to the CAPP. The Athabasca River is the main source of water for the oil sands mining projects, with 179 million cubic metres of water used in 2009. Oil sands producers recycle between 80 and 95 percent of the water they use, according to the CAPP. That does not satisfy the objections of groups opposed to the oil sands mining, who say that billions of litres of contaminated water is dumped into Alberta's groundwater, while mining contributes to acid rain over Alberta and Saskatchewan, and oil produced from the sands is three times more greenhouse-gas intensive than conventional oil. They cite academic studies that indicate pollutants from the industry enter the Athabasca River and its tributaries. There have been various accidents over the past four decades.

In June 1970, a CGOS pipeline released over 3000 cubic metres (19,000 barrels) of oil that reached the Athabasca River. The oil slick was visible all the way down to the Athabasca Delta 250 km downstream. The oil slick persisted for two weeks and the water supplies for Fort McKay and Fort Chipewyan and the commercial fishery in the Athabasca Delta were interrupted. [9]

Irrespective of the environmental pros and cons, there is big money in oil sands. The Alberta government estimates that over the next 25 years, more than $2 trillion will come from new oil sands projects in estimated investments, reinvestments, and revenues. It expects production to increase from 1.31 million barrels a day in 2008 to 3 million barrels a day by 2018, with much of this destined for export to the United States. For its future sustainable development policy, the government relies in part on an expert panel report by the Royal Society of Canada released in December 2010, which sought to identify the environmental and health aspects of the oil sands industry.[10] The expert panel found "no credible evidence" of harmful contaminants reaching residents downstream of the oil sands, and said the industry's activity was "not a current threat" to the Athabasca River system. But it found shortcomings in tailings pond operation, in the rate of land reclamation, and release of noxious odours. Greenhouse gas emissions, while improving, created a "major challenge" for Canada, and there needed to be a better environmental regulatory performance. Alberta has since framed a development policy that reflects the panel's findings.

For Canada and its main oil and gas customer, the United States, one big issue is the future of the $7 billion Keystone XL (extension) pipeline that is designed to deliver Canadian oil as far south as U.S. refineries in Houston on the Gulf of Mexico. The Canadian pipeline and energy company, TransCanada Corp., has already built the first part of the Keystone project, a $6 billion crude oil pipeline that runs 3,467 km (2,154 miles) from Hardisty in Alberta to refineries in Illinois, and on to Cushing, Oklahoma. First oil to the Wood River/Patoka markets in Illinois flowed in June 2010, followed by the Cushing extension in February 2011. What remains is the U.S. Gulf Coast Expansion, a 2,673 km (1,661 miles) extension of the pipeline that TransCanada says is its largest and most ambitious project. TransCanada CEO Russell K. Girling says that once the Gulf Coast expansion (or "Keystone XL") is operational—now expected to be late-2014—Keystone's capacity will rise to 1.1 million barrels a day and could expand further to 1.5 million barrels a day as Canadian and

U.S. supplies grow. But the pipeline has attracted the ire of environmentalists, who fear what would happen to the Ogallala Aquifer if there should be oil spillage along Keystone's initial proposed route through the Nebraska sand hills. The Aquifer, which is vital to the health of the American Midwest farming community, covers 450,000 sq km of land in parts of eight U.S. states—South Dakota, Nebraska, Wyoming, Colorado, Kansas, Oklahoma, New Mexico, and Texas. In January 2012, the Obama administration rejected TransCanada's initial application. The company said immediately it would reapply for a permit and would consider other routes through Nebraska, delaying the project's start to at least 2013.

TransCanada already owns and runs 57,000 km of gas pipelines across Canada and the United States, including the Alberta system, the Canadian Mainline system, and the 17,000-km ANR pipeline from Texas to the Midwest and Great Lakes, plus a host of smaller pipelines in which it holds an interest. It owns or has a stake in 19 power stations with a capacity of about 11 gigawatts. It also has interests in wind power and the Bruce nuclear power plant in Ontario. If TransCanada's Keystone XL project is again deferred, there is another proposal in the wings: Calgary-based Enbridge, Canada's No. 2 pipeline operator, has its Northern Gateway pipeline project, which would take oil from Alberta west to a tanker port at Kitimat in British Columbia, for export to Asian markets. Enbridge's backers include China's Sinopec, but the Northern Gateway project faces many of the same environmental hurdles as Keystone XL and is no certainty to proceed. Like TransCanada, Enbridge already runs a network of oil and gas pipelines across North America, including its 1,607 km (1,000-mile) Alberta Clipper line linking Hardisty, Alberta, to Superior in the U.S. state of Wisconsin. The line's initial capacity is 450,000 barrels of crude a day, expandable to 800,000 barrels.

Canada has deepwater oil fields off the east coast, and emerging shale gas regions in Alberta, British Columbia, and Saskatchewan that have attracted attention. For example, separate to its investment in Syncrude, a unit of China's Sinopec agreed in October 2011 to buy Calgary-based oil and gas explorer Daylight Energy for $2.1 billion. Daylight has oil and gas fields in Alberta and British Columbia. Canadian natural gas company Encana is producing from gas fields at Bighorn, Cutbank Ridge, and Greater Sierra in the Alberta-British Columbia area, and from its Deep Panuke field off the Nova Scotia coast. As well, there are potential oil reserves above the Arctic Circle, as identified in the 2008 USGS appraisal. There has been some production in the Beaufort Sea off the Mackenzie Delta, where BP, Chevron, and Imperial Oil are exploring.

Qatar Fires up Its LNG Trains

In the past, Qatar used to be famous for its pearl hunting activities, but when the Japanese invented artificial pearls, so to speak, this caused a lot of poverty and deprivation in Qatar. . .
—*Sheikh Hamad bin Khalifa Al Thani, Emir of Qatar (quoted in transcript of interview in the* Financial Times, *24 October 2010)*

Between April 2009 and March 2011, something amazing happened in the global LNG industry, courtesy of the emirate known as Qatar. This tiny country, the home of global broadcaster Al Jazeera and host nation for the 2022 World Cup football tournament, made a quantum leap in its ability to influence world gas supply. In just 24 months, Qatar Petroleum's two gas subsidiaries QatarGas and RasGas added six LNG processing trains, each with a capacity of 7.8 million tonnes, to bump the country's LNG export capacity from just over 30 million tonnes a year to 77 million tonnes. It was a mammoth engineering and construction exercise, and a staggering increase for a country that had no gas processing industry just 15 years earlier. But there will be no new LNG capacity for some time to come, with any increased output having to come from improvements to the 14 existing trains. That follows Qatar's 2005 decision to put a moratorium on any further gas developments from its massive North Field, other than those already approved. The moratorium was extended in 2011 until at least 2014, based on the view of Qatar's ruler, the Emir Sheikh Hamad bin Khalifa Al Thani, and his advisors that they needed a better understanding of the potential life of Qatar's major gas field, and where global LNG prices might be headed. In 2009 and 2010, Qatar awarded three new exploration and production licences for areas outside the North Field to CNOOC of China, JX Nippon Oil & Gas of Japan, and China National Petroleum Corp. (CNPC) in partnership with Shell.

Qatar shares its gas riches with Iran, drawn from what is one of the world's largest gas condensate fields in the Persian Gulf spread over an area of 9,700 sq km. About 6,000 sq km of this is in Qatari territorial waters and is known as the North Field or North Dome, while the remaining 3,700 sq km in Iranian waters is known as South Pars. The International Energy Agency estimates the entire field holds 51 trillion cubic metres (1,800 trillion cubic feet) of in-situ gas and about 50 billion barrels of condensate. While Qatar is a relative newcomer to gas, its search for hydrocarbons goes back more than 70 years. Its first oil well, Dukhan 1, was drilled onshore in 1939. It began exporting crude in 1949, and in 1960 its first offshore fields were discovered, culminating in the big Bul Hanine oil field coming on line in 1972. It has about 15 billion barrels of oil reserves and about 26 trillion cubic metres of gas reserves, the third largest in the world behind Russia and Iran. State-owned Qatar Petroleum was set up in 1974 and the first gas was drawn from the North Field in 1989, but it was not until the second half of the 1990s that the first LNG was produced for export. The projects embarked on by Qatar Petroleum's two gas subsidiaries have attracted plenty of suitors since the first processing trains were built in late 1996. While Qatar Petroleum has between 65 and 70 percent of each of the 14 trains, the remaining equity is shared by various combinations that include Total, ExxonMobil, Mitsui, Marubeni, Korea Gas, LNG Japan, ConocoPhillips, and Shell. Russia's Gazprom is interested in being involved in future projects after 2014. China and India are substantial buyers of Qatari gas, but as yet, no Chinese or Indian energy companies have taken equity in any of the QatarGas and RasGas projects. India's ONGC Videsh signed up in 2005 to explore for oil in a Qatari offshore block but relinquished it in 2008.

Qatar's sovereign wealth fund, the Qatar Investment Authority, took a stake in the Industrial and Commercial Bank of China (ICBC) at the time of its initial public share offer in 2006, and ICBC subsequently set up a branch in the Qatari capital Doha. In July 2007, Qatar Petroleum began sending natural gas via a pipeline to the United Arab Emirates and from October 2008 to Oman. Qatar Petroleum describes this $5 billion project, known as Dolphin Gas, as one of the largest energy-related ventures in the Middle East. In November 2011 Qatar Petroleum and partner ExxonMobil launched the $10 billion Barzan project to supply gas to the Qatari domestic market from 2014. Qatar is a relatively small country of about 11,500 sq km. The Qatari peninsula juts about 160 km into the Persian Gulf, meaning that the country's only land border is with Saudi Arabia to the south. The Dukhan area in the west holds Qatar's onshore oil deposits, while the gas fields are offshore to the northwest. The oil and gas sector contributes almost half of Qatar's national budget, and has given its 1.7 million inhabitants (only 300,000 of whom are Qatari citizens) one of the highest per capita incomes in the world. Like other countries in the Gulf, Qatar's need for labour in the construction and service industries draws hundreds of thousands of migrant workers from India, Pakistan, Nepal, Bangladesh, and other parts of Asia. According to a 2011 report by Deutsche Bank, Qatar's economy may follow its 15 percent growth figure in 2010 with 19.5 percent in 2011, the fastest pace in the world. About \$250 billion is earmarked for infrastructure spending and other projects leading up to the 2022 World Cup—a substantial figure for a country with a GDP of only \$125 billion. After a period as a British protectorate, Qatar became independent in 1971. The current ruler, Sheikh Hamad, replaced his father in 1995.

Kazakhstan's Fields of Dreams

The Kashagan field, named after a nineteenth-century Kazakh poet from Mangistau, is one of the world's largest oil discoveries of the last 40 years.[11]

—*North Caspian Operating Company*

The final country in the BRACQK equation is Kazakhstan, which has large oil and gas resources in its western regions, particularly in Caspian Sea territorial waters. According to the U.S. Energy Information Administration, Kazakhstan has proven oil reserves of 30 billion barrels, and the capacity to become a top-five producer within the next decade. Its Kashagan field in the northern part of the Caspian Sea may well be the world's largest offshore oil field, with minimum reserves of 7 to 9 billion barrels. But whether Kashagan will ever be developed to its full potential is the \$160 billion question. Cost blowouts and disputes with the partners and the Kazakh government have delayed the start of production from an initial estimate of 2005 until 2012 or 2013. Full production, which would see oil flowing at a rate of 1.5 million barrels a day, is unlikely much before 2020.

The field, discovered in 2000 in shallow waters with a reservoir depth of 4,200 metres, is undeniably a world-class oil asset that has attracted the attention of global energy majors. Shell, ExxonMobil,

ConocoPhillips, Total, Italy's Eni, and Japan's Inpex are the current stakeholders with Kazakhstan's state-owned Kazmunaigas in the Kashagan consortium known as the North Caspian Operating Company. Early investors BP and Norway's Statoil sold out in 2001. BG Group also was part of the original investor group and sought to sell its 16.67 percent stake in 2003 to the Chinese oil companies CNOOC and Sinopec, but was required instead to sell half to Kazmunaigas and the rest to other consortium members. Eni is the operator for phase 1 of Kashagan, with a target of 370,000 barrels a day initially. In late 2011, it said phase 1 was "90 percent complete." Phase 2, led nominally by Shell, is supposed to lift that eventually to 1.5 million barrels a day.

Kashagan epitomizes the problem Kazakhstan faces in getting its oil and gas out to world markets. There are financial hurdles, political pressures, competing interests, technical challenges and the difficult logistics of developing a high-pressure field in shallow waters that are frozen for part of the year. As well, there is only a six-month window during the year to get heavy equipment to the site via the Volga Don Canal and the Baltic Sea-Volga waterways. Then there's the neighbourhood—Russia to the north, China to the east, and Kyrgyzstan, Uzbekistan, and Turkmenistan to the south, and beyond them, Tajikistan, Afghanistan, Pakistan, and India. Russia has long been Kazakhstan's dominant economic partner, but China is keen to be involved in developing its oil, gas, and mineral resources that include uranium, coal, copper, lead, zinc, gold, chromium, nickel, manganese, and iron ore. India also wants Kazakhstan's uranium, and its state-owned ONGC is a stakeholder with Kazmunaigas in another Caspian Sea oil exploration area, the Satpayev block. South Korea and Japan are other investors in the energy mix, while Kazakhstan must maintain stable relations with the other Central Asian "stans" if it wants to transport its oil and gas safely.

So far, President Nursultan Nazarbayev has managed to keep his landlocked nation's economy on a growth trajectory, largely on the back of revenues from oil and gas, plus uranium, coal, and copper. Nazarbayev, who has been in power since 1991, was reelected for another five-year term in April 2011 and has no obvious successor, though a health scare a few months later revived the succession debate. His son-in-law, Timur Kulibayev, was a key figure in the national holding company Samruk-Kazyna, which owns various state-owned companies, including Kazmunaigas and the nuclear fuel company

Kazatomprom. A former son-in-law Rakhat Aliyev, once married to the president's eldest daughter Dariga and seen as a potential successor to Nazarbayev, was removed as Kazakhstan's ambassador to Austria in 2007 after accusations he was involved in a bizarre kidnapping of executives at Nurbank, a bank he controlled. Kazakhstan unsuccessfully sought Aliyev's extradition; a court later convicted him in absentia and sentenced him to 20 years in prison. Aliyev lives in exile in Austria.

> "I will give only one integrated index of the country's progress. In 1994, Kazakhstan's GDP per capita was slightly above $700. By January 2011, it has reached more than 12 times that and exceeds $9000—a level we had planned to reach only by 2015."
> —*President Nursultan Nazarbayev, address to the nation*
> (*"Building The Future Together,"* Astana, *28 January 2011*)

China is the biggest recent investor, helping finance and build the 2,228-km (1,384 miles) Kazakhstan-China oil pipeline that runs from Atyrau port on the Caspian Sea to Alashankou in China's Xinjiang region. The line, completed in 2009, is a joint venture between Kazmunaigas and China National Petroleum Corp. (CNPC) and has a capacity of 200,000 barrels a day that may be doubled by 2013 under a second-stage development. The line could also carry oil from the Kashagan field in future. The country's other main export line is the Caspian Pipeline Consortium (CPC) pipeline, which takes oil from the Tengiz and Karachaganak fields to the Russian port of Novorossiysk, about 1,500 km (940 miles) away on the Black Sea. Daily capacity is about 600,000 barrels of Kazakh oil and 140,000 barrels of Russian oil. A proposed expansion could lift capacity to about 1.34 million barrels by 2014. Partners in this line include Russia's Transneft, Kazmunaingas, Chevron, LUKArco, ExxonMobil, Rosneft-Shell, Eni, and BG Group.

There is also a 600,000-barrel a day northbound pipeline from Atyrau to the Russian city of Samara, which then connects to the Black Sea. This line carries oil from the long-running Karachaganak field, which joint operator BG Group describes as "one of the world's largest gas and condensate fields" with an initial estimated 9 billion barrels of condensate and 1.36 trillion cubic metres (48 trillion cubic feet) of gas in place. BG's partners in Karachaganak, where production began in 1984, are Eni, Chevron, LUKOIL, and Kazmunaigas, which took a 10 percent stake in the project in

December 2011 for $1 billion plus a settlement that ended long-running disputes over tax and project costs.

The listed company Kazmunaigas Exploration Production (KMGEP), which is held 59 percent by Kazmunaigas and 11 percent by China Investment Corp., produces about 500,000 barrels a day from its fields in Kazakhstan, including Uzenmunaigas, Embamunaigas, and its stakes in the Kazgermunai joint venture, the CCEL venture with China's Citic, and PetroKazakhstan.

The International Energy Agency said in its most recent world energy outlook that the Caspian Sea region has the potential to make a "significant contribution to ensuring energy security in the rest of the world, by increasing the diversity of oil and gas supplies." But potential barriers to developing the Caspian's oil and gas reserves include "the complexities of financing and construction transportation infrastructure passing through several countries, the investment climate and uncertainty over export demand."[12]

In the IEA's New Policies scenario, Caspian oil production jumps from 2.9 million barrels a day in 2009 to a peak of around 5.4 million barrels between 2025 and 2030, before falling back to 5.2 million barrels by 2035. The IEA envisages that Kazakhstan will contribute all of this increase, ranking fourth in the world for output growth to 2035 behind Saudi Arabia, Iraq, and Brazil. Caspian gas exports also are projected to grow rapidly, reaching almost 100 billion cubic metres in 2020 and 130 bcm in 2035, up from less than 30 bcm in 2009.[13]

For all this to come to pass, President Nazarbayev and Kazmunaigas will have to convince skittish investors that costs can be controlled, infrastructure can be created on time, and corruption can be kept in check. While Nazarbayev is often portrayed as a ruthless, greedy dictator whose family is immensely rich (his second daughter Dinara and her husband Timur Kulibayev are on the Forbes billionaires list), Transparency International rates Kazakhstan the least corrupt (after China) in the region. The global watchdog's 2011 corruption perception index ranks Kazakhstan at 120 out of 182 nations on the list, with a score of 2.7 out of 10.[14] That puts it ahead of Azerbaijan and Russia (both 143), Tajikistan (152), Kyrgyzstan (164), and Turkmenistan and Uzbekistan (both 177 with a score of 1.6).

As part of an anticorruption drive launched in the late 2000s, the former chairman of Kazmunaigas, Serik Burkitbayev, was convicted of abuse of power in March 2009. As a former Soviet republic,

Kazakhstan has seen its share of oligarchs under Nazarbayev's 20-year rule. In the metals and mining sphere, the trio of Alexander Mashkevich, Alijan Ibragimov and Patokh Chodiev are prominent as the founders of controversial London-listed miner Eurasian Natural Resources Corporation (ENRC). Kazakhstan's richest man is Vladimir Kim, who is chairman and the largest shareholder in copper miner Kazakhmys. Bulat Utemuratov, lead investor in private equity firm Verny Capital and a close friend of Nazarbayev, will see his fortune grow further when Swiss commodity trader Glencore completes its $3.2 billion purchase of Verny's 42 percent stake in miner Kazzinc. Ahead of Glencore's 2011 initial public offer, the exiled Rakhat Aliyev issued a warning to investors in which he claimed President Nazarbayev was the secret ultimate beneficiary of the stake held in Kazzinc by Utemuratov, and of the ENRC stakes held by Mashkevich, Ibragimov, and Chodiev.

A notable investor in Kazakhstan is Indian tycoon Lakshmi Mittal, who bought the former government steelworks Karmet in 1995 for his global steel empire, which is now ArcelorMittal. Separately, Mittal had a stake in a Caspian Sea oil venture with LUKOIL and Kazmunaigas, which he sold to Sinopec in 2010.

Notes

1. USGS Fact Sheet, "Circum-Arctic Resource Appraisal: Estimates of Undiscovered Oil and Gas North of the Arctic Circle," 2008.
2. Press release, "Novatek First to Navigate the Northern Sea Route in 2011," Moscow (15 July 2011). http://www.novatek.ru/en/press/releases/index.php?id_4=414.
3. ExxonMobil, "Rosneft and ExxonMobil to Join Forces for Development of Arctic and Black Sea Resources," Sochi, Russia (30 August 2011). http://www.businesswire.com/portal/site/exxonmobil/ index.jsp?ndm ViewId=news_view&ndmConfigId=1001106&newsId=20110830006157& newsLang=en.
4. Presentation by Eduardo Molinari, E&P Strategy Coordinator, Petrobras, "Overview of the Brazil upstream Presalt development and downstream business fundamentals," at Platts 4th annual crude oil markets conference, London, 13 May 2011.
5. Royal Dutch Shell, Prelude project, www.shell.com.au/home/content/aus/aboutshell/who_we_are/shell_au/operations/upstream/prelude/ and Island Navigation Corporation Alumni Association, "The C.Y. Tung Biography," www.islandnavigation.org/cyTung.asp.

6. International Energy Agency, "World Energy Outlook 2010" (9 November 2010), www.iea.org/weo/2010.asp.
7. Ibid.
8. Canadian Natural, "Horizon Oil Sands." Accessed 1 September 2011. www.cnrl.com/operations/north-america/horizon-oil-sands.html.
9. Royal Society of Canada Expert Panel, *Environmental and Health Impacts of Canadian Oil Sands Industry* (Ottawa, Ontario: The Royal Society of Canada, December 2010).
10. Ibid.
11. North Caspian Operating Company. Accessed 5 September 2011. www.ncoc.kz/en/default.aspx.
12. International Energy Agency, World Energy Outlook 2010.
13. Ibid.
14. Transparency International, "Corruption Perception Index 2011," 1 December 2011. Accessed 10 December 2011. http://cpi.transparency .org/cpi2011/.

CHAPTER 14

The Up and Comers

Turkey, Iran, Indonesia, Mexico

In 2030, the world's four biggest economies almost certainly will be China, the United States, India, and Japan. The next five are likely to be, in no particular order, Russia, Germany, Brazil, France, and the United Kingdom. No surprises so far. But who will fill that tenth spot, and which countries will make up the second tier, in the ranking 11 to 20? In the view of long-term forecasters such as investment bank Goldman Sachs, it will be Mexico. The IMF, the World Bank, and other banks also believe that even with the dreadful scourge of its drug-related violence, Mexico is headed for top-ten status by 2030—and maybe even a top-five slot by 2050—on the strength of its petroleum resources, growing population, and proximity to the big North American market.

Mexico is one of four new names likely to be among the world's 20 largest economies within two decades; the other three are Turkey, Iran, and Indonesia, forming what we might call the up-and-coming TIIM. They will join advanced economies such as Italy, Canada, and South Korea, while the remaining spots will be shared among incumbents such as Spain, Australia, and Argentina, and emerging candidates Egypt, Saudi Arabia, Nigeria, Malaysia, Vietnam, the Philippines, and Venezuela. Goldman Sachs sees Indonesia joining Mexico in the top 10 by 2050, but global bank HSBC has a somewhat different perspective. It sees Indonesia in the 16 spot, with Turkey at No. 11, Mexico at No. 8, and Iran well back at No. 25.[1]

Of course, this is just a global guessing game that tries to factor in such variables as economic growth forecasts, demographic changes, resource availability, technological advances, and trade and investment patterns. What the crystal ball gazers cannot foresee is the political situation 20, 10, or even 5 years from now, and how that can affect a country's prospects. Will Mexico overcome the drug cartels, will Turkey reach an accord with its Kurdish minority, will Indonesia defeat endemic corruption, and will Iran tread a development path that eases its neighbours' fears? All four members of our new TIIM have their share of political risk, but they also share the essential ingredient for growth: youngish populations, meaning more people with potentially longer income-earning years ahead of them—assuming there are jobs to be had and their societies are not convulsed by the sort of mayhem that can send an economy spiraling into recession. Mexico's population is expected to grow from 114 million now to 130 million by 2030. Indonesia is already the world's fourth most populous country, with 240 million now and an expected 300 million by 2030. Iran and Turkey now have about 75 million people each, and should see their populations grow to about 85 to 90 million by 2030.

Mexico, Iran, and Indonesia are rich in energy resources. Iran, for example, has the world's third-largest proven oil reserves after Saudi Arabia and Venezuela, though the OPEC figures on which this claim is based are viewed with skepticism in some quarters.[2] Indonesia is a leading exporter of LNG and thermal coal, and has considerable geothermal capacity. Mexico is the world's sixth-largest oil producer, and its giant Cantarell field in the Gulf of Campeche was second only to Saudi Arabia's Ghawar field at peak production in the early 2000s. Turkey is the odd man out when it comes to energy resources; it must import 90 percent of its energy, mainly from Russia and Iran. But it does have its own special resource—water, or, more properly, the control of the water that flows from the Tigris and Euphrates rivers into Syria and Iraq. It is also an important energy transit point between suppliers in Central Asia and their key European markets, giving it a degree of influence as an alternative supply route to those offered by Russia. Plus, there is the likelihood it will seek a role in how the energy reserves of the eastern Mediterranean—essentially the oil and gas fields discovered between Israel, Lebanon, and Cyprus—are developed.

Their growth outlook makes our four-member TIIM potentially an attractive target for resource-hungry China and India, though the sanctions on Iran limit the investment opportunities there. Both China and India want to be part of the gas pipeline networks emanating from Central Asia, including possibly a stake in Turkey's petrochemicals sector. In Indonesia, ethnic Chinese traders and entrepreneurs have long played a big role in its business sector—sometimes with disastrous consequences for them, such as during the 1965–1966 riots and again in 1998—while India is keen to upgrade its role from resource buyer to co-venturer. In Mexico, there are silver, gold, copper, and lead mining possibilities, and oil exploration ventures are becoming a possibility. China has already identified Mexico's potential as an investment destination for export manufacturing, with companies such as telecoms equipment maker Huawei Technologies and computer maker Lenovo setting up factories there that can gain access to the North and South American markets. Chinese car and truck plants are also planned.

Turkey: A Pivotal Position

> Econometric analyses show that per capita income (in Turkey) will reach only 80 percent of the current European Union average if we achieve 10 percent growth every year until the centennial of our republic in 2023.
>
> —*Turkish President Abdullah Gul,*
> *address to parliament, 1 October 2011*

Turkey expects its primary energy consumption to rise from 126 million tonnes of oil equivalent in 2010 to 222 million tonnes by 2020.[3] Almost 90 percent of its electricity comes from oil, gas, and coal-fired plants, with about 10 percent hydro and 1 percent renewable. It has about 2.6 billion tonnes of coal reserves, plus small amounts of oil and gas. That means its energy self-sufficiency ratio is only 30 percent, and it must make up the remainder through imports of oil and gas, mainly from Russia, Iran, Azerbaijan, and Saudi Arabia. Egypt, Iraq, and Algeria are other suppliers. Turkey's main oil and gas reserves are in the Hakkari Basin, in the southeast, where the major producers are state oil company TPAO (Turkiye Petrolleri Anonim Ortakligi), Shell, and ExxonMobil. There is also exploration in the Black Sea, where TPAO, Chevron, and

ExxonMobil are all active. Total, ConocoPhillips, Eni, and Austria's OMV also have a presence. Turkey may have extensive oil and gas in the Aegean Sea, but tensions with Greece over Cyprus are likely to make any fields there difficult to exploit (Cyprus is an EU member, with only Turkey recognizing the breakaway northern half of the island). To ease its reliance on imported oil and gas, Turkey planned to have three nuclear plants operating by 2023 and as many as 20 by 2030, but that ambitious program is unlikely following the Fukushima nuclear disaster in Japan. The first 4,800 MW nuclear plant is earmarked for Akkuyu, on the eastern Mediterranean Sea.

Turkey sees itself as "a natural energy bridge" between the source countries in the Caspian Sea and Middle East, and the big consumer markets of Europe.[4] A key component of this is the BTC oil and natural gas pipeline network that runs for 1,768 km (1,099 miles) from the Caspian Sea city of Baku in Azerbaijan to Tbilisi in Georgia and on to the port of Ceyhan in Turkey on the Mediterranean Sea. BP operates the 1 million barrels a day oil pipeline and is the major shareholder in a consortium that includes international oil companies Chevron, Total, ConocoPhillips, Eni, Inpex, and Statoil, plus TPAO and SOCAR (State Oil Company of Azerbaijan Republic). The BTC pipeline moved its first Azeri oil in 2006; oil from Kazakhstan was shipped across the Caspian Sea to Baku and into the pipeline from 2008. Ceyhan is also connected by a 1.6 million barrels/day pipeline to Kirkuk in Iraq, which allows Iraqi oil to reach Europe. Ceyhan appears likely to become an important energy hub; apart from its pipelines, gas liquefaction plant and export terminal, a consortium led by Calik Enerji has a refinery project there. In 2007 Indian Oil Corp. also said it planned to build a refinery at Ceyhan, but the proposal faded in 2010.

Turkey's gas connection with Europe became operational in 2007 with the Turkey-Greece Interconnector, which, in turn, will link with Italy. Turkey also supports the Nabucco natural gas pipeline project, which is designed to move Caspian Sea gas via Turkey through Bulgaria, Romania, and Hungary to Austria from 2017, and would further loosen Russia's grip as Europe's main energy supplier. Gas for Nabucco would come from Azerbaijan's Shah Deniz field and Turkmenistan's extensive fields.

Turkey defines its objective as becoming Europe's fourth main artery of energy supply after Norway, Russia, and Algeria—part of its push for greater visibility within Europe ahead of its long-sought membership of the European Union. Turkey has been seeking to join the EU since 1987; it began full negotiations for entry in 2005, with 2013 the earliest possible date for its entry.

But Turkey continues to have problems with its neighbour Greece over the divided island of Cyprus, and at home with its large Kurdish minority. About 15 million of its 75 million people are Kurdish, some of whom support the Kurdistan Workers Party (PKK), an insurgent group that seeks a separate Kurdistan state. Since 1984, Turkey has been fighting a violent battle with the PKK, which operates from northern Iraq. There are about 5 million Kurds living in northern Iraq and a similar number in Iran.

Iran: Rich in Oil and Gas, but Lacking Technology and International Friends

> Who used the mysterious September 11 incident as a pretext to attack Afghanistan and Iraq—killing, injuring and displacing millions of people in two countries—with the ultimate goal of bringing into its domination the Middle East and its oil resources?
>
> —*Iranian President Mahmoud Ahmadinejad, speech to the UN General Assembly, New York, 22 September 2011*

With its virulently anti-U.S. stance, its nuclear ambitions, and its professed goal of exporting a Shi'a revolution to the region, Iran is the wild card in the international energy deck. Its oil reserves are rated the third largest in the world after Venezuela and Saudi Arabia, and it ships more oil abroad than any country other than Saudi Arabia and Russia. Its biggest trading partners include China, India, Japan, South Korea, Russia, Turkey, Germany, and the UAE. China and India between them account for a third of Iran's oil exports and want to be more closely involved in how Iran develops its oil and gas fields. China's state-owned oil companies, in particular, have sought a prominent role there. According to OPEC figures, Iran's crude oil output in 2010 was just over 3.5 million barrels a day, and exports were 2.5 million barrels a day, worth about $72 billion for the year.[5] Production in 2011 was in the range of 3.5 to 3.6 million barrels a day, according to OPEC's January 2012 monthly oil report.

But Tehran's political stance and opaque nuclear power program have made it a target for U.S. and UN sanctions that keep its production capacity and technological capabilities below par. Those sanctions, and the difficulties that ensue for big customers China and India in paying for Iranian oil and gas, are a turnoff for most investors. Still, Iran has some powerful attractions: the massive South Pars/North Dome gas field that it shares with Qatar, and the equally impressive new oilfields such as Azadegan in the south-western province of Khuzestan. This part of Iran, which borders Iraq's Basra province and the Persian Gulf, looks to be awash in oil. Along with Azadegan's reserves of 42 billion barrels of oil, there are three other large fields in Khuzestan—Ahwaz (already producing, boosted by gas injection), Yadavaran, and Soussangerd—that between them may hold another 50 billion-plus barrels. Production from these fields—assuming the infrastructure and maintenance requirements can be met—would complement long-serving reservoirs such as Gachsaran and Marun (both producing about 500,000 barrels a day) and the large Esfandiar offshore field that Iran shares with Saudi Arabia. A number of Iran's other oil and gas fields are shared with neighbours Qatar, Iraq, Kuwait, Oman, UAE, Saudi Arabia, and Turkmenistan.

Before the 1979 revolution and the overthrow of the Shah, Iran was producing more than 5 million barrels a day of oil. That figure dropped during the debilitating 1980–1988 war with Iraq—a conflict that had its origins in part over control of the Shatt al-Arab waterway (known as the Arvand Rud in Iran) used by both countries for their oil exports. In the assessment of the U.S. Energy Information Administration, a combination of the "war, limited investment, sanctions, and a high rate of natural decline in Iran's mature oil fields have prevented a return to such production levels."[6]

China, India, Russia, Japan, Venezuela, and oil majors such as Shell, Total, Eni, and Statoil have all been keen to play a greater role in revitalizing Iran's oil industry, but among the major players, only China, India, and Venezuela have retained their enthusiasm in the face of sanctions. China's Sinopec signed an agreement in 2007 with state-owned National Iranian Oil Co (NIOC) to develop the Yadavaran field with first production in 2013, and in 2011 Iran's Petroleum Engineering and Development Co. (PEDEC) said Iran and China would jointly invest $12 billion to develop the Azadegan field over the next 10 years. The first phase is targeted for completion by 2016 and will add 600,000 barrels a day to Iran's output. That follows two agreements between China National Petroleum

Corp. (CNPC) and NIOC in 2009 covering development of the north and south parts of Azadegan, respectively. Japan's Inpex pulled out of its part of the Azadegan project in October 2010 because of U.S. sanctions.

In September 2011, Gazprom Neft, the oil arm of Russia's Gazprom, was dropped by NIOC as a partner in developing the Azar oil field that Iran shares with Iraq. NIOC cited long delays in getting a final decision from Gazprom Neft about its level of involvement. Instead NIOC said it would work with an Iranian contractor to bring the field into production. Belorusneft, the Belarus state-owned oil company that was sanctioned by the United States in April 2011 over its Iran involvement, later in the year withdrew from a proposed development of the Jofeir oil field with NIOC. All of this suggests the operating environment for non-Iranian companies is a challenge.

Iran's South Pars and Qatar's contiguous North Dome (also known as North Field) represent what is regarded as the world's largest gas field, with an estimated 51 trillion cubic metres of gas and 50 billion barrels of gas condensates, according to the International Energy Agency (IEA). Qatar began gas production from the North Dome in 1989, but since 2005 has had a moratorium on further development until 2012. Even so, Qatar's North Dome gas output in 2012 is expected to be up to 760 million cubic metres a day. NIOC subsidiary Pars Oil & Gas Co. has been producing gas from South Pars since 2002, but the sheer scale of the field means Iran and its partners will need to invest $15 billion a year over the next 10 years to develop its part of the resource in as many as 30 phases. According to Iran's Oil Ministry, South Pars gas could be adding $100 billion a year to Iran's export income by 2015. A string of the world's oil and gas companies have worked on different phases of the project, but because of sanctions the field has narrowed since 2010 to CNPC, Venezuela's PDVSA, Angola's Sonangol, and various domestic contractors. India's state oil company ONGC was interested in taking a stake in South Pars phase 12 in 2009–2010, but nothing came of it. Earlier ONGC, Indian Oil, and Oil India were partners in exploring the Farsi offshore block for Iran's Farzad gas field. China's CNOOC struck an agreement with NIOC in 2006 to develop the smaller North Pars gas field, but the deal was suspended in 2011. India's Petronet LNG, set up by a consortium of state-owned energy companies ONGC, BPCL, GAIL, and Indian Oil, has identified Iran as a possible future gas supplier. It currently buys its gas from Qatar.

Indonesia: Growing Spending Power

> As a developing nation, we prioritize the promotion of growth and the eradication of poverty. But we will not achieve these goals by sacrificing our forests. . . forest management is tightly intertwined with the livelihood of our people, with our food security, with the availability of wood and fuel.
> —*Indonesian President Susilo Bambang Yudhoyono,*
> *Jakarta, 27 September 2011*

Despite the depredations of illegal loggers, Indonesia hosts a tropical forest area that is the third largest in the world, its biodiversity a source of wonderment to naturalists and a green resource to be treasured for future generations. Beneath the tropical canopy is another set of resources—food, water, minerals, and energy—that offers economic opportunity and the chance for better living standards, including for the 25 percent of Indonesia's 240 million people who live below or just above the poverty line. Indonesia's economy is among the fastest growing in Asia in 2011–2012, but little more than a decade ago the country was locked in a high-inflation, low-growth pattern that followed the 1997–1998 economic crisis. To make the most of its resources, Indonesia needs better infrastructure, better government services, better education, more jobs for its young people, better health care, a greater emphasis on upgrading human skills and, in the eyes of many investors, better corporate governance to encourage more finance and technology from outside. Despite the efforts of President Susilo Bambang Yudhoyono's administration since 2004, corruption remains entrenched in the bureaucracy, and the country ranks 100th on Transparency International's 2011 corruption perception index. The World Bank ranks it 122nd in "ease of doing business," well behind China (but ahead of India). Even so, it is a country of immense possibilities and is by far the most important economy in Southeast Asia.

Indonesia's volcanic activity—it sits on the Pacific "ring of fire"—gives it extensive geothermal potential, though bringing that onstream requires new policies, pricing, and infrastructure. More importantly in the short term, Indonesia has substantial oil and gas resources, and is one of the world's top three exporters of LNG—though its own energy needs are growing so rapidly it may become a gas importer within a few years, which would require regasification terminals. For LNG exports, state-owned Pertamina runs an eight-train gas liquefaction facility at Bontang in East Kalimantan, with annual capacity of 22.6 million tonnes, which is among the largest in the world. BP's 7.6 mtpa two-train Tangguh plant in West Papua, which started shipments in 2009, may be expanded to as many as eight trains over the next decade. Pertamina also accounts for about 15 percent of total gas production, drawing on fields in the Natuna Sea, where its partners include ExxonMobil, Total, and Petronas of Malaysia. Another U.S. oil major, Chevron, is working on the country's first deepwater gas project, Gendalo-Gehem, with China's Sinopec and Eni of Italy. Sinopec is investing $680 million for an 18 percent share of Gendalo-Gehem, which sits off the coast of East Kalimantan. Chevron already operates the Minas and Duri oil fields on the east coast of Sumatra and is the country's biggest crude oil producer, ahead of Pertamina. ExxonMobil is working with Pertamina to develop the large Cepu oil prospect off East Java, with peak production expected in 2014. BP, Shell, ConocoPhillips, and Inpex also are active. Separately, Pertamina is working on geothermal and coal-bed methane (CBM) exploration and production, in keeping with Indonesia's target energy policy, which calls for the share of oil to fall to 26.2 percent by 2025. Coal's share is expected to rise to 32.7 percent, with natural gas at 30.6 percent, geothermal at 3.8 percent, and other renewables to reach 4.4 percent by 2025.

> In the area of energy security, our forests are home to potential sources of energy such as microhydro, geothermal, and bio-energy. We are increasing the portion of alternative sources of energy in our energy mix. Forest ecosystems offer competitive advantage by making possible the replacement of conventional fuels by renewable energy sources.
> —*Indonesian President Susilo Bambang Yudhoyono,*
> *27 September 2011*

Though Indonesia is strong in hydrocarbons, much of the recent energy focus has been on the country's emerging role as a supplier of thermal (steaming) coal. In the global competition for coal, China and India are the big buyers, along with traditional users Japan and South Korea, while Indonesia itself is becoming a substantial coal consumer. By 2015, two of the world's top three thermal coal exporters will be the Indonesian companies Bumi

Resources and Adaro Energy, in the view of mining and energy consultants Wood Mackenzie (Swiss-based Xstrata is the largest exporter, drawing on its coal mines in Australia, while Rio Tinto is currently ranked third). According to Wood Mackenzie coal analyst Rudi Vann, 6 of the 10 largest projects for thermal coal mine expansion are in Indonesia, and Bumi and Adaro each have mines in this category. These mines, along with greenfield projects, will see Indonesia accounting for the largest share of growth in thermal coal exports over the next decade, Vann says.[7]

Bumi Resources, Asia's largest thermal coal exporter from its stakes in the giant Kaltim Prima Coal (KPC) and Arutmin mines in Kalimantan—the Indonesian part of the island of Borneo—is controlled by the Bakrie Group, a large conglomerate headed by Aburizal Bakrie, a businessman turned politician who one day may be Indonesia's president. The group, established by Bakrie's father, Ahmad Bakri, in 1942 as a spice trading company, has interests in coal, oil and gas, property, telecoms, infrastructure, and agribusiness. Aburizal Bakrie stepped down as group chairman in 2004, but retains influence as head of the family. His younger brothers Indra and Nirwan have taken larger roles in recent years. Aburizal, now chairman of the Golkar political party, has seen his family's business come close to ruin on more than one occasion over the last 20 years, most recently in 2008 after the global financial crisis, and in 1997–1998 when the Asian financial crisis rocked Indonesia's currency and brought down the Suharto regime. Bakrie continues to carry a heavy long-term debt load, with China Investment Corp. among its creditors. Aburizal Bakrie was an unsuccessful contender to be Golkar's candidate for the presidency in 2004, and may seek to run again in 2014. In 2010, UK financier Nathaniel Rothschild joined forces with the Bakrie family and Indonesian private equity investor Rosan Roeslani to form London-listed Bumi Plc as a vehicle to hold stakes in Bumi Resources and Roeslani's own big thermal coal producer in Kalimantan, Berau Coal Energy. Another resources investor, Samin Tan of Borneo Lumbung Energi, subsequently bought half the Bakries' stake in Bumi Plc for $1 billion. Berau, which has reserves of 470 million tonnes, originally was set up by Mobil Oil and Japanese trading company Nissho Iwai in the 1980s. Roeslani's Recapital Group acquired Berau in 2009. Likewise, Bumi Resources' Kaltim Prima Coal has foreign antecedents, having been set up by Rio Tinto and BP in 1992, while Arutmin was established by BHP Mineral

Exploration in 1981. India's Tata Power has stakes in KPC and Arutmin and uses Indonesian coal in its Indian power generation.

Indonesia's other big coal exporter is Adaro Energy, controlled by a group of investors led by CEO Garibaldi Thohir. A key figure in Adaro's emergence over the last 20 years as the No. 2 exporter is Edwin Soeryadjaya, who was one of the founding investors. Soeryadjaya comes from a long business background— his father William Soeryadjaya and uncle Tjia Kian Tie set up Astra International in the 1950s as a trading company, gradually building it into Indonesia's biggest automotive retailer. Astra also had interests in agribusiness and equipment (United Tractors), finance, IT, and infrastructure. Soeryadjaya led the financial restructuring of Astra from 1987 and its subsequent initial public offering in February 1990, but the family was forced to sell out in 1992 because of debts related to the now-defunct Bank Summa. Other influential figures at Adaro are Sandiaga S. Uno, who co-founded private equity firm Saratoga Capital with Edwin Soeryadjaya in 1998; Edwin's cousin Theodore "Teddy" Rachmat, who was president director of Astra International from 1984 to 1998; and Benny Subianto, another Astra executive who ran United Tractors and later served as president commissioner of Berau Coal.

From 1 million tonnes in its first year of production in 1992, Adaro has grown to an operation of 50 million tonnes a year, drawn mainly from its Tutupan and Wara deposits near Tanjung in south Kalimantan. Adaro trucks coal along an 80 km private road from its mines to a crushing terminal at Kelanis, where it is barged down the Barito River to a loading point for customers in China, India, Japan, South Korea, and Taiwan. Adaro says its proximity to these markets gives it a significant geographic advantage over suppliers from Australia, South Africa, Russia, and Colombia. Adaro's growth plan includes acquiring coal mines in south Sumatra to replicate its success in Kalimantan.

There is much more to Indonesia's mining sector than just coal; it is the world's biggest tin exporter, and has extensive copper, gold, silver, nickel, and bauxite deposits. U.S. miner Freeport McMoRan holds 90.6 percent of Freeport Indonesia, which runs the giant Grasberg open-pit copper and gold mine in West Papua. The Indonesian government has the remaining 9.4 percent. Another U.S. company, Colorado-based Newmont Mining, operates the Batu Hijau copper and gold mine on Sumbawa island, with partners

Sumitomo Corp. and the provincial government. Two important state-owned miners are Timah, Indonesia's largest tin producer, and Aneka Tambang (Antam), which mines and refines nickel, gold, silver, and bauxite.

Mexico: Exploiting the Potential

> The question many people ask is obviously valid: Should this head-on confrontation with criminals continue or stop? For me, the answer is clear: This fight must go on. Mexico must go on. We must go on fighting criminals and we will destroy them.
> —*Mexican President Felipe Calderon,*
> *State of the Union address, 3 September 2011*

Mexico's resource base is impressive: the No. 6 crude oil exporter, the world's biggest producer of silver (its Fresnillo underground silver mine has operated since 1554), among the top 10 producers for lead, zinc, copper, and gold, and a recoverable coal base of 1.3 billion tonnes. Grupo Mexico, Industrias Penoles, and Grupo Carso subsidiary Empresas Frisco are the main domestic mining players, while London-listed Fresnillo Plc (spun-off from Penoles in 2008) and Canadian miners such as Goldcorp (which owns Luismin) lead the way among overseas names. The United States and Australia are the next most active, while Japan, China, and India also are present in the sector.

But it is a different story in the oil and gas sector, where state-owned oil monopoly Petroleos Mexicanos (Pemex) calls the shots. With 2010 turnover of $104 billion, Pemex is already one of the largest companies of its type in the world; among national oil companies only China's Sinopec and CNPC, Saudi Arabia's Aramco, Brazil's Petrobras, and Russia's Gazprom had a greater turnover.[8]

The Mexican government relies heavily on direct payments and taxes from Pemex, with up to a third of total government revenue coming from the oil industry. Given the importance of Pemex to Mexico's economy and its pivotal role in the oil and gas industry, there is little chance of major advances into its territory by the world's biggest oil companies. There have been few opportunities so far for Chinese or Indian investors in Mexico's petroleum sector, beyond some exploration and drilling work by CNPC as a Pemex contractor, and a tie-up between Sinopec and oil services provider Grupo Diavaz.

India's Reliance Industries is a possible service provider as Pemex steps up work in 2011–2012 on its $9 billion refinery at Tula, Hidalgo. The 310,000 b/d refinery, the first to be built in Mexico for 30 years, is due for completion in 2015.

Pemex has had a monopoly on oil and gas exploration since Mexico's then-President Lazaro Cardenas nationalized foreign oil assets in 1938, but in March 2011 the Mexican government opened the door a little to private and overseas oil companies. In a move to gain access to better production technology, it allowed Pemex to begin a series of licensing rounds for performance-based contracts on existing oil blocks. Twenty blocks were offered to international bidders. Eventually, Pemex hopes these licences will cover new deepwater prospects. Pemex says the new regulations are shifting it into a "corporate business model" that will allow it to increase crude oil production from 2.576 million barrels a day in 2011 to 3 million barrels a day by 2018. It wants to be producing crude oil from new discoveries by 2013, and to be sourcing deepwater gas by 2015.[9] Although output from its Cantarell field has slipped from 2.1 million barrels a day in 2004 to 460,000 barrels now, Pemex is boosting production from other fields such as Ku-Maloob-Zaap (KMZ) and Crudo Ligero Marino Litoral Tabasco. In late 2011, it said its dependence on Cantarell had fallen significantly, down from 63 percent of total production in 2004 to just 19.0 percent. It said that excluding Cantarell, its growth in crude oil output between 2005–2010 was 9 percent, the highest of all crude producers.[10]

Pemex has identified the onshore Chicontepec Basin northeast of Mexico City as having strong potential, with 19 billion barrels of recoverable reserves. But much of it is heavy crude, making it a costly and complex development. There are also shale oil deposits in the north of the country.

Outside Mexico, Pemex increased its stake in Spanish oil company Repsol YPF to almost 10 percent in late 2011, in part to see if they could work together on deepwater projects. Pemex also has a half share of Shell's Deer Park refinery in Texas, the sixth-largest refinery in the United States with capacity of 334,000 barrels a day.

Mexico may have the oil and gas fields of the Gulf of Mexico and proximity to the U.S. market as its greatest advantage, but it suffers terribly from its image of violence. More than 40,000 people have died in drug-related violence since President Felipe Calderon launched his crackdown on the drug cartels in 2006, and a 2011 poll reaffirmed crime, the drug war, and negative assessments of the economy as the major causes of dissatisfaction among Mexicans. Short of some sort of dramatic breakthrough, it seems this will be Mexico's millstone.[11]

Notes

1. HSBC, The World in 2050, Hong Kong, January 2011. www.research .hsbc.com/midas/Res/RDV?p=pdf&key=ej73gSSJVj&n=282364.PDF.
2. OPEC, Annual Statistical Bulletin, Vienna, July 2011. www.opec.org/ opec_web/static_files_project/media/downloads/publications/ ASB2010_2011.pdf.
3. Government of Turkey, "Energy, Water & Environment Directorate," Turkey's Energy Strategy, January 2009. www.mfa.gov.tr/data/ DISPOLITIKA/EnerjiPolitikasi/Turkey's%20Energy%20Strategy%20 (Ocak%202009).pdf.
4. Ibid.
5. OPEC, Annual Statistical Bulletin, Vienna, July 2011.
6. U.S. Energy Information Administration, "Iran Country Analysis Brief" (January 2010), www.eia.gov/countries/country-data.cfm?fips=IR.
7. Presentation by Wood Mackenzie at Coaltrans Asia conference, Bali, Indonesia, 31 May 2011.
8. Petroleos Mexicanos, Annual Report 2010, Mexico City, September 2011. www.ri.pemex.com/index.cfm?action=content&sectionID=135& catID=12320#2010.
9. Ibid.
10. Ibid.
11. Global Attitudes Project, *Crime and Drug Cartels Top Concerns in Mexico* (Washington, DC: Pew Research Center, 31 August 2011).

CHAPTER 15

What Happens Next

A Host of Global Opportunities

China cannot develop itself in isolation from the rest of the world, and global prosperity and stability cannot be maintained without China.

—China's State Council white paper on peaceful development, 7 September 2011

China is the world's largest energy user, having overtaken the United States in 2009. As a consequence, even with 20 to 25 percent hydropower in its energy mix, China consumes more thermal coal than any other nation. It is the No. 2 oil user behind the United States and by 2030 it will also be one of the world's biggest natural gas consumers. Already it is the biggest user of coking coal and metals such as iron ore, copper, tin, zinc, lead, nickel, aluminum, chromium, and a host of rare metals. In food, it is the biggest consumer of wheat, rice, pork, chicken, apples, and palm oil, to name just a few items. It uses more potash fertiliser than anyone else, and consumption will continue to rise as Chinese farmers move up the food value chain.

Although this makes it the mother of all import markets, it is a prodigious supplier in its own right. For example, it is the world's biggest food producer, particularly of vegetables, wheat, rice, pork, and chicken. It is also the biggest coal producer, and it may well end up having the world's biggest shale gas reserves. It is the main supplier for a variety of rare-earth elements and other scarce metals such as antimony, tungsten, mercury, carbon (graphite), and bismuth.[1] That gives it enormous weight in any discussion of what happens next. The United States, Europe, Japan, and India are all big consumers of various commodities and in some cases—such as coal, conventional oil and shale oil/gas in the United States, and coal in India—have substantial supply capacity. But none will dominate global supply chains in the way that China seems likely to do, over the next 20 years. This presupposes, of course, that there is no social implosion in China that leads to a splintering of the country into coastal, hinterland, northern or southern empires. The major long-term task of the expected new team of Xi Jinping and Li Keqiang when they take over as president and premier in 2012–2013 will be to manage continued high economic growth without any further breakdown in social harmony.

To a degree, the same applies in India, where incumbent Prime Minister Manmohan Singh has the popular but untested Rahul Gandhi waiting in the wings for a 2014 election run. His opponent could be the Gujarat Chief Minister Narendra Modi, whose business-friendly policies are offset by the legacy of the 2002 Gujarat anti-Muslim riots. India's many divisive issues include caste, colour, ethnicity, religion, and gender discrimination, allied to a growing gulf between rich and poor, and a Maoist-style domestic insurgency known as the Naxalite movement that picks away at the rural social fabric. On top of this, India's myriad growth challenges range from corruption to poor infrastructure, inadequate health, education and job training, child labour exploitation, power-sharing tensions between the central and state governments, a degraded environment with water, soil and air quality problems, and a troublesome neighbourhood with attendant external terrorism risks.

Whichever paths China and India—and Russia and Brazil, too—follow as they seek to draw level with the United States, Europe, and Japan, the intensity of the resources war is likely to be undiminished. Economic information and insider access will be highly valued. Consider this observation by the U.S. national counterintelligence chief, Robert Bryant, in assessing the economic espionage outlook in late 2011: "We judge that the governments of China and Russia will remain aggressive and capable collectors of sensitive U.S. economic information and technologies, particularly in cyberspace."[2] According to Bryant, China's "Project 863" provides money and guidance for efforts to "clandestinely acquire U.S. technology and sensitive economic information." Bryant's report also cites a cyber attack on United States and international energy companies that began in November 2009, identified by computer security company McAfee as emanating from Chinese IP addresses.[3]

At a regional security forum known as the Shangri-La Dialogue held in Singapore in June 2011, Chinese Defense Minister General Liang Guanglie delivered what he called Beijing's "solemn pledge" to the international community. China, he said, "will never seek hegemony or military expansion," and was committed to peace and stability in the South China Sea.[4] Two months later, when Japan expressed concern about China's level of military spending, China scolded Japan as "irresponsible," and told it to think about its past military misdemeanors.[5] The following month, September, it was India's turn for a tongue-lashing, with China warning it about cooperating with Vietnam in looking for oil off the latter's coast. China's sovereignty, rights, and relevant claims over the South China Sea "have been formed in the long course of history," the Chinese Foreign Ministry declared to the world in general.[6]

China and India have a large and growing economic relationship, they share a long border and a historical connection in the spread of Buddhism. But China also knows it has India's military measure—India told it so back in 2009, when Admiral Sureesh Mehta, then India's Chief of Navy, offered the assessment that "in military terms, both conventional and non-conventional, we neither have the capability nor the intention to match China, force for force."[7] Since then, China has rebuilt and relaunched the old Russian aircraft carrier it acquired from the Ukraine in the 1990s, and has begun the long march to acquiring its own carrier-building and operating expertise. India has one ex-British carrier that is 60 years old and is due to get a refurbished ex-Russian carrier by the end of 2012. It also aims to have its own indigenous carrier launched by 2014. Russia plans to have two aircraft carriers based in the Russian Far East in 2013, while the U.S. Seventh Fleet operating out of Japan always has at least one carrier in its lineup. Japan itself has two helicopter carriers.

A thriving America is good for China and a thriving China is good for America. We both have much more to gain from cooperation than from conflict.
—*U.S. Secretary of State Hillary Clinton, November 2011*

National leaders may make soothing noises about peaceful cooperation, but given the level of mistrust between China and India, China and Japan, and China and the United States, it's far from inconceivable to see future clashes in the East and South China Seas or the Indian Ocean trade routes as China seeks to safeguard the resources it believes belong to it, and to manage its sea lanes of communication. That rationale applies to scores of other hotspots around the globe—Cuba looking for oil 100 km (60 miles) off the coast of Florida irritates the United States, as does Venezuela's own version of resources diplomacy. Neighbourhood squabbles over subsea oil and gas field rights range from the Mediterranean to the Caspian Sea, the Persian Gulf, and Africa's Gulf of Guinea. In Central Asia, the routes taken by pipelines to key markets in Russia, China, Europe, and South Asia are a focus of negotiation and security tension. Resource-rich Africa is a mine of opportunities, but militancy, carpetbaggers, and corrupt governments detract from its appeal and heighten the risk. In South America, landlocked Bolivia growls at Chile over its lack of access to the Pacific Ocean, while Argentina and Uruguay have had various spats over water use.

Significant Developments Ahead

Against this background, these are some of the most significant energy, metals, food, and water developments we are likely to be hearing about in the years ahead:

1. The North American shale fields such as Bakken, Utica, Niobrara, Marcellus, Eagle Ford, Haynesville, Barnett, Horn River, and Montney. Further into this decade, the North Slope shale fields in Alaska may become economically viable. One consequence of the North American gas glut will be an increase in pipeline connections and, from 2015 onward, the likelihood of LNG exports from terminals in Louisiana and Kitimat on Canada's west coast.
2. The Chinese shale fields in the Sichuan Basin, where PetroChina and Sinopec have Shell and Exxon helping them

explore. But Sichuan is also a big food-producing area, and farmers may object to fracking and the possible impact on water quality. Shale field developments in the Tarim Basin in Xinjiang and in Inner Mongolia are also likely.

3. The Argentinian shale fields in Patagonia and Neuquen provinces, where Repsol YPF, Total, Exxon, Apache, and Americas Petrogas are active. Argentina's shale reserves may be the third largest, behind China and the United States. Poland and Germany are likely to emerge as Europe's top shale sites.

4. The Tavan Tolgoi coking coal mine, Mongolia. With reserves of 7 billion tonnes, it is the largest undeveloped coal deposit in the world. The United States, Chinese, Russian, Japanese, and South Korean companies want to help Mongolia's state-owned Erdenes Tavan Tolgoi bring the project into full production by 2014.

5. The Oyu Tolgoi copper and gold mine, also in Mongolia. Rio Tinto, through Ivanhoe Mines, is developing what Rio calls "this incredible mine" in partnership with the Mongolian government. Production is expected to start in 2013.

6. The ultra-deepwater pre-salt oil fields off the coast of Brazil, headlined by the Lula field. Expensive and technically challenging for state-owned Petrobras, the pre-salt fields contain high-quality low-sulfur oil, and by 2020 could be contributing more than 40 percent of Petrobras's domestic oil output.

7. The Kashagan oil field in Kazakhstan's part of the Caspian Sea. It may be the world's largest offshore field with up to 9 billion barrels of reserves, but full production is unlikely before 2020 because of funding and ownership issues. Italy's Eni is the first-phase operator.

8. The gas fields of Turkmenistan, including South Yolotan, the second-largest field in the world behind Iran's South Pars. Turkmen gas would enhance the viability of the Nabucco pipeline project from the Caspian Sea to European markets. But equally the gas could go east to China; state-owned China National Petroleum Corp. won a 2009 tender to help develop South Yolotan.

9. The Kamoto copper mine in Africa's Democratic Republic of Congo, majority-owned by commodity trader Glencore. Kamoto may have production capacity of 300,000 tonnes of copper and 30,000 tonnes of cobalt by 2015.

10. The Olympic Dam uranium-copper-gold mine expansion, Australia. Another of BHP Billiton's "100-year" mines, with a new open pit likely to take six years to dig. Eventual copper output will exceed Chile's massive Escondida mine, also owned by BHP.

11. The Gorgon and Pluto LNG projects, North West Shelf, Australia. At $43 billion, Chevron's Gorgon three-train project is the North West Shelf's single biggest development, with first gas to Asian customers expected in 2014. Before then, Woodside should have its first Pluto gas going to Japan in 2012. Prelude and Wheatstone are other LNG projects in the queue.

12. The Yamal Peninsula and Kara Sea oil and gas fields in the Yamal-Nenets region of Russia's western Siberia. The single biggest field is Bovanenkovskoye. Gazprom, Rosneft, Novatek, and LUKOIL are active, while Total has 20 percent of Novatek's Yamal LNG project and Shell, Statoil, and Mitsui may become involved. Gazprom plans a 2,400-km pipeline to ship Yamal gas to central Russia.

13. The oil and gas fields of the Krishna-Godavari (KG) Basin, Bay of Bengal, India. Reliance Industries is developing India's biggest field there and has brought BP in as a partner. Further into the future is the potential of seabed methane gas, or gas hydrates.

14. The Simandou high-grade iron ore deposits in Guinea, Africa. After a complex set of negotiations with the Guinea government, Rio Tinto has aligned itself with Aluminium Corp. of China (Chinalco) to develop one half of the prospect, while Brazil's Vale is working with Geneva-based BSG on the other half.

15. The thermal coal deposits of Indonesia, led by Bumi Resources' Kaltim Prima Coal operation and Adaro Energy's Tutupan mine.

16. Expansion of the Pilbara iron ore region in Western Australia, where BHP Billiton, Rio Tinto, Fortescue Metals Group, and Hancock Prospecting could lift combined output to almost 1 billion tonnes a year by 2020. Chinese and Japanese groups are major investors.

17. The Mount Weld rare earths mine, Western Australia. Along with Molycorp of the United States, Lynas Corp. is considered

the most likely of the many rare earth miners outside China to get finished product into the global supply chain.

18. The brine-based lithium deposits of the "Lithium Triangle," where Bolivia, Chile, and Argentina meet. Salar de Atacama in Chile is the most productive salt pan, but Bolivia has high hopes for its Salar de Uyuni.

19. The Belo Monte dam in Brazil, due for completion after 2015. Hydropower is a big contributor to Brazil's energy mix, but Belo Monte raises environmental hackles in the same way as China's Three Gorges Dam and the various Upper Mekong dam projects.

20. Turkey's Southeast Anatolia Project (GAP in Turkish), which includes the Ilisu Dam on the Tigris River. The dam, due for completion by 2015, will have a 1,200 MW power station, but will see 40,000 to 60,000 people relocated and the ancient city of Hasankeyf flooded.

21. The offshore wind farms of Europe, particularly Germany and the United Kingdom. Bigger turbines, fewer environmental issues and the capacity to create a pan-European smart power grid will keep wind on top of Europe's renewable list.

22. The glut of cheap PV solar panels, led by Chinese makers. This gives a pricing edge to concentrating PV power, but long term the advantage is likely to lie with more advanced concentrating solar thermal power plants. Rooftop solar panel installations across the United States and China are other areas to watch.

23. More investment interest in niobium, the metal used to strengthen steel in cars and gas pipelines. Steel companies from China, Japan, and South Korea have taken stakes in Brazil's Companhia Brasileira de Metalurgia e Minerao, the world's biggest producer of niobium.

24. The opening up of the potash supply chain now dominated by Canpotext—the marketing arm of the three North American producers Potash Corp. of Saskatchewan, Mosaic, and Agrium—and Belarusian Potash Co., owned by Russia's Uralkali. Global miners BHP Billiton, Rio Tinto, and Vale all have ambitions in this segment. China and India are the biggest users of the fertiliser.

25. The cost of grain and other food staples in India, China, and Africa, where weather extremes and poor supply systems can

have a big impact on rural consumers. The International Rice Research Institute is working on ways to lift yields, while still keeping rice prices at about $300 a tonne.

26. The North Dome/South Pars gas field of Qatar and Iran. Qatar has set itself up as the LNG exporter to the world, while Iran says South Pars will be fully developed over the next decade. China's CNPC is involved, as is Venezuela's PDVSA.

27. The rise of urban mining in Japan and Europe. As recycling systems improve, the electronic leftovers from consumers' discarded appliances will release more metals such as gold, silver, chromium, nickel, and palladium. Beligum-based Umicore is the world's biggest recycler of batteries and precious metals. Australia-based Sims is the global leader in metals and electronics recycling and is targeting China and India.

Survive and Prosper

These are just some of the areas where we can expect to see change. In the nineteenth century, Charles Darwin used the phrase "survival of the fittest" to mean that it was not the strongest species that survived, but the ones best able to adapt to their immediate—and changing—environment. In the late twentieth century, Intel co-founder Andy Grove refined that into the mantra "only the paranoid survive." So who will survive and prosper in the first half of the twenty-first century, when the competition among 7 billion people for access to food, water, minerals, and energy will be acute? Japanese business strategist and globalisation pioneer Kenichi Ohmae suggested in 1995 that the end of the nation state was nigh—that countries were dinosaurs waiting to die, and in their place would arise "new engines of prosperity" based on natural economic zones.[8] He identified some of them as northern Italy, the upper Rhine, Silicon Valley/Bay Area, Hong Kong/southern China, Singapore-Johore-Batam, Pusan, and Fukuoka, San Diego, and Tijuana. Some of this regionalisation has come to pass—notably the Pearl River Delta encompassing Hong Kong and southern China—but equally we have seen countries keen to form supranational groupings and unions over the past 15 years: G8, G20, G77, APEC, GCC, Mercosur, the expanded EU (see Exhibit 15.1).

1. Argentina	11. Italy
2. Australia	12. Japan
3. Brazil	13. Mexico
4. Canada	14. Russia
5. China	15. Saudi Arabia
6. European Union	16. South Africa
7. France	17. Republic of Korea
8. Germany	18. Turkey
9. India	19. United Kingdom
10. Indonesia	20. United States

Exhibit 15.1   Group of 20 membership

Russian leader Vladimir Putin has created a Common Economic Space with Belarus and Kazakhstan and has even spoken of a Eurasian Union that would bring back into the fold some of the Central Asian nations that went their own way after the breakup of the Soviet Union in 1991. "We are not talking about recreating the USSR. It would be naive to try to restore or copy what was in the past. But time dictates that we should have closer integration based on values, politics and economics," Putin said in outlining his Eurasian Union concept.[9]

Russia under Putin may be the energy player to watch over the next decade, because quite possibly it has more conventional oil and gas than anywhere else. OPEC rates it sixth for oil and first for gas in proven reserves, but that assessment does not include potentially huge fields in Arctic waters and eastern Siberia. In 2011, Russia was the world's biggest oil producer (10.5 million barrels a day) and second biggest exporter with 4.8 million barrels a day, behind Saudi Arabia's 6.6 million barrels a day.[10] It also has the world's second biggest coal reserves behind the United States. But much of its energy and metals capacity has been inhibited by a lack of technology. With Putin pushing for modernisation and the likelihood of an investment-driven spurt in productivity ahead, plus the completion of a range of pipelines that tie in Caspian and Siberian production and add to its east-west "swing" supply capability, Russia is potentially the most important energy and metals player in the world.

Certainly its ambition is to change its role from raw material supplier to one where high added-value products are a bigger part of the mix, and where energy markets such as China, Japan, Korea, and India become more important to it. Under its 2030 Energy Strategy approved by Putin in 2010, the goal is that Russia will "not only retain its position as the largest energy supplier in the world, but will also qualitatively change its presence on the world energy market by diversifying its commodities structure and destinations of energy export, actively developing new international energy business and increasing the presence of Russian companies abroad."[11] The success of that strategy will depend on how well Putin keeps his Tsarist tendencies in check, and how skillfully he manages the country's oil and gas oligarchs and their foreign suitors. Endemic corruption remains the biggest bugbear for outside investors, but is rarely acknowledged by Moscow.

Short of a calamitous global natural disaster, widespread social upheaval, or a world war, we can be reasonably sure for the next two decades that the richest people with the best access to resources will live in Western Europe, North America, Japan, Korea, Australasia, and city-states such as Singapore, Hong Kong, Dubai, and Abu Dhabi. By dint of their massive populations, China and India will be the world's biggest and third-biggest economies respectively, though their per capita income levels will be mid- to low range. They will be big, powerful, and relatively poor, creating a set of geopolitical circumstances the world hasn't encountered before. There are plenty of economists who believe China's level of real growth is overstated, its spending on property and infrastructure is wasteful, its price advantage is waning and its export-driven focus is unsustainable, with the implicit warning that a sharp slowdown lies ahead. Equally, other economists point to the momentum generated by China's industrialisation and urbanisation; there may be lower real growth rates in the future, they argue, but the size and growing appetite of China's middle and lower classes will ensure a continued demand for resources. Indeed, the economist Ross Garnaut maintains the world will be surprised at how quickly China moves ahead. In his 2010 report on how China will develop over the next 20 years, Garnaut wrote:

> People in China and abroad who focus on conventional measures of national output will find that China catches up with the world's most productive economies in output per person— and with the United States in total output—much more quickly

than they had been expecting from extrapolation of differentials in national growth rates.[12]

Setbacks are inevitable; China's expensive and hugely ambitious program to create a 16,000 km high-speed rail network by 2020 was put on hold after a train ran into the back of another near the city of Wenzhou in July 2011, leaving 40 people dead and posing questions about safety procedures, construction standards, corruption, and the integration of technology from different suppliers. Even so, China already has by far the world's largest network of 300 km/h rail services.

In sharp contrast to the speeds reached in China, India's fastest train, the Bhopal Shatabdi express, has a theoretical maximum of 160 km/h on its relatively sedate 700 km, eight-hour journey between New Delhi and Bhopal. There are no bullet trains on the horizon for the 8 billion passengers who use the Indian railways every year. Nonetheless, advances in transport and power generation, allied with industrialisation and urbanisation, are important parts of the Indian growth story. India will have close to 600 million people living in its cities and towns by 2030, according to a 2010 McKinsey report.[13] The urban infrastructure required to cope with 68 Indian cities with populations above 1 million is of a massive scale: McKinsey estimates $1.2 trillion of capital investment is needed to ensure future urban dwellers are not condemned to the life that is the norm today for many inhabitants of India's biggest city, Mumbai: slums, poor water and power services, bad roads, transport gridlock, and general urban decay. In July 2009, a retired Indian civil servant named Ashok Vichare became something of a media star when he took delivery in Mumbai of the first Tata Nano, an Indian-built super-cheap small car with a 624cc engine and fuel economy of just 4 litres per 100 km. But even with the frugality of the Nano and other economical cars in India, automotive demand is so strong that the country's oil consumption is destined to rise to about 4.2 million barrels a day by 2020, up from 3.1 million in 2011. The imperative to source energy resources for an urbanising India drives state-owned companies such as ONGC, Indian Oil, Oil India, and private entities Reliance, Essar, Videocon, and Vedanta in the search for oil and gas assets as far afield as Africa, Australia, and the Americas. Likewise, on the coal front, Indian companies are following the Chinese abroad in seeking to own, control or have a substantial stake in the entire supply chain, from mine to rail line to port to domestic power plant.

Challenges for China, India Replicated

The challenges facing an urbanising China and India are replicated on a smaller scale in what are known as the "growth" or emerging economies. By 2050, 19 of the world's top 30 economies are expected to come from the emerging ranks—countries such as Mexico, Turkey, Indonesia, Iran, Egypt, Thailand, Malaysia, Vietnam, and energy producers Venezuela and Colombia.[14] Current members of the G20 such as Australia, Argentina, Saudi Arabia, and South Africa will also vie for a top-30 place. The Nobel-winning economist Michael Spence says some of the developing countries already are starting to take over the kind of high-value-added components that 30 years ago were the reserve of the advanced economies. "This climb is a permanent, irreversible change," he wrote in 2011.[15] All of this amounts to what the Australian analyst Michael Wesley calls a global environment of "rivalrous interdependence," where the name of the game is endless manoeuvring and competitive cooperation.[16] Events such as the eurozone's financial crisis, or the chaos that attends the remaking of Arab nations across North Africa and the Middle East attest to how quickly the international situation can change. London-based Jan du Plessis, chairman of Rio Tinto, the mining group that has the most globally dispersed set of assets, found his view of Europe "almost unreservedly negative" as the eurozone crisis unfolded near the end of 2011. But he was more positive about the United States, calling it "a pragmatic nation that doesn't give up easily, and has the determination and the optimism to keep trying new things until it solves a problem." As for China, du Plessis had little doubt that its long-term growth rate remained in place, "keeping China firmly in position as the world's primary engine of growth."[17]

This is the human element of the Earth wars, but there is a natural element at play as well. In classic chaos theory, tiny differences at the start of a sequence of events lead to vastly different outcomes— the so-called *butterfly effect* popularised by the U.S. mathematician and meteorologist Edward Lorenz in his work on computerised weather prediction in the 1960s. Lorenz, a professor emeritus at Massachusetts University of Technology (MIT) when he died in 2008 at the age of 90, wrote a paper in 1972 titled "Predictability: Does the Flap of a Butterfly's Wings in Brazil Set Off a Tornado in Texas?" to explain his theory of sensitive dependence on initial conditions. Modern business has long been sensitive to its dependence on the weather. Whether it is a tsunami delivering a killer blow to Japan's nuclear power industry, a hurricane shutting down oil rigs in the Gulf of Mexico, floods swamping auto component factories across Thailand's industrial heartland, volcanic ash closing air space across Europe, or cyclonic rains deluging the Australian coalfields, the power of nature to significantly disrupt the global supply chain is a constant risk factor for business.

The interconnectedness of the world's economies is such that security of supply is even more of an imperative than it was in the twentieth century. It is what compels nations and business groups to constantly diversify and to test new strategies that might strengthen their supply chains. They seek to forge new alliances, they scour the world for new materials and new technology, and they make investments and acquisitions that they hope will give them some measure of control over their destinies. In the ongoing Earth wars of the twenty-first century, the things they fear most are to be sidelined by a loss of supply, overtaken by a competitor with better access, brought undone by an unforeseen political twist, or put out of business entirely by a whole new process or product.

Notes

1. British Geological Service, "BGS Risk List 2011," October 2011, www
.bgs.ac.uk.
2. Robert Bryant, U.S. National Counter Intelligence Executive, report to Congress, "Foreign Spies Stealing U.S. Economic Secrets in Cyberspace," October 2011.
3. McAfee Labs, "Global Energy Cyberattacks: Night Dragon," Santa Clara, 10 February 2011.
4. Chinese Defense Minister General Liang Guanglie, speaking at Shangri-La Dialogue, Singapore, 5 June 2011.
5. Chinese Foreign Ministry spokesman Ma Zhaoxu, "China Expresses Strong Dissatisfaction with the Irresponsible Remarks Against China's National Defence Building in Japan's New Defence White Paper," 3 August 2011.
6. Chinese Foreign Ministry spokesperson Hong Lei, "China's Sovereignty, Rights and Relevant Claims over the South China Sea Have Been Formed

in the Long Course of History and Persistently Upheld by the Chinese Government," 19 September 2011.

7. Admiral Sureesh Mehta, India's then-Chief of Navy, address on "India's National Security Challenges," New Delhi, 10 August 2009.

8. Ohmae, Kenichi, *The End of the Nation State: The Rise of Regional Economies* (London: HarperCollins, 1995), 214 pp.

9. Russian Prime Minister Vladimir Putin, "A New Integration Project for Eurasia," Moscow, *Izvestia* (3 October 2011).

10. Organization of Petroleum Exporting Countries, *Annual Statistical Bulletin 2010–2011,* 18 August 2011, and Russian Energy Ministry, 3 October 2011.

11. Russian Energy Ministry, "Energy Strategy of Russia for the Period up to 2030," Moscow, 2010.

12. Ross Garnaut, *China: The Next 20 Years of Reform and Development* (Canberra: Australian National University E Press, 2010).

13. McKinsey Global Institute, "India's Urban Awakening: Building Inclusive Cities, Sustaining Economic Growth," Mumbai, April 2010.

14. HSBC, *The World in 2050,* Hong Kong, 4 January 2011.

15. Michael Spence, "Globalization and Unemployment," *Foreign Affairs* (July/August 2011).

16. Michael Wesley, *There Goes the Neighborhood: Australia and the Rise of Asia,* extract (Sydney: Lowy Institute, 3 May 2011).

17. Rio Tinto chairman Jan du Plessis, address to Australian Institute of Company Directors, "A global business perspective on managing for growth in a volatile international environment," Sydney, 4 November 2011.

Conclusion

A World So Changed

So who will emerge victorious in the Earth wars? If you listen to the global miners, they have absolutely no doubt that China is and will remain the defining market for energy and resources, and they make their 10-, 20-, and 100-year business plans accordingly. Some of the miners liken China's position now as akin to North America's in the late nineteenth century, when the great surge of development began that took the United States to global preeminence for 100 years or more. The demand and development momentum, the miners argue, has irrevocably moved from West to East, and the world must get used to that. North American entrepreneur Robert Friedland, the founder of Ivanhoe Mines and one of the intriguing and controversial characters of modern-day mining, goes further. In his view, Africa will be the next frontier of greatest promise, after China, India, Indonesia, and Asian resource-rich countries like Kazakhstan and Mongolia have provided the impetus for many millions of new middle-class consumers to emerge.

But equally, there are plenty of economic forecasters who see no inevitability about the rise of China and the decline of the West. Being the mother of all markets or having access to the fantastic resource potential of a Congo, Mozambique, Zambia, or Liberia is not the same as being an Earth Wars winner. There are matters of technology, logistics, markets, skills, and funds to resolve, plus the ever-present risk of cultural conflict, social breakdown, and natural catastrophe. Institutional, legal, and financial reforms within China are moribund. And, the economists argue, if fundamental human rights and the rule of law are lacking, can any nation claim to be a winner? Plus, there is a sting in the tail of China's urban one-child policy. This is a complex and controversial issue, but essentially since the late 1970s, the policy has saved China from having to feed an extra 400 million mouths. Now that demographic dividend might be turning against it, as fertility falls and the population ages. Consumer demand is rising, of course, but a society without siblings is likely to be a sorry situation.

In contrast, by rights, India's democracy, demography, and dynamic diaspora should deliver it a large chunk of economic good fortune over the next few decades. According to the UN's latest population projections, India will have more people than China by 2025, when China's population will peak at just under 1.4 billion. India's youngish population will keep on growing until 2060, when it peaks at 1.72 billion. By then, its economy may even be bigger than China's. That means that by the middle of this century, the world will have two large and powerful Asian nations as economic leaders, just as it had in the sixteenth century. But the difference this time is that while China and India will be big, they will still be poor in per-capita incomes, relative to North America, Europe, Japan, South Korea, Australia, and parts of South America, Asia, and the Middle East.

There will be an elite of several million super-rich, while hundreds of millions of Indians and Chinese will move to middle-class status, with a concomitant appetite for food, water, metals, and energy on a grand scale. Yet equally, many millions of their fellow citizens will remain trapped in poverty, with little in the way of job prospects or access to the good life they might see around them. A rising tide may have lifted all boats, but some will be riding much higher. How much disaffection will this inequality breed, particularly when information will be mobile, ubiquitous, and largely free? In effect, will power and poverty prove a dangerous mix?

That depends on two things: (1) how rigidly the Communist Party of China (CPC) keeps its hands on the levers of control at the local and provincial level; and (2) how successfully democratic India reins in its alarming propensity for self-harm.

Economically, India has all the ingredients for success: business enthusiasm, domestic demand, access to science, technology, labour and capital, and international linkages. But—with some honourable exceptions—it is let down badly by its politicians, bureaucrats, and law enforcers at national, state, and local levels. Corruption is the poison that daily eats away at its institutions of government, law and order, and justice. That plays out in the form of massive shortcomings in infrastructure, health, education, environmental protection, social justice, and general security—all to the detriment of its civil society and to the investors who want to bring food, water, energy, and resources projects to fruition. External and internal terrorism add an unhappy overlay to this dispiriting outlook.

China, of course, has its own widespread problems of venality, black money, and "pay to play" corruption among its administrators and law enforcers. But China's state security apparatus is much more ruthless than India's chaotic and multilayered approach. The CPC aims to keep problems mainly in house; it will catch and kill its own, occasionally making an example of fallen party members through public executions of corrupt officials and other "economic criminals" who have transgressed.

At the national level, the iron fist of the CPC so far has kept most social disturbances under control and out of sight, though separatist sentiments in the west, food inflation, concerns over pollution, housing strains, migratory labour, joblessness, the rural-urban divide, and its attendant ills are all testing the party's chain of command out to the provincial and county level.

Just as in India, continued economic growth in China is the government's key objective. But to some observers, China's economic miracle of the past 30 years is built on unsustainable foundations that include export dependency, a too-cheap currency, inadequate labour safeguards, a state-directed banking system that has a clear preference for state enterprises over small and medium businesses, rampant speculation in hot sectors such as property and construction, and a disregard for intellectual property rights and the environment. Beijing's response is that it has the right policy mechanisms to deliver continued GDP growth of 8-plus percent to support its focus on domestic stability, and it is also doing the heavy lifting as a global growth engine. In effect, it is a "put up or shut up" riposte to the less-than-dynamic economies of Europe, North America, and Japan.

Nor should corruption and misallocation of resources be seen as the preserve of India, China, and the dictators of Africa. Among the big resource-rich economies, Russia (ranked a lowly 143 out of 182 countries on Transparency International's 2011 corruption perceptions index), Brazil (ranked 73), Mexico, and Indonesia (both ranked 100) continue to see their share of crony capitalists, government ministers, and officials with snouts in the public trough. In the United States (ranked 24, well behind Australia, Canada, Germany, Japan, and the United Kingdom), corruption in government and big business is almost an art form—think Enron, lobbyist Jack Abramoff, financier Bernie Madoff, hedge funds Long-Term Capital Management and Galleon, and former Illinois Governor Rod Blagojevich, to name just a few.

But the United States has a number of redeeming features, including its ability to renew itself in the face of adversity or threats to its position, and its willingness to shine a light on corporate and political skulduggery. It has technology, innovation, infrastructure, deep capital pools, well-defined markets, a business environment that encourages investment and rewards risk-taking, and an abundance of enthusiasm and confidence. It would be foolish to write off America in the Earth Wars, particularly when its expertise and resources in shale oil and gas, and in gas-to-liquids conversion, are rewriting the North American energy scenario.

Equally, Europe cannot be dismissed simply because of its recent political and economic incompetence. It retains the intellectual capacity, vision, R&D, and engineering skills to make its investments in renewable energy pay off in the long run. Its energy hardware and systems might be more cheaply manufactured in India and China, but its mastery of design, process, and distribution (such as supranational power grids and pipelines) will keep it relevant. Germany, Scandinavia, the Benelux economies, France, the United Kingdom, Italy, and Spain all have particular skills in energy, metals processing, and food production. Much the same applies in Japan and South Korea, where some of the most advanced thinking is taking place on solar, wind, hydro, wave, and battery power.

That leaves the pure food, metals, and energy suppliers, some of whom are big consumers, too. With economies of scale at their disposal, the resource-rich countries of Australia, Brazil, Canada, Qatar, and Kazakhstan are clear winners in some or all of these categories. The same goes for Saudi Arabia, UAE, and Kuwait among the oil suppliers. Iran could be a winner, but its outlook is clouded by its pariah status and its willingness to butt heads with perceived enemies. In neighbouring Iraq, Baghdad's ability to redeem its oil wealth is some years away yet, and is dependent on fresh technology and the security situation. And just as the world gets ready for what the International Energy Agency says is a new "golden age of gas" predicated on supplies from Central Asia, Qatar, Iran, and Australia, who should emerge but Khalid A. Al-Falih, CEO of the world's most valuable company, Saudi Aramco, to tell us that a petroleum renaissance awaits. If so, the biggest winner may not be Saudi Arabia, but Russia—home of Putin, the oligarchs, and some of the biggest but most inhospitable oil fields on the planet. If Russia can keep its kleptocrats in line, solve the logistics of Arctic oil and gas, get its pipeline networks to Europe and China humming, and satisfy its foreign investors, it will be a genuine Earth Wars winner. But all of that is a tough ask for a country where the rule of law and judicial independence and transparency are concepts honoured in the breach.

Like the United States, Canada, and Brazil, Mexico could be a big Earth Wars winner from the Americas. It has resources, a young population, and the important benefit of North American market access. But like Iran and Russia, it has big hurdles to overcome—in its case, the challenge to society posed by violent criminality.

In Southeast Asia, Indonesia looks a likely winner. Its young population will grow to a peak of 293 million by 2050, consolidating its status as the world's fourth most populous country. Rich in oil and gas, thermal and coking coal, palm oil and other foodstuffs, it is on a high-growth path. Its proximity to the big energy markets of North Asia gives it a transport advantage over most of its rivals.

At the corporate level, the global contest comes down to this: the big miners and oil companies have the advantage of incumbency for now, but the cashed-up national oil and metals companies of China, India, and Russia have the money to change that by acquisition. They are likely, though, to take a more cooperative approach than the hostile takeover or the go-it-alone attitude. We can expect to see more partnerships that bring together technology, funding, market access, and political connections to exploit new resources.

If the Earth wars were a sporting contest, here's how the half-time score might stand at the beginning of 2012: United States 10, China 8, Europe and Japan 6, Russia and India 5, Brazil 4, Mexico, Canada and Australia 3, Saudi Arabia, Qatar, Kuwait and UAE 2, South Korea, Indonesia, South Africa, Nigeria, Turkey, Iran, Central Asian Republics and Mongolia 1. But contests can throw up unexpected results: Vietnam, Venezuela, Colombia, Chile, and parts of Africa could force their way onto the scoreboard before the decade is out.

Bibliography

A New Water Politics: World Water Council 2010-12 Strategy. Paris: World Water Council, 2010.

"Africa's Path to Growth: Sector by Sector," *McKinsey Quarterly* (June 2010).

Alaska North Slope Oil and Gas: A Promising Future or an Area in Decline? Fairbanks, AK: National Energy Technology Laboratory, US Department of Energy, April 2009 update.

Asia 2050: Realizing the Asian Century. Manila: Asian Development Bank, 4 May 2011.

Asia Pacific Executive Brief. Sydney: IMA Asia, October 2011.

Austin, Greg, and Alexey D. Muraviev. *Red Star East: The Armed Forces of Russia in Asia.* Sydney: Allen & Unwin, 2000, 402 pp.

Backman, Michael. *Asian Eclipse.* Singapore: John Wiley & Sons (Asia), 1999, 412 pp.

Basrur, Rajesh M. *Minimum Deterrence and India's Nuclear Security.* Stanford: Stanford University Press, 2006, 264 pp.

Bijapurkar, Rama. *Winning in the Indian Market: Understanding the Transformation of Consumer India.* Singapore: John Wiley & Sons (Asia), 2008, 226 pp.

Bribe Payers Index 2011. Berlin/Brussels: Transparency International, November 2011.

Calder, Kent E. *Asia's Deadly Triangle.* London: Nicholas Brealey Publishing, 1996, 253 pp.

Central Asia: Border Disputes and Conflict Potential. Brussels: International Crisis Group, 4 April 2002.

Chaze, Aaron. *India: An Investor's Guide to the Next Economic Superpower.* Singapore: John Wiley & Sons (Asia), 2006, 321 pp.

China and India, 2025: A Comparative Assessment. Santa Monica, RAND Corporation, 22 August 2011.

Circum-Arctic Resource Appraisal: Estimates of Undiscovered Oil and Gas North of the Arctic Circle. Menlo Park, CA: U.S. Geological Service, 2008.

Conflict with China: Prospects, Consequences and Strategies for Deterrence. Santa Monica, RAND Corporation, October 2011.

Corruption Perceptions Index 2011. Berlin: Transparency International, 26 October 2011.

Cunningham, Fiona, and Rory Medcalf. *The Dangers of Denial: Nuclear Weapons in China-India Relations.* Sydney: Lowy Institute, 18 October 2011.

Diamond, Jared. *Collapse: How Societies Choose to Fail or Survive.* London: Penguin Books, 2005, 575 pp.

Diamond, Jared. *Guns, Germs, and Steel.* London: Vintage Books, 2005, 480 pp.

Dupont, Alan, and Graeme Pearman. *Heating up the Planet: Climate Change and Security.* Sydney: Lowy Institute, June 2006.

Earth, Fire, Wind, and Water: Economic Opportunities and the Australian Commodities Cycle. Sydney: ANZ Bank, August 2011.

East Asia Analytical Unit, Australian Department of Foreign Affairs and Trade. *India: New Economy, Old Economy.* Canberra: Department of Foreign Affairs and Trade, 172 pp.

East Asia Analytical Unit, Australian Department of Foreign Affairs and Trade. *Indonesia: Facing the Challenge.* Canberra: Department of Foreign Affairs and Trade, 2000, 172 pp.

East Asia Analytical Unit, Australian Department of Foreign Affairs and Trade. *China Embraces the Market.* Canberra: Department of Foreign Affairs and Trade, April 1997, 428 pp.

Energy Strategy of Russia for the Period up to 2030. Moscow: Ministry of Energy, 2010.

Energy Technology Perspectives: Scenarios and Strategies to 2050. Paris: International Energy Agency, 2010.

Engardio, Pete (ed.). *Chindia: How China and India Are Revolutionizing Global Business.* New York: McGraw-Hill, 2006, 384 pp.

Environmental and Health Aspects of Canada's Oil Sands Industry. Ottawa: Royal Society of Canada Expert Panel, December 2010.

Fairbank, J. K., Reischauer, E. O., and Craig, A. M. *East Asia: The Modern Transformation.* Boston & Tokyo: Houghton Mifflin Tuttle, 1965, 955 pp.

Foo, Check Teck. *Reminiscences of an Ancient Strategist: The Mind of Sun Tzu.* Aldershot, UK: Gower Publishing, 1998, 535 pp.

Foreign Spies Stealing US Economic Secrets in Cyberspace. Washington DC, US National CounterIntelligence Executive report to Congress, October 2011.

Friedman, Thomas L. *The World Is Flat: The Globalized World in the Twenty-First Century.* London: Penguin Books, updated edition 2006, 600 pp.

Garnaut, Ross. *Australia and the Northeast Asia Ascendancy.* Canberra: Australian Government Publishing Service, 1989.

Garnaut, Ross. *China: The Next 20 Years of Reform and Development,.* Canberra: Australian National University E Press, Department of Foreign Affairs, 2010.

Global Brazil and US-Brazil Relations. New York: Council on Foreign Relations, July 2011.

Global Economic Prospects 2011. Washington, DC: World Bank, 7 June 2011.

Global Energy Cyberattacks: "Night Dragon." Santa Clara, CA, McAfee Inc., 10 February 2011.

Global Gas: A Decade of Two Halves. New York/London: Morgan Stanley, 14 March 2011.

Gordon, Sandy. *India's Unfinished Security Revolution.* New Delhi: Institute for Defence Studies and Analyses, August 2010.

Growing Food for 9 Billion. Rome: Food and Agriculture Organization, 2010.

Hiscock, Geoff. *Asia's New Wealth Club.* London: Nicholas Brealey Publishing, 2000, 348 pp.

Hiscock, Geoff. *Asia's Wealth Club.* London: Nicholas Brealey Publishing, 1997, 312 pp.

Hiscock, Geoff. *India's Global Wealth Club.* Singapore: John Wiley & Sons (Asia), 2008, 294 pp.

Hiscock, Geoff. *India's Store Wars.* Singapore: John Wiley & Sons (Asia), 2008, 208 pp.

Human Development Report 2011. New York: United Nations Development Program, November 2011.

IEA Statistics: CO_2 Emissions from Fuel Combustion. Paris: International Energy Agency, 2010.

Independent Investigation into the Grounding of the Panamanian Bulk Carrier Pasha Bulker. Canberra: Australian Transport Safety Bureau, May 2008.

India in the Super-Cycle. London/Mumbai: Standard Chartered Bank, 25 May 2011.

India: The Growth Imperative. McKinsey Global Institute, September 2001.

India's Urban Awakening: Building Inclusive Cities, Sustaining Economic Growth. McKinsey Global Institute, April 2010.

International Energy Outlook 2011. Washington, DC: U.S. Energy Information Administration, 19 September 2011.

Jobim, Nelson, Minister of Defense, Brazil. *Brazil and the World—Opportunities, Ambitions, and Choices.* Rio de Janeiro/London: Chatham House, 7 April 2011.

Kaplan, Robert D. *Monsoon: The Indian Ocean and the Future of American Power.* New York: Random House, 2010, 366 pp.

Kaye, M. M. (ed.). *The Golden Calm: An English Lady's Life in Moghul Delhi.* New York: Viking Press, 1980, 217 pp.

Key World Energy Statistics 2011. Paris: International Energy Agency, October 2011.

Kristof, Nicholas D., and Sheryl WuDunn. *Thunder from the East.* London: Nicholas Brealey Publishing, 2000, 377 pp.

Lamb, Alistair. *Asian Frontiers.* Melbourne: F. W. Cheshire Publishing, 1968, 246 pp.

McDonald, Hamish. *The Polyester Prince: The Rise of Dhirubhai Ambani.* Sydney: Allen & Unwin, 1998, 273 pp.

McGregor, Richard. *The Party: The Secret World of China's Communist Rulers.* New York: HarperCollins, 2010, 320 pp.

Magnus, George. *Uprising: Will Emerging Markets Shape or Shake the World Economy.* London: John Wiley & Sons, 2011, 358 pp.

Mech, Michelle. *A Comprehensive Guide to the Alberta Oil Sands.* Ottawa: Green Party of Canada, May 2011.

Medcalf, Rory, and Raoul Heinrichs. *Crisis and Confidence: Major Powers and Maritime Security in Indo-Pacific Asia.* Sydney: Lowy Institute, 28 June 2011.

Medium-term Oil and Gas Markets 2011. Paris: International Energy Agency, 16 June 2011.

Menzies, Gavin. *1434. The Year a Magnificent Chinese Fleet Sailed to Italy and Ignited the Renaissance.* New York: William Morrow, 2008, 368 pp.

Mine 2011: The Game Has Changed. Melbourne: PricewaterhouseCoopers, May 2011.

Ohmae, Kenichi. *The End of the Nation State: The Rise of Regional Economies.* London: HarperCollins, 1995, 214 pp.

Ohmae, Kenichi. *The Invisible Continent: Four Strategic Imperatives of the New Economy.* London: Nicholas Brealey Publishing, 2000, 262 pp.

O'Neill, Jim, Dominic Wilson. Roopa Purushothaman, and Anna Stupnytska, *How Solid Are The BRICs?* Goldman Sachs Global Economic Paper No. 134, December 1, 2005.

Oppenheimer, Stephen. *Eden in The East.* London: Weidenfeld & Nicholson, 1998, 560 pp.

Osborne, Milton. *The Paramount Power: China and the Countries of Southeast Asia.* Sydney: Lowy Institute, 2006.

Overseas Investments by Chinese National Oil Companies. Paris: International Energy Agency, February 2011.

Parfitt, Ben. *Fracture Lines: Will Canada's Water be Protected in the Rush to Develop Shale Gas?* Toronto: Munk School of Global Affairs, University of Toronto, 15 September 2010.

Piramal, Gita. *Business Legends.* New Delhi: Penguin Books, 1998, 654 pp.

Piramal, Gita. *Business Maharajas.* New Delhi: Viking Penguin Books, 1996, 474 pp.

Podder, Tushar, and Eva Yi. *India's Rising Growth Potential.* Goldman Sachs Global Economic Paper No. 152, January 22, 2007.

Pursuing Sustainability: 2010 Assessment of Country Energy & Climate Policy. London: World Energy Council, January 2011.

Rajadhyaksha, Niranjan. *The Rise of India: Its Transformation from Poverty to Prosperity.* Singapore: John Wiley & Sons (Asia), 2007, 176 pp.

Rawson, Philip. *The Making of the Past: Indian Asia* (Oxford, UK: Elsevier-Phaidon, 1977, 152 pp.

Renewables 2011: Global Status Report. Paris: REN21, July 2011.

Report on the State of Food Insecurity in Urban India. Chennai: M. S. Swaminathan Research Foundation, September 2010.

Rosen, Daniel H., and Thilo Hanemann. *An American Open Door: Maximising the Benefits of Chinese Foreign Direct Investment.* Asia Society, May 2011.

Sanghvi, Vir. *Men of Steel.* New Delhi: Roli Books, 2007, 109 pp.

Schwarz, Adam. *A Nation in Waiting: Indonesia's Search for Stability.* Sydney: Allen & Unwin, 1999, 533 pp.

Strategic Plan 2011–15. Vientiane/Phnom Penh: Mekong River Commission, 2011.

Streifel, Shane. Development Prospects Group, World Bank. *Impact of China and India on Global Commodity Markets: Focus on Metals & Minerals and Petroleum.* World Bank, 2006.

Sun, Shuyun. *A Year in Tibet.* London: HarperCollins, 2008, 242 pp.

Technology Roadmap: Biofuels for Transport. Paris: International Energy Agency, May 2011.

Thapar, Romila. *A History of India, Volume One.* New Delhi: Picador, 1966, 381 pp.

The Super-Cycle Report. London: Standard Chartered Bank, 16 November 2010.

The United States and the Rise of China and India. Chicago: The Chicago Council on Global Affairs, September 2006.

The World Copper Fact Book 2010. Lisbon: International Copper Study Group, 6 October 2010.

Thirwell, Mark. *India: The Next Economic Giant.* Sydney: Lowy Institute, 2004.

Top Trends in Indian Retail Sector. New Delhi: Technopak Retail Outlook, Vol. 1, October 2007.

Toynbee, Arnold (ed.). *Half the World: The History and Culture of China and Japan.* New York: Holt, Rinehart & Winston, 1973, 368 pp.

Upstream Dialogue: The Facts on Oil Sands. Calgary: Canadian Association of Petroleum Producers, June 2011.

Verhoeven, Harry. *Black Gold for Blue Gold? Sudan's Oil, Ethiopia's Water and Regional Integration.* London: Chatham House, April 2011.

Ward, Karen. *The World in 2050: Quantifying Shifts in the Global Economy.* Hong Kong: HSBC Global Research, January 2011.

Water in a Changing World: UN World Water Development Report 3. Paris: UNESCO, 2009.

Wesley, Michael. *There Goes The Neighbourhood: Australia and the Rise of Asia.* Sydney: NewSouth Books, May 2011, 224 pp.

Wilson, Dominic, and Roopa Purushothaman. *Dreaming with BRICs: The Path to 2050.* Goldman Sachs Global Economic Paper No. 99, 1 October 2003.

World Economic Outlook. Washington, DC: International Monetary Fund, September 2011.

World Energy Outlook 2010. London: International Energy Agency, 9 November 2010.

World Energy Outlook 2011. London: International Energy Agency, 9 November 2011.

World Oil Outlook 2010. Vienna: Organization of Petroleum Exporting Countries, August 2011.

World Oil Outlook 2011. Vienna: Organization of Petroleum Exporting Countries, November 2011.

World Nuclear Industry Status Report 2010–2011: Nuclear Power in a Post-Fukushima World. Paris, Berlin, Washington, WorldWatch Institute, April 2011.

Acknowledgments

The concept for this book had its origins in an invitation to speak about India and China consumer demand to a gathering of Asian agribusiness leaders in Singapore in November 2010. The two-day discussion helped crystallise my thinking about the nexus between rising incomes in emerging markets and the global consumption of food, water, energy, metals, and other resources, and prompted me—with the encouragement of Wiley's Singapore publisher Nick Wallwork—to begin work on *Earth Wars*. I would like to thank the two people most responsible for that invitation, John Baker of Rabobank International in Singapore, and Rex Holyoake, editor and publisher of *Asian AgriFood* magazine.

Some of the content of this book draws on my reporting and analysis of India, China, Japan, Korea, Indonesia, and other (mainly Asian) economies during my time as international business editor of *The Australian* newspaper 1995–2000, then as Asian business editor of CNN.com International 2001–2006, and as a freelance business writer since 2007. I would like to thank former colleagues at *The Australian* and CNN, including Grant Holloway, Bruce Dover, Ian Macintosh, Geoff Elliott, Susan Kurosawa, Lyndall Crisp, and Helen Trinca, for their continued support.

Professor M. S. Swaminathan and his colleagues at the M. S. Swaminathan Research Foundation in Chennai were generous with their time in explaining the intricacies of Indian food security and the supply chain. More broadly, I was able to use information gathered for two earlier books on India in writing about the food, water, and energy situation there, and I want to acknowledge my debt to the many people I interviewed during Indian assignments between 2000 and 2011. Likewise, for China, Japan, Indonesia, Korea, Europe, the Middle East, and North America, I drew on interviews and other material gathered during reporting assignments from the 1990s onward.

Jack Lifton and Gareth Hatch of Technology Metals Research in the United States helped me gain a better understanding of the many factors that go into the global rare earths story and its intricate supply chain.

On the energy front, Kathleen Tanzy at energy and metals information provider Platts in New York gave me access to industry leaders at the Platts 2011 London oil and gas conference, and to a subsequent treasure trove of information that extended from hydrocarbons to coal and renewables. Dr. Leo Drollas of the Center for Global Energy Studies shared his perspective on China, while Professor Saul Estrin of the London School of Economics painted the big picture on emerging markets.

Dr. Klaus Rave, Steve Sawyer, and Angelika Pullen of the Global Wind Energy Council ensured I had the latest wind power information, and T. F. Jayasura of the Indian Wind Turbine Manufacturers Association helped me make the most of the Wind Power India 2011 gathering in Chennai.

In Sydney, the Lowy Institute has produced a stream of valuable reports and papers on economic, political, and social interactions in the Asia-Pacific, and I have made full use of these. Richard Martin of the Asia-focused strategic consultancy IMA Asia and his India-based colleague Adit Jain have continued to be supportive with access and insights on the region's economic outlook. Two ex-Japan colleagues, Denis Gastin and Warren Reed, kindly reviewed some of my material dealing with trading organizations.

The ubiquity and mobility of the Internet in recent years has revolutionized information access for business writers like me. Company reports and presentations, regulatory filings, prospectuses, share market data, and commodity prices are available from around the world, including from previously hard-to-get markets such as China, Russia, the Middle East, and Central Asia. Mainstream media sites such as the *Wall Street Journal, Financial Times,* Bloomberg, Reuters, Nikkei, *Economic Times,* Caixin, *Moscow Times, Al Jazeera,* and *O Globo* provided me with a first taste, supplemented by a host of other sites that cover everything from think tanks and bloggers to social media and special interest groups. These yield a level of information that would have been inconceivable two decades ago. As always, the challenge is to sift what is relevant and reliable from the avalanche of available material.

For statistics and background information, I have referred mainly to quasi-government bodies and industry associations, including the International Monetary Fund, the World Bank, the Asian Development Bank, UN-Water, the UN Food & Agriculture Organization, the International Water Resources Association, the Organization of Petroleum Exporting Countries, the International Association of Oil & Gas Producers, the World Nuclear Association, the Solar Energy Industries Association, the World Coal Association, the World Steel Association, the World Energy Council, the International Energy Agency, the International Atomic Energy Agency, the U.S. Energy Information Administration, the International Copper Study Group, REN21, Earth Policy Institute, and other environmental groups. I also referred to industry outlooks and forecasts by consultants (McKinsey, BCG, KPMG), energy majors such as Royal Dutch Shell, ExxonMobil, BP, and banks HSBC, Standard Chartered, Goldman Sachs, Morgan Stanley, and Nomura. A full list appears in the footnotes and Bibliography.

A final thank you goes to Nick Wallwork, Jules Yap, Cynthia Mak, Cindy Chu, and the rest of the Wiley team in Singapore, who have given me great support in getting this book into production, as have Emilie Herman, Stefan Skeen, and Cheryl Ferguson at the Wiley office in the United States.

About the Author

Australian journalist Geoff Hiscock has been writing about Asian and international business for more than 30 years from bases in Hong Kong, Tokyo, Bangkok, and Sydney. He is the author of two recent books on India—*India's Global Wealth Club* (2007) and *India's Store Wars* (2008), both published by John Wiley & Sons, Singapore. Earlier, he wrote *Asia's Wealth Club* (1997) and its follow-up, *Asia's New Wealth Club* (2000), the key books that first brought many of the region's billionaires to the attention of an international audience. He served as Sydney bureau chief and Asia business editor for CNN .com Asia Pacific from 2001 to 2006, and as international business editor of *The Australian* daily newspaper from 1995 to 2000. Earlier in his career, he worked for newspapers that included the *Sydney Morning Herald*, the *Bangkok Post* and the *Hongkong Standard*. Since 2007, he has been a freelance business writer and author based in the Hunter Valley, north of Sydney.

Index